Historical Association Studies

The Causes of the English Civil War

3/4

Historical Association Studies

General Editors: Muriel Chamberlain, H. T. Dickenson and Joe Smith

The Causes of the English Civil War

Norah Carlin

BLACKWELL
Publishers

The right of Norah Carlin to be identified as author of this work has been asserted in accordance with the Copyright, Designs and Patents Act 1988.

First published 1999

2 4 6 8 10 9 7 5 3 1

Blackwell Publishers Ltd
108 Cowley Road
Oxford OX4 1JF
UK

Blackwell Publishers Inc.
350 Main Street
Malden, Massachusetts 02148
USA

British Library Cataloguing in Publication Data

A CIP catalogue record for this book is available from the British Library.

Library of Congress Cataloging-in-Publication Data

Carlin, Norah.
    The causes of the English Civil War/Norah Carlin.
        p.   cm. – (Historical Association studies)
    Includes bibliographical references and index.
    ISBN 0-631-20450-4 (acid-free paper). – ISBN 0-631-20451-2
        (pbk.: acid-free paper)
    1. Great Britain – History – Civil War, 1642-1649 – Causes.
        2. Great Britain – Politics and government – 1603-1649.   I. Title.
    II. Series.
DA415.C28   1999
942.06'21 – dc21   98-39044
                                                                                       CIP

Typeset in 11 on 13 pt Times
By Avocet Typeset, Brill, Aylesbury, Bucks.
Printed in Great Britain by TJ International Ltd, Padstow Cornwall.

This book is printed on acid-free paper

Contents

Outline Chronology

Note: at the time, the new year began on 25 March, but this chronology adheres to the modern practice of beginning on 1 January.

1603 March	James VI of Scotland succeeds Elizabeth as James I of England.
1604 March–July	First session of James's first parliament, which turns down proposals for closer union with Scotland; the Commons prepare (but do not deliver) an 'Apology' defending their traditional privileges.
1605 November	Catholic 'Gunpowder Plot' to blow up the king and parliament discovered.
1605–6 November–May	Second session of the parliament elected in 1604.
1606	Bate's Case: judgement is given in favour of the king's right to levy impositions on trade.
1606–7 November–July	Third session of the parliament elected in 1604.
1610 February–July and October–December	Further sessions of the parliament elected in 1604 fail to reach agreement with James over finance, and protest about impositions.
1612 November	Death of Prince Henry; James's second son, Charles, becomes his heir.
1614 April–June	'Addled Parliament' clashes with James over impositions.
1617 January	George Villiers, the king's new favourite, created Earl of Buckingham (to become Duke in 1623).
1618	War between Holy Roman Emperor (Habsburg) and German Protestant princes begins; this becomes in retrospect the start of the Thirty Years' War.
1619 May	British delegates attend the Dutch synod at Dort, where they oppose Arminianism.
1621 January–June and November–December	James's third parliament; this ends with a row over the Commons' Protestation concerning freedom of

	discussion in parliament.
1622	James issues injunctions on preaching, restricting discussion of political and theological questions from the pulpit.
1623 March–October	Visit of Charles and Buckingham to Madrid results in breaking off of Spanish marriage negotiations, which is greeted with public rejoicing in England.
1624 February–May	James's fourth parliament. Money granted for war against Spain is made accountable to House of Commons.
1625 March	Death of James and accession of his son Charles I.
May	Marriage of Charles and Henrietta Maria, sister of Louis XIII of France.
June–July	Charles's first parliament meets in London, and delays the usual grant of tonnage and poundage to the king.
August	Second session of parliament meets in Oxford, but still does not grant tonnage and poundage; the attack on Buckingham begins.
September	Buckingham's attack on Cadiz fails miserably.
October	Charles revokes all grants of church land in Scotland since 1540 into his own hands.
1626 February	York House conference polarizes opinion over Arminianism.
February–June	Charles's second parliament; Buckingham is attacked by both houses.
September	Charles begins the levy of a forced loan.
1627 October	Buckingham's expeditionary force is defeated at La Rochelle.
November	Judges in the Five Knights' case rule that the king can imprison subjects without stating the cause.
1628	William Laud becomes Bishop of London.
March–June	Charles's third parliament meets.
June	Charles accepts the Petition of Right drawn up by parliament.
August	Assassination of Buckingham by John Felton, a soldier, at Portsmouth.
1629 January–March	Further session of Charles's third parliament, which ends with angry scenes as members of the Commons try to prevent its dissolution and pass resolutions against royal policies. Leaders of this protest, including Sir John Eliot, are imprisoned.
March	Charles issues a proclamation forbidding discussion of future parliaments.
March–May	Many merchants refuse to pay tonnage and

	poundage, declared illegal by the recently dissolved parliament.
March and May	Grain riots at Maldon in Essex are treated with exceptional severity; three leaders, including one woman, are executed.
1630 November	Peace with Spain.
1631	New 'Book of Orders' is issued to guide the work of Justices of the Peace.
1632 January	Sir Thomas Wentworth is appointed king's lord deputy in Ireland.
November	Death in prison of Sir John Eliot.
1633	Charles visits Scotland for coronation and attends parliament in Edinburgh.
August	William Laud becomes Archbishop of Canterbury.
1634 October	Ship Money is levied on coastal counties only.
1635 June	Ship Money is levied on all English counties for the first time.
1637 June	Puritan pamphleteers Prynne, Burton and Bastwick are punished with mutilation.
July	Riots against the new Scottish prayer book break out in Edinburgh.
November	The trial of John Hampden for refusal to pay Ship Money results in a judgement narrowly in the king's favour.
1638 February	The Scottish National Covenant is launched, and gains wide support.
November	The general assembly of the Scottish kirk abolishes bishops.
1639 June	The first 'Bishops' War' against the Covenanters ends in truce after a few skirmishes only.
1640 January	Wentworth, returned from Ireland, is made Earl of Strafford.
April–May	The Short Parliament meets, demands to deal with outstanding grievances before moving to a settlement, and is dissolved.
August	The Scottish Covenanters defeat the English army at Newburn and occupy Newcastle.
September	The great council of peers meets at York and advises calling a new parliament.
November	The 'Long Parliament' (not finally dissolved until 1660) meets.
December	London citizens present the 'root and branch' petition to parliament, demanding the abolition of bishops in England.
1641 February	The Triennial Act makes the summons of parlia-

	ment every three years obligatory.
March–May	The trial, attainder and execution of Earl of Strafford.
May	Act against the dissolution of the present parliament without its consent.
June	Ten Propositions are agreed by parliament as a basis for negotiations with the king.
July–August	Acts abolishing prerogative courts such as Star Chamber, and Ship Money.
August–November	Charles visits Scotland, settles with the Scottish parliament, and is suspected of involvement in 'the Incident', a plan to kidnap covenanting leaders.
October	Second session of the Long Parliament begins; the Irish rebellion breaks out.
November	The Commons' Grand Remonstrance is passed by a small majority.
December	The old ruling oligarchy is defeated in London city elections; demonstrations outside parliament turn into violent clashes.
1642 January	Charles's attempt to arrest five members of the House of Commons and one peer fails, Londoners defend parliament, and the king leaves London for York.
February	Act excluding bishops from parliament is passed.
March	Militia Ordinance is passed by both houses of parliament.
April	Charles is refused access to arms magazine at Hull.
2 June	Parliament presents the Nineteen Propositions, which are rejected by the king.
11 June	Charles issues commissions of array.
July	Parliament votes to raise an army under the Earl of Essex.
July–September	Local skirmishes over control of the militia and county arms magazines.
August	Charles raises his standard at Nottingham.
September	Essex's army leaves London.
October	The first major battle of the civil war takes place at Edgehill.

England and Wales in 1640

1

The Problem of Causation

Historians have been investigating the causes of the English civil war since almost as soon as it was over. The royalist Earl of Clarendon, for example, thought that the causes were short-term political ones, while the republican James Harrington believed that the war was the result of major changes in society during the previous hundred years. These seventeenth-century writers began a debate which has continued ever since (Richardson, 1988). The search for the causes of events has long been an important part of historical investigation, and in the mid-twentieth century it was mainstream thinking for a standard work on the nature of history to argue that 'the study of history is a study of causes' (Carr, 1961, p. 87). In recent years, however, this thinking has been challenged, especially by the postmodernist school of thought which stresses the philosophical difficulties involved in making any statement about the causes of complex historical events. As a result, some historians have been prepared to abandon the subject of causes altogether, or at least to recommend that they be abandoned, because they are 'a constriction on historical thought' (Vincent, 1996, p. 49). Before embarking on a discussion of the causes of an event such as the English civil war, therefore, it is nowadays necessary to explain the problems and justify the approach. This is, on balance, an improvement on the days when students were expected to study causation automatically in order to answer standardized questions in examinations. It need not be the case that historians' only response to such problems is to stick their heads in the sand or fall back on their professional traditions (Jenkins, 1991, pp. 50–3).

Fortunately, a sophisticated understanding of postmodernist theory is not required in order to understand the most common pitfalls in dealing with the causes of the English civil war, which have frequently been discussed by historians over the last few decades. The first of these is the temptation to present developments which followed the event as if they were causes which preceded it. For example, it is sometimes assumed that the growth of republicanism must have been one of the causes of the civil war, simply because we know that the outcome was the execution of Charles I and the setting up of a republic. In fact, you would look long and hard to find anyone in England at the outbreak of the civil war who did not believe in the necessity of monarchy in England, and recent historians have made out a very good case for the argument that republicanism played very little part in the events leading to Charles I's execution, and that in so far as it did grow it was a result of the war rather than one of its causes. The problem is similar with regard to the question of religious freedom. Was freedom of religious opinion or worship one of the aims envisaged by the opponents of Charles I and Archbishop Laud, or was it an unintended outcome of their attempts to take over and change the established church? We have to take seriously the possibility that our knowledge of the outcome may have distorted our understanding of the origins of the conflict, and try to correct this.

The second basic problem is the type of interpretation that was identified by Geoffrey Elton thirty years ago as the 'high road to civil war', in which signposts or milestones are picked out along the route to the eventual outcome and everything else ignored (Elton, 1966). According to Elton and those who have followed him, the dominant interpretation of the English civil war from the 1920s to the 1970s, as a struggle for sovereignty between crown and parliament, had been developed by a process of rather narrow selection by historians. A series of statements about the constitution drawn up in the House of Commons in the early seventeenth century had been formed into a coherent story in which the House of Commons proceeded by stages to 'win the initiative' in a conflict with the monarchy. But these documents, Elton argued, were not all equally significant, did not form a coherent series, and did not mark any real progression of the House of Commons from relative powerlessness to a position of strength. When they are put into perspective, Conrad Russell claims, it seems that there were no fundamental conflicts between crown and parliament, and that between 1604 and 1629 'the House of Commons was not powerful and it did not contain an opposition' (Russell, 1976).

Revisionists of this kind have been so successful at constructing alternative perspectives, by selecting events and documents that run counter to the traditional assumptions about the conflict, that they have sometimes been congratulated on explaining why there was no civil war in mid-seventeenth century England and the execution of Charles I did not take place! Pointing to evidence which makes these events harder to explain is potentially very useful, but a negative exercise which constructs an alternative selection aimed at destroying previously accepted explanations of the evidence may have its own built-in bias, which ignores or plays down events that might support the previous interpretation. It has been suggested, for example, that Conrad Russell's revisionist history of the parliaments of the 1620s is guilty of this at times (Thompson, 1986). A fuller understanding of seventeenth-century England and its problems has to take both these selective 'histories' (and potentially, many others) into account and try to explain the contradictions and paradoxes presented by those surviving traces of seventeenth-century experience which we call evidence.

A third type of explanation which presents serious problems is the claim that an event such as the English civil war was the result of long-term, impersonal processes of which people at the time were unaware. To attribute the political conflicts of the period to underlying 'forces' such as modernization, progress or the rise of capitalism seems to run the risk of making human beings the passive agents of abstract processes over which they have no control. Many of our problems in explaining events such as the English civil war in fact spring from the belief of nineteenth- and early twentieth-century historians that their main business was to identify and justify impersonal forces like these in history, whereas most late twentieth-century historians doubt that this is a legitimate enterprise (Appleby, Hunt and Jacob, 1994, pp. 52–90). But in some cases phrases such as the 'rise of' democracy, or individualism, or capitalism' may be useful generalizations about changes in history which have been the outcome of human choice and action, rather than indicating commitment to a theory of impersonal forces governing human affairs. Structures and patterns, discerned by the historian in retrospect, may be necessary tools for shaping any historical narrative or analysis, provided that they do not come to be seen as predetermined ends which shaped people's actions before the consequences appeared (Burgess, 1990). An example of such misuse of developmental concepts is Christopher Hill's assertion that Puritan insistence on Sunday observance anticipated the work rhythms of modern industrial society (Hill, 1969, p. 142). However, concepts such as the rise of capitalism can be legitimate tools for explaining historical events, if they are appropriately defined and critically applied. The argument that such explanations would not have made sense to the participants in the events at the time does not necessarily invalidate them: after all, no one at the time would have understood the explanation that the outbreaks of bubonic plague from which they suffered were caused by a bacillus. There is less difficulty with concepts such as the rise of capitalism than there is with explanations in terms of the rise of ideas, such as liberty. When we are dealing with ideas, there should be a rigorous obligation on historians to locate concepts in their contemporary context, because it is important not to attribute to people of the past thoughts which they could not have had (Skinner, 1969).

Is it possible to have a scientific theory of historical causation which would resolve all these problems and lead to a satisfactory agreement among historians about the causes of the English civil war? The belief that history is a 'social science'which could and should aspire to the kind of certainty which natural science is often believed to offer was a powerful influence on historical writing for most of the twentieth century, but has been shaken to its foundations by changing views about the nature of science, as well as by arguments about whether scientific aims can be achieved in history (Appleby, Hunt and Jacob, 1994, pp. 160–97). Perhaps the most important point for students approaching a problem such as the causes of the English civil war is to be aware that there is no question of 'proving'a particular cause (or even a particular complex of causes) to be valid. This is not only because, however much we recover by the hard work of researchers into the past, we will never know 'all the facts'about the situation that led to the English civil war. Even if we did know all the facts (and it is hard to know where we would draw the line), their meaning and relevance would still be matters for debate. Most historical situations are too complex for causes to be identified by using any set of scientific laws or logical rules, or indeed by the application of any theory which would predict the relation between causes and specific effects. This is in fact true of many situations in the natural world also. Though it is easy to explain why a water pipe has burst by the simple and well-known law that water expands when it freezes, causal explanation is not so simple when it comes to a complex medical problem such as cancer: there are too many possibilities and too few certainties among the potential causes that are known, and a strong probability that there are many others we do not yet know.

It is as difficult to talk of disproving suggested causes of historical events as it is to talk of proving them. Existing arguments for a theory can be criticized, but it is always possible that better arguments could be put forward, or the theory itself developed and improved. That the testing of a theory may lead to its being modified rather than abandoned is evident from the whole history of natural and social science. That is why it is wrong, for example, to claim that the theory of history as class struggle has been 'disproved' (Kishlansky, 1986, p. ix), though to say that this or any other explanation of the civil war is unproven would merely be stating the obvious. Some revisionist historians seem to think that demonstrating a new cause disproves all previously accepted ones. Thus some interesting ideas and discoveries, such as the changing political culture of the Renaissance aristocracy (Farnell, 1977) or the secret dealings of some of the nobility with the rebellious Scots in 1640 (Russell, 1993a), have been used to argue that the House of Commons played only a passive role in the events leading up to the war and that there was no English revolution at all. But to search for a single, sufficient cause which would make all other explanations unnecessary is to pursue an illusion.

Lawrence Stone argued in the 1970s that the application of sociological methodology to the problem of revolutions could produce a general theory which could then be used to explain seventeenth-century English events. He therefore began his classic work on the causes of the English revolution with an examination of various general theories formulated by mid-twentieth century sociologists (Stone, 1972). One problem with all such theories (apart from their changing fashion more rapidly even than historical explanations) is that they depend on relatively simple generalizations which as they become wider become more remote from what we know of the historical reality. Few seventeenth-century specialists would now accept, for example, that the people who led the English revolution could be described, along with eighteenth-century Jacobins and twentieth-century Maoists, as 'fanatics, extremists, zealots ... prepared to smash through the normal constraints of habit, custom and convention' (Stone, 1972, p. 13). Such sweeping statements almost always seem more useful for the events about which the reader knows less, and more dubious in relation to the events about which one knows more. But there is also a general problem about the search for laws of history, analogous to laws of nature, whether they use sociological theory or any other method. The experimental and investigative methods developed by natural and social science in pursuit of general laws are virtually impossible to carry out in historical studies because we do not have the same kind of access to the past that we have either to the material world or to people in present-day societies.

Stone divided the causes of the English civil war into long-term 'preconditions', shorter-term 'precipitants' and immediate 'triggers' which produced the specific actions and reactions leading to war and revolution. The major current dispute about the origins of the English civil war is whether it had long-term causes at all. One recent writer, arguing that Stone's long- and medium-term perspectives are superfluous, has said that all that is really necessary is to determine 'what was required ... to convert a poorly engineered motorway and a faulty vehicle into an actual accident' (Maclachlan, 1996, p. 167). The analogy of an accident investigation is a useful one, for such investigations are indeed concerned with more than the immediate causes of collisions. Accident blackspots may be identified, and if large numbers of cars of a particular make are found to be involved in accidents, the makers may come under pressure to recall them. An overall increase in road accidents may also be caused by the unprecedented numbers of vehicles on the roads, which you may believe to be due to the manufacturers' relentless drive for profits, or to the growth of individualism and consumer choice, depending on your political perspective. However, these wider causes become visible only when road accidents of a similar kind are studied in large numbers, and large numbers of events of a similar kind are what we do not have in history. This does not mean that events like the English civil war did not have general and long-term causes, only that they are harder to distinguish and very much more difficult to agree on.

Most revisionist historians argue that the English civil war was the result of a series of decisions made by a very few people, above all by Charles I, in a short period of time (1639 to 1642), and that the kinds of social change or systemic political breakdown often categorized as preconditions of revolution cannot be found in the 'unrevolutionary England' of the years preceding the outbreak of civil war (Russell, 1990a, 1990b). Others recognize the important contribution of economic and social change in shaping the outcome, but insist that these changes were not causes. However, when one historian says that 'massive changes in the economic, social and cultural structures' meant that 'the consequences for England of a breakdown of order in the 1640s were very different from those that would have resulted from a breakdown of order in the 1540s', he is describing what many historians would call a necessary but not a sufficient cause of the civil war (Morrill, 1993, p. 283; Evans, 1997, pp. 157–8). A discussion about causation can admit several different kinds and levels of causes. There seems to be no justification for 'cutting out' of the theoretically endless chain of causes in 1625, the date of Charles I's accession. For one thing, the immediate causes may themselves require longer-term explanations (Morrill, 1993, pp. 254–5). How far back we pursue the chain of causes is a matter of judgement on which historians differ, and on which students may make their own decisions according to their judgement of the issues.

Those historians who believe that the civil war had only short-term causes are more likely to deploy the dramatic strategy of envisaging 'might have beens'. This is basically a legitimate exercise: any statement about causation implies that without a certain factor, the outcome would have been different; and since we cannot conduct laboratory experiments in history in which we change the circumstances and measure the result, there seems to be nothing essentially wrong with 'thought experiments' – a method, after all, which Einstein used in developing his theory of relativity. In history, however, we lack the natural laws and mathematical formulae on which Einstein based his arguments. But we should at least maintain a regard for the normal standards of historical evidence and reasoning, which some of the most entertaining speculations may fail to satisfy. The suggestion, for example, that if the Irish rebellion had been delayed for three weeks the Long Parliament might have agreed to go home and the civil war would have been avoided, begs a host of questions, as will be seen below (Russell, 1990a, p. 213). Another of Russell's speculations, that 'if Charles, instead of [the earl of] Bedford, had died of the smallpox in May 1641, it is hard to imagine anything worse than a confused regency resulting,' ignores the possibility that parliament would have increased its powers during the regency, and faced a further conflict with Charles II when he came of age (ibid., p. 212). Most historians find that imagining what might have happened if things had been slightly different tends to lead to the conclusion that 'it is unlikely that the overall pattern of events would have diverged totally from what actually happened'(Evans, 1997, pp. 132–3). This is a pointer to the multiplicity of causes in a situation like the outbreak of the civil war: removing only one of them would have limited effects.

It has been argued that all judgements in history are subjective, depending on nothing more than the individual historian's prejudices or position in relation to the historical establishment (Jenkins, 1991). In so far as this is saying that the study of history is not an isolated intellectual pursuit, but is itself part of the history of society and is constructed by those who practise it, it has a great deal of validity. But the inadequacy of rejecting a historical judgement because of its ideological implications or because of the position of the person advocating it can be shown by a couple of examples from this history of this period. One is the suggestion that Charles I dealt with his parliaments in the mid-1620s in an authoritarian way because his newly married wife,

Henrietta Maria, refused to attend his coronation, and he was compensating for his lack of authority in his own home by treating parliament in a high-handed manner (Carlton, 1995, pp. 78–83). One initial reaction to this might be that it is unacceptable because it is misogynistic – an example of an all too common male bias towards blaming women for things that go wrong in history. However, the misogynistic aspect of the explanation should make it more rather than less plausible in this case, because in the early seventeenth century explicit parallels between authority in the family and in the state were very common, and male fears about the disorderliness of women were frequently linked to fears about change in society and the state (Underdown, 1996, pp. 45–67). In the case of Conrad Russell's views on the origins and nature of the English civil war, which he sees as an aristocratic rebellion rather than a struggle for constitutional government involving the wider political nation, these views cannot be rejected simply on the grounds that this historian is a hereditary English peer and a descendant of the Earl of Bedford, a central figure in this attempted aristocratic coup. There is plenty of common ground on which we can argue about whether these explanations are better or worse than others. It is this search for better explanations, rather than the unattainable 'correct' explanation, that spurs historians on to uncover more evidence, more documents which do or do not fit a particular explanation, and to engage in more discussions about the meaning of the past and the present.

Few people could disagree that the debates of the past quarter century have led to a greater knowledge and understanding of the English civil war and its causes. Certainty can never be achieved in debates about historical causation, but this is not a problem, so long as we are continually trying to improve and refine our historical studies, along with our understanding of human affairs in general. The alternatives seem to be either total scepticism, which would give up on any attempt to understand why wars and revolutions, for example, have happened; or total relativism, which would recognize many different explanations but would forbid their supporters to argue with one another about whether some are better than others (Jenkins, 1991, pp. 64–8). The consequence of either of these choices would surely be to hand control over human affairs to the cynical and the powerful, who will continue to draw their own conclusions from history even if historians do not. The study of causation has seemed to historians from Herodotus in the fourth century BC to revisionists in our own day to be central to the kind of enquiry that history is. Moreover, it is still wars, civil wars and revolutions that attract the most intense debates about their causes; perhaps they are found to be the most interesting precisely because their causes are infinitely debatable.

This work will aim, therefore, at continuing the debate on the causes of the English civil war. The next chapter will examine the course of political events in Britain in the five years before the outbreak of the English civil war, which is important to both long-term and short-term causal explanations of the conflict. For those historians who regard it as an accidental war, or one caused largely by external events in Scotland and Ireland, the narrative of these years is so fundamental that it is sometimes presented as self-explanatory, the pressure of events producing further events. But a grasp of the short-term crisis is equally essential in investigating the long-term causes of the civil war, for however deep the strains and tensions which economic and social change, religious conflict or political polarization may have put on English society by 1637, if the events which precipitated the crisis had not happened as and when they did, then we have to assume that the outcome would have been different, in some ways if not in every way. For the longer-term perspective, the immediate crisis opens up further questions, rather than closing them off.

Starting with the events of 1637–42 should also help to meet another criticism which has been addressed to many previous accounts of the causes of the English civil war: that accounts of the causes of the upheavals of this period differ partly because they are trying to explain different things (Burgess, 1990, pp. 621–3). Although it has been suggested that the title of a book on this period can be a clue to its interpretation – Marxist historians referring to the English 'revolution' and revisionists being inclined to use more cautious terms such as 'rebellion' or 'civil war' (Hughes, 1991, pp. 2–3) – the title of this book is intended to indicate only that it is an attempt to explain the outbreak of the war in 1642, and not the revolutionary events of 1647–9 which followed the war. To attempt the latter would require an additional examination of the ways in which the experience of civil war itself transformed the situation, of the development of new ways of thinking and new political alignments among the victors, and of the unprecedented role played by the parliamentarian army, all of which helped to create a further political breakdown and a revolutionary solution. Instead, the next chapter will attempt only to describe and explain the crisis which began in Scotland in 1637 and led, five years later, to civil war in England. It is true that an account of the causes of the 1647–9 revolution might well involve an examination of those long-term factors which, it will be argued in the later chapters of this book, destabilized English society and politics in ways that help us to explain the crisis of 1640–2. But readers who wish to use these chapters for this further purpose will have to develop their own ideas about the connections between political, religious and social developments before 1642 and the events which came later, for they are not examined here.

While following the course of events from 1637 to 1642 in some detail, the next chapter will therefore attempt to explain why the English state was thrown into crisis by events in Scotland and Ireland, why a parliament that met in late 1640 with the aim of making peace came to make war on the king within two years, and why both sides in the conflict were able to acquire the political and material support that made civil war possible. The three chapters which follow will raise longer-range questions related to these years of crisis: whether religion was the main destabilizing factor in England, whether the conflict between Charles I and the English parliament was related to long-term problems in their relationship since the accession of the Stuarts in 1603, and whether the divisions in the nation can be explained by economic and social change in the preceding century. The last chapter will assess three approaches to the causation of the civil war which have tended to dominate the discussion for decades, if not for centuries: the responsibility of Charles I as an individual, the concept of a conflict of ideas, and the part played by social change. Each of these requires some consideration of more theoretical approaches, which the preceding chapters will on the whole avoid.

2

The Crisis of 1637–42

The events of the five years before the outbreak of the English civil war are crucial to any discussion of its causes. It is usual to open a narrative of these events with a brief outline of English society, religion and politics in 1637, avoiding so far as possible the long-term problems which will be discussed later. From this perspective, the country was apparently peaceful and prosperous, with the population and price increases of the previous century levelling off and trade expanding. Overwhelmingly rural and hierarchical, English society appeared stable and orderly by comparison both with a century earlier and with other European societies which were troubled by war and internal revolts. There had been no popular rebellions since 1549, and no seriously threatening aristocratic ones since 1569. Rising prices and outbreaks of plague in 1636–7 caused concern, but central and local government co-operated to carry out agreed policies for relieving distress, ensuring food supplies and avoiding disorder.

Following the Reformation in the sixteenth century, England had developed an identity as a Protestant nation, and like most European countries had one national church closely identified with the state. The king was recognized as its supreme head on earth, by all except a few tens of thousands of Roman Catholics who led an underground religious existence. Dissenting Protestant congregations outside the national church had no more than a few thousand members between them. There were many Protestants who wished to see the doctrine, worship or structure of the Church of England reformed, but accepted that their future lay within and not outside it. Even the most bitter of these critics within the Church of England in 1637 did not challenge the view that authority over the church should be identified with rule over the state: the king's use of his authority in the church was criticized in England, but it was not widely disputed in principle, as it was in Scotland.

England in 1637 was ruled, as it had been for centuries, by a monarch advised by a council of nobles and administrators, and local government was carried on by Justices of the Peace drawn from the local landowning class in each county. The English parliament, which brought the monarch, the hereditary nobility and the representatives of the localities together to consult on matters of policy and to make laws, had not met since 1629, and the king appeared to have no plans for calling another meeting in the near future. But regular meetings of parliament were not essential to the day-to-day running of the country, gaps as long as seven years had been known before, and successful meetings of the Scottish and Irish parliaments in the 1630s suggested that Charles I was not averse to parliaments in principle. In the absence of parliaments the royal court was, as always, the centre of official political activity. Since the parliaments of the late 1620s had been argumentative and the last had ended with unpleasant scenes of disruption and confrontation, many people accepted that the absence of parliaments would be prolonged, though not permanent. There was discontent, especially over taxation being raised in the form of Ship Money without parliamentary consent, but the vast majority of taxpayers shut up and paid up once the judges had ruled, in 1637, that it was legal . One observer wrote that the taxpayers 'only privately breathe out a little discontented humour and lay down their purses', and revisionist historians have tended to judge the English people in the 1630s by their deeds, as consenting in practice to Charles's rule (Cope, 1987, pp. 11–33, 118).

There were in the England of 1637 no political parties, no organized opposition movements and no revolutionaries. Discontent was mostly expressed in conservative terms such as dislike of innovation, or in disputes over procedure and individual cases, and not in general arguments. Did the crisis which led to the English civil war come, therefore, out of the blue, disturbing the peace of a society in which there was little or no previous potential for conflict and rebellion? Royalists looking back after the civil war thought so, but the king's advisers were not unanimous at the time. When, in 1638, Charles I was contemplating the unprecedented action of fighting a war against his Scottish subjects without calling the English parliament, the Marquis of Hamilton predicted that the English would rebel. But even in May 1640, the Earl of Strafford thought that whatever the king did, 'the quiet of England will hold out long' (Russell, 1991, pp. 56, 126).

Any narrative of 1637–42 is necessarily selective, and any selection constitutes an analysis. For over a hundred years the standard narrative selected events which supported the story of a constitutional revolution carried out by a determined and far-sighted House of Commons, seeking to prevent any recurrence of the arbitrary exercise of royal power such as there had been since 1629. Since the 1970s, however, this narrative has been challenged in three major ways. The first (and long overdue) way has been to question its anglocentrism. Many past historians showed little interest in Scottish or Irish affairs except as producing 'external' events in 1637–9 and 1641–2, but there is now much more interest in the period as a British crisis. The importance of events in Scotland and Ireland, however, sometimes seems to be considered a reason for denying that the English civil war had any causes in England.

The second challenge to the constitutional narrative focuses on the significance of the House of Lords rather than the House of Commons. Aristocratic factions, it is said, dominated the political scene, using the upper house and their personal influence over members of the lower one to pursue their own political aims, which were 'to get themselves taken into office, and thereby to force radical changes of foreign and religious policy on Charles I, without substantially changing the existing constitution' (Russell, 1973, p. 28). The civil war is even portrayed as a baronial revolt, with the House of Commons playing a very much reduced part and the driving force being 'a revived, baronial view of the nobility's role as a counterpoise to the arbitrary power of kings'(Adamson, 1990).

The third approach is a shift of focus from parliament to the wider political nation. This began with an interest in the politics of the 'country' alliance which opposed court candidates in the elections of 1640 (Zagorin, 1969), and developed into studies of the county community in various shires, which were at first concerned almost entirely with the gentry class (Everitt, 1966). There is now a wider interest in the 'middling sort of people' in the counties and towns, who were also an influential part of the political nation, and in the popular political culture of the time (Underdown, 1996). Events outside parliament, such as local riots or petitioning campaigns, have thus come to feature as more than a side-show to the main drama at Westminster (Manning, 1991).

Though each of these alternative approaches may enrich our understanding of the causes of the English civil war, they also risk producing new selective narratives with their own tendency to distortion. The British approach may evade discussion of long-standing tensions in England, the baronial account can only be sustained by ignoring most of what went on in the Long Parliament, and some studies of local politics argue that what happened at Westminster was unimportant compared with local rivalries and factions. The account given here will attempt to combine and compare the traditional narrative and alternatives, and to show that even among those historians who insist that the civil war had only short-term causes, there is no consensus and no single answer to questions about causation.

The Three Kingdoms, 1637–42

Since 1603 England, Ireland and Scotland had been ruled by one monarch as three separate states. When James VI of Scotland succeeded to the English throne as James I, his desire for a closer political and institutional union was rejected by the English and Scottish parliaments. Meanwhile, English monarchs had ruled Ireland as a kingdom, though a subordinate one, since the 1540s, but closer union was not on the agenda. It has been said that the main thing the three kingdoms had in common in 1637 was being ruled by the same man, James's son Charles Stuart, who had succeeded him in 1625. Charles I's rule over his three kingdoms had some political coherence despite the different institutional and religious contexts. His policies centred on royal authority over other goals, and as he tried to bring the three kingdoms into greater institutional and religious uniformity by the direct exercise of this authority, he was prepared to bypass representative institutions which might stand in his way.

Did the British crisis reflect the problems which all rulers of multiple kingdoms in early modern Europe experienced when they attempted to enforce uniformity in religion, law or institutions (Russell, 1991, pp. 27–8, 524)? Up to a point, the Scottish and Irish rebellions do resemble the Catalan and Portuguese revolts against the Spanish monarchy in the 1640s (Macinnes, 1991, pp. 43–5; Clarke, 1981). But what happened in England was unique among multiple kingdoms: the Catalan and Portuguese rebellions provoked no Spanish civil war, and the heartlands of Austria were not torn apart by the Habsburgs' attempts to impose Catholicism on their German empire. The situation of England was not simply 'pig in the middle', and the connections between political problems in the three kingdoms were complex. Russell has described the relationship as a 'billiard ball effect', since English reactions to the Scots rebellion had a crucial influence on discontent in Ireland, and the Irish rising brought matters in England to a head (Russell, 1990a, p. 27). But this does not address questions about the long-term causes of these problems, nor explain why each kingdom was vulnerable to being knocked sideways by events in the others.

Serious opposition to Charles I came first from Scotland in 1637, in a nationwide revolt against the new church service book he tried to impose. The traditions of the Scottish Protestant kirk, closer to continental Calvinism than the English church, clashed with the king's preference for a more ceremonial type of worship, which many Protestants associated with Catholicism. But it was not only over church ceremonies that Charles's ecclesiastical policy clashed with Scottish preferences, powerful though the implications of ceremonial and symbolic behaviour were in seventeenth-century society. Religion was inextricably intertwined with politics in Scotland because the quarrel was also about the government of the kirk by bishops and by the king. Scotland had a Presbyterian movement, deeply rooted in the parish kirk sessions and regional presbyteries or synods, and Presbyterians at heart believed that hierarchy in the church (though not in society) was wrong, and that no Christian church should be dependent on the state (Brown, 1992, pp. 48–9). This movement had coexisted with bishops and the royal supremacy for decades under James VI, and the kirk's pro-Presbyterian general assembly had not met since 1618, but the opposition still had roots in the localities (ibid., pp. 47–51, 73–9).

Religion was not the only source of disaffection in Scotland. The regal union of 1603 had left Scotland with an absentee monarchy. James VI and I was surrounded by Scottish courtiers in London, and boasted that he governed his native kingdom by the pen. But he was becoming increasingly insensitive to Scottish opinion on religious matters, and already by 1621 the Scottish parliament showed signs of polarization between court and country (Goodare, 1995). Charles I was more seriously out of touch with Scotland, which he had left at the age of four. He had few Scottish courtiers, was reluctant to consult his English advisers about Scottish affairs, and was remote from his Edinburgh council. His first visit to Scotland as king, in 1633, aroused antagonism by the elaborate religious ceremony of his coronation (Morrill, 1990), and by his ostentatious intervention in parliamentary proceedings. His projects of 'modernizing' reform for Scotland, such as the Act revoking former church lands out of the hands of lay feudal lords in 1625, a common fishing policy which satisfied neither the English nor the Scots, and the attempt to import English forms of local government, discredited his rule because they failed, and different layers of Scottish society learned from the experience of collaborating locally to obstruct them (Macinnes, 1991, pp. 49–127; Brown, 1992, pp. 101–11).

Scotland was a very different society from England in the early seventeenth century, though it was not the backwoods enclave of medievalism and bigotry described by some English historians (Trevor-Roper, 1967). The aristocracy was powerful and independent, the system of landholding was still feudal, and mercantile interests were largely of the old-fashioned corporate privileged kind, but Scotland was nevertheless experiencing change (Macinnes, 1991, pp. 32–4). The economic situation of lesser landlords and larger farmers was improving, and both landowners and merchants had considerable political importance in the parliamentary 'estates' of barons, lairds and burgesses. In the central lowland belt, noble political influence on lesser land-lords in parliament was weak by the early 1620s (Goodare, 1995). The Protestant clergy enjoyed an influence partly due to their social role in town and countryside, where responsibility for social discipline was in the hands of the ministers and elders of the parish kirk session. Some historians have argued that social power in Scotland was shifting downwards, away from the feudal nobility (Makey, 1979, pp. 1–15). The rebellion of 1638–40 was indeed led by the nobility; but some would say that their power and credibility had come to depend on their identification with the political and religious interests of the nation as a whole, rather than on their old feudal position (Macinnes, 1991, pp. 1–25).

The National Covenant, launched by Presbyterian nobles and clergy in February 1638, had political as well as religious implica-tions. Though its signatories declared their loyalty to the king, this was so closely linked to 'the preservation of the laws and liberties of the kingdom'that it could be regarded as a conditional statement of allegiance (Donald, 1990b, pp. 97–8). It called for immediate meetings of the parliament and general assembly, and the organiz-ers set up a committee of the estates which were represented in par-liament, to watch over the government of Scotland until the full parliament should meet. The Covenanters rapidly suppressed regional pockets of opposition, organized an army for the defence of the country, and summoned a general assembly of the kirk which abolished bishops. By 1640 Charles had been forced to recognize the reforms of a general assembly and a parliament which he had initially refused to summon, and in 1641 he accepted that the Scottish parliament should nominate his council in Edinburgh. Religious and constitutional change had gone hand in hand in Scotland, and some of the Covenanters' strategies for restraining royal power, such as the Act for triennial parliaments, were to be imitated later in England. One of the most significant effects of the northern revolution may have been to provide Charles I's English opponents with a model for constitutional reform, 'an education and an inspiration for disaffected people in England' which 'demonstrated that the king could be successfully resisted and his policies reversed'(Macinnes, 1991, p. 198; Young, 1997, p. 133).

Early in 1639 Charles decided to raise an army in England to fight the Scots. He believed that the sizeable surplus in his treasury, together with the customary charges for raising the county militias and a revival of the nobility's feudal military obligations, would make the calling of a parliament unnecessary (Sharpe, 1992, p. 794). This enterprise was less than a total success: fewer soldiers were mobilized than expected, and 'the troops were mostly untrained, pay scarce and morale low' (Fissel, 1994, p. 24). The collection of local militia charges proved difficult, and reduced payment of the simultaneous Ship Money levy. The peers summoned to attend the king at York were unenthusiastic, and some explicitly demanded a parliament in England (Russell, 1991, pp. 84–5). In the first 'bishops' war' of June 1639, a small English force crossed the border, but retreated when it encountered the Covenanters' army. A pacification which both sides regarded as temporary was agreed, and Charles began to plan a major assault on Edinburgh by land and sea.

The parliament Charles called in England to finance this 1640 campaign was a political disaster. Expectations were raised that the grievances which had built up since the last meeting in 1629 would be dealt with, especially Ship Money and the religious policies which many saw as a drift towards Catholicism. The elections stimulated an unprecedented amount of political discussion, and in many places opposition to candidates seen as courtiers was organized by local élites who were normally keen to avoid contested elections (Kishlansky, 1986, pp. 108–11). Debates in the House of Commons were dominated by discussion of the subjects' grievances, and leading speakers argued that the king must remedy these before they would agree to any taxation. Charles's attempt to get the House of Lords to press the Commons to grant money backfired, because their right to intervene in taxation matters was questioned . After less than three weeks he dissolved the assembly, which came to be known as the Short Parliament. It is possible that he misjudged the mood of the majority and missed the opportunity for at least an initial political compromise (Sharpe, 1992, pp. 875–6).

The political crisis in England deepened over the summer of 1640. The king's councillors were divided, and Charles chose to take advice from hard-liners such as the Earl of Strafford and Archbishop Laud, who advised him to thrash the Scots and forget about parliaments (Russell, 1991, pp. 125–7). His decision to summon the militia again, from the southern as well as northern counties, led to more widespread tax refusal and a high level of substitution, whereby trained men sent others in their places. The resulting army not only suffered humiliating defeat, but created its own mayhem, with soldiers rioting for pay, attacking images and altar rails in churches, or destroying hedges and fences around recently enclosed land, while two officers believed to be Catholics were murdered (Fissel, 1994, pp. 264–86). Disaffected members of the nobility made contact with the Scots, encouraging them to invade England and even promising to bring a number of militia regiments over to them in the hope of preventing Charles from fighting back (Donald, 1989; Russell, 1993a). This did not happen, however, and the Scots defeated Charles at Newburn in Northumberland, and on the same day twelve peers in London signed a petition for another parliament. The Scots occupied Newcastle and demanded negotiations with a new English parliament, while the king agreed to raise money to pay their expenses rather than have them plunder the Northumbrian countryside. Mistakenly believing that the war had shaken his subjects out of their disloyalty, and that he would now get the funds he needed, Charles bowed to pressure from his moderate councillors and called another parliament, which met in November 1640 (Russell, 1984b).

The impact of the Scottish rebellion on English affairs in 1639–40 is controversial. Some English historians have seen the Scots as arrogantly determined to impose their own religious preferences on the larger and more modern English nation (Trevor-Roper, 1967). But it has been doubted whether the British perspective was in itself of much importance to the Covenanters, their calls for a parliament and further religious reform in England arising from their need to secure their gains in Scotland rather than being a fundamental aim (Morrill, 1990, pp. 15–19). Their proposal for a federal union of Britain was one in which their English sympathizers never showed much interest. The main advantage which the Scots derived from the British dimension was that as Charles's problems in England became more critical, he was readier to compromise with them, recognizing constitutional and religious changes which he had earlier rejected as reducing him to a mere figurehead.

The English peers and gentlemen who allied with the Covenanters in 1640 to get Charles to call a second parliament have been castigated by Russell as treasonous and dishonourable (1991, pp. 149–53). The documentary evidence for this plot offers the Scots the support of several English regiments who will declare themselves 'armies for the commonwealth', and expresses the desire for 'a speedy parliament for redress of the grievances and composing the war without blood'(Donald, 1989, pp. 227–8). Some of the king's opponents in England were clearly contemplating a form of rebellion in 1640, though their immediate aim was to stop rather than to incite bloodshed, and they planned to appeal to the concept of the commonwealth, or public good (Donald, 1989, pp. 227–9). Moreover, the opposition to Charles I was more than a 'fifth column'for the Scots, and it was not a simple case of Puritan co-religionists joining the Covenanters' rebellion. A study of the Yorkshire gentry's resistance to mobilization in 1640 has suggested that they were motivated by dissatisfaction with Charles's policies in England rather than by pro-Scots feeling, while some of the king's opponents disapproved all along of 'encouraging a foreign nation proud and subtle, against their natural prince' (Scott, 1997). Behind the opposition to Charles in England lay a growth of national political awareness, and the king's leading opponents were trying to use both the Scottish invasion and this heightened political consciousness to advance a programme of religious and constitutional reform in England. The Scottish invasion of 1640 was in a sense the first stage of civil war in England, though the next two years were spent mostly in trying to prevent its going any further.

Ireland was the third element in the British crisis, and the one which most directly triggered the English civil war of 1642. Already in 1638 Charles was drawing Ireland into British affairs, arming Ulster Catholic chieftains ready for action against the Scottish Covenanters (Fitzpatrick, 1988, pp. 77–108). Both Scots and English began to fear an invasion from Ireland, and many believed the Irish army was part of a plot involving Charles, the pope and the Spanish to recapture England for Catholicism (Hibbard, 1983, pp. 104–8). The Earl of Strafford was later accused of advising the king to use this army to 'reduce' one of his other kingdoms, though it has never been clear whether he meant Scotland or England (Russell, 1991, pp. 125–7). But instead of overawing his Scottish and English opponents, the king's Irish army brought them together and heightened their anti-Catholic fears.

Religion was a crucial factor in the Irish rising of October 1641, which had a further major impact on the situation in England. The established church in Ireland was Protestant and the government was dominated by English courtiers and Protestant settlers; but the native Irish and the 'old English' descendants of medieval settlers still adhered to the semi-clandestine Catholic church, and a large proportion of the population were in constant breach of the anti-Catholic laws. Religious differences were, however, intertwined with property and other issues. For eighty years the policy known as 'plantation' had transferred land confiscated from the native Irish into mainly English and Scottish Protestant hands. The Irish parliament was increasingly dominated by the new English, who were the main beneficiaries of plantation, but the old English and native Irish were not fully displaced. There were even native Irish landowners who co-operated with plantations and benefited from the land market. By the late 1630s this regime seemed to be working, and Ireland appeared more peaceful than it had been for some time (Clarke, 1970).

Recent historians have emphasized that the 1641 rebellion was started by native landlords who had collaborated with the Dublin government and plantations, rather than by the dispossessed (Clarke, 1981). The English parliament currently in session was threatening to step up the punishment of Irish Catholics, and was claiming rights over the Dublin parliament which had previously been exercised by the king. Those who started the 1641 rebellion claimed that they were defending the king and his royal prerogative as well as their own religion. They even claimed – disastrously for their image in England – that the king had authorized them to raise an army to defend him. The old English soon joined the rising, persuaded that they were defending both monarchy and Catholicism (Clarke, 1981; Russell, 1991, pp. 372–99).

The Irish rebellion was more than a conservative reaction against recent political developments, however. Native Irish resentment against the plantations, which had produced bitter rebellions in the sixteenth century, still simmered. In Ulster, English and Scottish planters had been extending their property by using their profits to buy up better land (Clarke, 1981, p. 37). Contemporary accounts of the rebellion in Ulster suggest that most of the native Irish who joined it were primarily concerned with recovering their land and regaining their lost position in society. This took the leaders by surprise, especially when Irish peasants turned violently against their Protestant neighbours after living peacefully alongside them for years, and these leaders turned to the Catholic clergy and the old English to re-establish control (Canny, 1995). It is doubtful whether the rising can be called nationalist in the modern sense, since the rebels never demanded independence from the Stuart monarchy, but native Irish hostility to the plantations of English and Scots Protestant settlers was an important factor. From early 1642, members of the native Irish nobility who had spent many years in exile in Europe, the celebrated 'wild geese' who had flown in 1607–10, began to return and play a leading military role in the rebellion with the aim of re-establishing native Irish dominance in the island.

The disaffection of the old English gentry in Ireland was also based on fears about their property. The policy of imposing English law and institutions on Ireland appeared to threaten all property held by Irish law (Perceval-Maxwell, 1994). Such fears had grown during the rule of Sir Thomas Wentworth (created Earl of Strafford in 1640) as head of the king's administration in Ireland during the 1630s, and early in 1641 the Irish parliament mounted an attack on Strafford as the chief cause of their problems, similar to the accusations made by their Scots and English counterparts (Russell, 1991, pp. 280–4). The Ulster rising of October 1641, however, soon realigned the Catholic gentry in Ireland decisively against the English parliament, while the English parliament, as will be seen, regarded the rising as proof of a secret Catholic conspiracy against England rather than a parliamentarian protest against the same 'evil counsellor' who had been their own first target.

The interconnections between events in Scotland, Ireland and England in the five years before the civil war were therefore complex. Rather than resembling self-contained, impenetrable spheres colliding on the historical billiard-table, the affairs of the three kingdoms were more like a tangled loom of highly charged cables, some shorter and some longer. Short-circuiting of the various strands – religion and politics, Scotland and Ireland, property and parliaments – produced dangerous sparks, but nothing could have been more likely to cause a general conflagration than the king's slashing about with the cutting edge of royal prerogative in the belief that this would solve his problems.

The Long Parliament from 1640 to 1642

The English parliament which opened in November 1640 is known as the Long Parliament, because it sat until 1653 and was finally dissolved only in 1660. Already in late 1640 it seemed likely to last longer than the Short Parliament, if it was to tackle the problems which had arisen at the earlier meeting. Ominously, Charles could not see this, thinking that the Scottish invasion would deliver a compliant parliament into his hands. His moderate councillors, the electorate who returned more anti-court candidates than ever before, and the leaders of Lords and Commons, all expected that the political arguments of the Short Parliament would be resumed, and hoped for a political as well as a financial settlement (Russell, 1984b).

No one in November 1640 expected civil war. The members of parliament came to make peace with the Scots, disarm the Irish and disband the English army, not to fight the king. They recognized that it was in their interests to grant money immediately to secure this demilitarization, and there is no evidence that they tried to delay the negotiations with the Scots so as to maintain the threat of military force (Fletcher, 1981, p. 18). The king did not in any case have enough political support to fight even if others had wanted war. The court was isolated and the 'country' was a broad, comprehensive alliance of all who felt Charles's rule had gone wrong and needed to be put right. Lords and Commons, and even the bulk of the king's privy councillors, remained largely united on most of the major issues up to mid-1641. It was only in late 1641 that fundamental disagreements came to dominate parliamentary debate. By November 1641, the Commons could pass the Grand Remonstrance, a summary of the grounds and aims of opposition to the king, by only 159 votes to 148 after prolonged and heated debate. By that time, Charles had begun to acquire a royalist party in both houses of parliament and in the political nation. Even this, however, did not make armed conflict inevitable, though it began to make it more likely. The civil war broke out only when all the possibilities of a peaceful political settlement of the crisis appeared to both sides to have been exhausted.

There is little agreement on what the initial priorities of the Long Parliament were, and who led them. The two main interpretations both present problems. The older one portrays the gentry in the Commons, led by John Pym, as determined to carry out a constitutional revolution, securing parliament's role for the future and limiting the royal prerogative in order to prevent a return to personal rule. The Long Parliament did pass some measures extending the role of parliament and limiting the royal prerogative in its first six months: the Triennial Act ensuring regular parliaments in future in February 1641, and a further Act in May protecting the current parliament from dissolution without its own consent. But legislation to abolish Ship Money and the courts of Star Chamber and High Commission began to be debated seriously only in May, and these, along with others abolishing unpopular financial expedients of the 1630s, were pushed through with some urgency only when it became clear in early July that the king intended to go to Scotland (Fletcher, 1981, pp. 22, 28, 30, 49). It is not clear whether such measures had been part of the 'ambitious plans' of the Commons' leadership from the start (Kenyon, 1966, p. 190), but nor were they 'random, piecemeal measures' (Kenyon, 1986, p. 176). A coherent constitutional programme to limit the royal prerogative and abolish the institutions believed to be connected with its extension did emerge in the spring of 1641 during the debates on a Bill designed to reform the proceedings of Star Chamber, whether it was planned in advance or not (Fletcher, 1981, p. 30).

As far as leadership is concerned, the fascination of many historians with John Pym is problematic. The leading accounts of Pym's role, whether admiring or deprecating his activities, devote as much effort to explaining why the Commons often did not follow his lead, and to distinguishing certain important measures as 'independent initiatives', as to celebrating his leadership and control of the house (Hexter, 1941; Fletcher, 1981, pp. 38–40). A recent reassessment, based on Pym's contributions to debate noted in parliamentary diaries, argues that although he was one of the most active members of the Commons, with a particular interest in anti-Catholic measures and the reform of the king's finances, and had important links with opposition peers, he did not take the policy initiatives which have frequently been attributed to him (Morrill, 1995). To many revisionists, Pym was essentially a humble dependant of the Earl of Bedford, furthering the plans of his patron and other peers with their own clients in the House of Commons, plans for an aristocratic coup modelled on medieval examples of baronial opposition to weak rulers (Russell, 1984a; Adamson, 1990). In this scheme, parliament was 'to be used more as a forum than as an agent', in order to impose on the king a new council which would change his policies and restore his credibility (Russell, 1991, pp. 207–8). Most active members of the House of Commons, it has been claimed, 'sat as the clients, relatives and friends of peers', acting as their 'dutiful subordinates'whose political actions were 'passive and instrumental' (Christianson, 1977, p. 577; Farnell, 1977, pp. 643–4). There is indeed a problem with historians who have seen the opposition peers as 'Pym's men' or Pym 'using the House of Lords as a stalking horse', but the theory of a planned baronial coup raises as many problems as this previous distortion (Fletcher, 1981, pp. 75, 261).

When some of the peers who had opposed the Scottish wars were appointed to the privy council in March 1641, they apparently did not attend regularly, and refused to give their opinions on matters currently under discussion in parliament, implying that they saw parliament as an agent rather than a mere forum (Fletcher, 1981, pp. 45–6). The same peers refused to compromise on the execution of the Earl of Strafford, though the king made it clear that any deal on new appointments would depend on his life being spared (ibid., p. 14). The so-called 'Bedford plan' for getting the opposition into office may have been an unsuccessful attempt by the king to buy Strafford's life by offering rewards to his opponents, since the rumours about it came from the court rather than from the peers themselves (Ashton, 1978, pp. 138–9). The appointments of Bedford's lawyer Oliver St. John as solicitor-general and Lord Saye as Master of the Wards fell short of the major changes which were rumoured before Bedford's sudden death on 9 May 1641. A careful reading of Russell's influential chapter on the negotiations between king and parliament in early 1641 would suggest that the evidence that these were masterminded by a group of peers seeking office for themselves is almost entirely second- or even third-hand, or even purely circumstantial, like St. John's notes on medieval legislation made many years before, or the fact that medieval state offices were named among those for which parliament wished to approve appointments (Russell, 1991, pp. 237–74, p. 151 n.; Morrill, 1993, pp. 10–13). It is quite possible that some of the opposition peers, such as the Earl of Essex, did indeed have in mind the medieval precedents for a noble *coup d'etat* (Adamson, 1990), but to suppose that this was the only motivation present among the parliamentary opposition is a somewhat blinkered approach.

The Commons recognized that it was the traditional role of nobles to advise the monarch, they criticized Charles for distancing himself from most of his nobility, and they showed support for those peers who opposed him, but they did not at first demand parliamentary control over the appointment of councillors. They were not even keen to name 'evil counsellors' once they had disposed of Strafford and Laud. When the matter was debated in June 1641, there was no attempt to claim control of appointments or even to exercise a veto over new ones, though Pym threatened to name the evil counsellors to be removed (Fletcher, 1981, pp. 56–8; Russell, 1991, pp. 350–4). Only in August 1641, when the king was about to leave for Scotland, did the Commons demand specific appointments for two peers, Pembroke and Salisbury, who had not been among the pro-Scots group or those who called for a parliament in 1640, though they had opposed Strafford. The House of Lords turned down this proposal, together with one for a regent to be appointed during the king's absence (Fletcher, 1981, pp. 58–9). If the Commons did have 'faith in the traditions of noble paternalism' the lords apparently did not encourage them (Morrill, 1993, p. 13).

In the Commons debates on the Grand Remonstrance in November 1641, the proposal that parliament should approve the king's advisers did not come from Pym or his circle. A court source claiming that it came from Pym suggested that he was inspired by the recent settlement in Scotland, rather than the interests of any patron (Fletcher, 1981, p. 142). The Grand Remonstrance itself, like the Ten Propositions in June, appealed to the king only to appoint 'such councillors ... as the parliament may have cause to confide in', though the remonstrance also suggested a possible parliamentary veto on future appointments (Gardiner, 1906, p. 231). Historians who see this as an attempt to take over the executive functions of government, whether for aristocratic or constitutional motives, have to argue that its supporters intended far more than they said in debate (Russell, 1991, p. 426). The Nineteen Propositions, in June 1642, included the first proposal that parliament should actually approve all appointments to the privy council and major offices of state. The first draft of this document seems to have originated with the Commons and to have been delayed by the Lords for several months (Fletcher, 1981, pp. 261–2). If Pym really was all along pushing an aristocratic plan to put opposition nobles in power, one would have to ask why it was so slow to make headway in either house of parliament, and whether this was why it failed, despite the presence of the Scots army in England, to coerce the king. The House of Commons acted significantly more like an independent institution than the instrument of an aristocratic faction in 1640–2, and by reducing events in the Long Parliament to a baronial plot, revisionist historians are falling more deeply into the same trap as previous historians who reduced it to a constitutional revolution. It makes more sense to see within the parliamentary opposition in 1640–2 an interplay of several different motivations and strategies.

In the first six months of the Long Parliament the trial of Strafford, together with proceedings against other royal servants and advisers and the compensation of victims of injustice, took up most of the Commons' time, indicating what their priorities were. First and foremost, they wanted a 'revolution' in the contemporary sense of a drastic change in government policies and personnel, rather than a change in the system of government or the structure of society. However, they wanted Strafford to die not only because he gave the king bad advice, but because they believed that he posed a threat to the 'fundamental laws' of the kingdom. Since he had apparently advised the king, after the Short Parliament, that he was 'loosed and absolved from all rules of government, being reduced to extreme necessity, everything is to be done as power will admit', their fears are understandable (Russell, 1991, p. 126). They had some difficulty in proving Strafford guilty of treason. They argued that his advice caused a breach between the king and his people which could endanger the monarch's life, that a number of non-treasonous acts could cumulatively amount to treason, and that to attack the fundamental laws was more serious than to attack the king's person. Eventually they secured his death by an act of attainder, which simply required the consent of king, Lords and Commons, rather than by a judicial decision (Russell, 1965). The parliamentarians were evidently reluctant to base their actions on the principle of resistance to the king, but they believed that behind Strafford and other evil counsellors lay a deliberate intention to change the basis of the English monarchy from a legal, constitutional regime into 'the civil tyranny of an arbitrary, unlimited, confused government,' as Pym put it (Kenyon, 1986, p.192).

The attack on Strafford also shows that, despite their frequent use of religious language, parliamentarians gave priority to politics. Archbishop Laud was a more obvious target for their religious concerns; but Laud was not arrested until March 1641, and tried in late 1644 (Fletcher, 1981, p. 6). The politics of religion in the early months of the parliament seem to have been handled cautiously and with a regard for unity. The new canons for the Church of England made by the convocation of the clergy in June 1640 were attacked on constitutional grounds, for implying that parliament had no authority to change the church and that the clergy could make laws (Russell, 1991, pp. 231–4). Though some MPs now believed that the only solution to the problem of Laudianism was to abolish episcopacy, they did not regard this as a non-negotiable issue. The Commons failed to reach agreement on abolition several times between May and September 1641, and prioritized removing bishops from the House of Lords instead. When it came to the Grand Remonstrance, a clause calling for the abolition of bishops was proposed, but according to one of its supporters, 'we saw that the party for episcopacy was so strong as we were willing to lay the clause aside without further trouble'(ibid., p. 426). The remonstrance as agreed proposed to deal with the bishops by 'removing them from their temporal power and employments, that so the better they might with meekness apply themselves to the discharge of their functions', and to leave further reform to a synod of theologians (Kenyon, 1986, pp. 215–16).

The main reason for the Commons' persisting with controversial religious proposals seems to have been pressure from outside, including the massive petition from London in December 1640, demanding the abolition of episcopacy 'with all its dependencies, roots and branches', and similar 'root and branch' petitions from nineteen counties during 1641 (Fletcher, 1981, pp. 91–107). There was also diplomatic pressure from the Scots, who now saw episcopacy in England as a threat to their security (Russell, 1991, pp. 168–70). A total of 900 petitions against 'scandalous ministers' were presented to the Commons from December 1640 onwards, but it was not until September 1641 that they issued a specific order against recent innovations in religious ceremonies and furnishings. By then an Anglican party, defending the bishops and the prayer book, had come into existence, and the House of Lords issued a more conservative order on church worship (Morrill, 1993, pp. 69–90; Fletcher, 1981, pp. 111–24). Religion was becoming a more divisive issue.

From the beginning of the Long Parliament, there was substantial agreement on the expulsion of Catholic priests and the implementation of the anti-Catholic recusancy laws. Many members believed that the presence of a papal agent at court, the prominence of certain Catholic courtiers, and the king's wholesale pardoning of

Jesuits, were further indications of an international Catholic plot against England. Fear of Catholicism was strong, but it must be seen in the context of developments at court, in Ireland and elsewhere, for which we have substantial evidence. It would be 'wrong to discuss the fears they expressed as either hypocritical or groundless'. We now know, for example, that Charles was during these months attempting to borrow money from the pope to help him raise an army (Hibbard, 1983, pp. 168–79). The behaviour of the House of Commons does not wholly support the view that they were dominated by fear of Catholicism: Strafford, their prime target, had possibly the strongest anti-Catholic record among the king's close advisers (Fletcher, 1983, p. 156). When we read in the Grand Remonstrance that the danger to England lies in 'a malignant and pernicious design of subverting the fundamental laws and principles of government, on which the religion and justice of this kingdom are firmly established', it is difficult to say whether government or religion has priority (Kenyon, 1986, p. 210).

After Strafford's execution, the parliamentarians went on to develop their programme of constitutional reform, and by the time the king left for Scotland in August, they seemed to have broken enough new ground to prevent any repetition of the personal rule of the 1630s. Why did the members not, then, go home and celebrate these achievements after a session which had already become the longest ever? This question has often been asked, especially by historians who stress the parliamentarians' limited aims and conservative thinking (Coward, 1980, pp. 160–2; Russell, 1990a, pp. 16–24). One explanation is that the parliamentary leaders mistrusted Charles, fearing that he would disregard the concessions he had made once they dispersed. There were good grounds for mistrusting the king, above all the evidence for the 'Army Plots'exposed to the Commons in the spring of 1641. It appears that Charles had been making contingency plans for a violent response to the condemnation of Strafford, and during the trial he sent a band of mercenaries under an Irish officer to occupy the Tower of London. This was prevented by a combination of the citizens of London, the lieutenant of the Tower, and the House of Lords (Russell, 1991, pp. 221–3). As the king journeyed from London to Edinburgh during August, he passed through his northern army, not yet wholly disbanded, and it was not unrealistic to fear that he might still use it against the parliament (Fletcher, 1981, p. 53). While in Edinburgh, he was almost certainly involved in a plot to capture and possibly kill the Marquis of Hamilton and the Earl of Argyll, known as the 'Incident' (Russell, 1991, pp. 322–8). The plots failed or fizzled out, and Charles I did not return to take London by force; but it is important to remember that even the best-informed people of the time could not be sure of this. The members of parliament were deeply alarmed by the possibility of a royal military coup when Pym told them of the 'Incident' in October. The idea that their concern was diminishing, and that the Commons were about to reject Pym's leadership, and would have settled with the king and dissolved themselves had the Irish rebellion not broken out (Russell, 1990a, p. 213), seems to be an echo in some historians' minds of royalist propaganda and wishful thinking (Fletcher, 1981, pp. 128–36).

Parliament also sat on in late 1641 because they were nowhere near to completing their plans for legislation. Though the major constitutional acts in which historians have shown most interest were completed, much was still not done. Among the outstanding constitutional matters were putting the militia on a legal footing and permanently settling the king's revenues. Since the beginning of the session they had granted Charles the customs revenue for two months at a time, and they could not reasonably dissolve themselves without a more permanent settlement. There were also many issues which had been urged on the members by their constituents, as remedies for the grievances which had accumulated during the personal rule. Even in the spring of 1642 the Commons were still trying to catch up with Bills on the control of new building, the relief of maimed and shipwrecked seamen, the draining of fenlands, and many other matters (Fletcher, 1981, p. 251).

From November 1641, however, conflict between the king and parliament intensified and divisions among the members deepened. News of the Irish rebellion convinced most parliamentarians that defence was now an urgent matter which they could not leave to the king. Pym proposed to the Commons that they should inform the king that they would not consider themselves obliged to help him to restore order in Ireland unless he removed his evil counsellors. After debate, they agreed on a statement that although they would not waver from their allegiance they would, if he refused to appoint better advisers, 'take such a course for the securing of Ireland as might likewise secure ourselves' (ibid., pp. 143–4).

They eventually did this, taking control of England's defences into their own hands through the Militia Ordinance of March 1642, and launching the 'adventurers' fund to raise money for combating the Irish rebellion, promising Irish land in return for English money (Bottigheimer, 1971).

These measures were not taken, however, until Charles had further damaged his own credibility by minor military actions which seemed to threaten far worse. Soon after the king's return to London in November 1641, the Earl of Dorset ordered the guards surrounding parliament to fire on a crowd of demonstrators, but was fortunately not obeyed. When in late December the king attempted to place the Tower of London in the hands of an officer of murderous reputation called Lunsford, the London populace were so alarmed that tens of thousands turned out on the biggest demonstrations yet, linking the threat to their own safety with the power of the bishops in the House of Lords and demanding their removal. When royalist officers drew swords against the demonstrators on 29 December, they were feasted by the king that evening. Charles's attempt to arrest one peer and five members of the House of Commons on 4 January 1642, attended by a force of 400 armed men, utterly discredited himself and his supporters, and led to such a threatening display of solidarity between the parliament and the London citizens that within days the king had fled London (Fletcher, 1981, pp. 172–84; Lindley, 1997, pp. 121–4).

The raising of the issue of the ultimate control of military force brought civil war nearer, and parliament passed an ordinance in March 1642 placing the militia throughout the country under the control of its own nominees. Charles made his way to York, making plans to raise an army and attracting an entourage of 'cavaliers', a nickname reflecting their unconcealed enthusiasm for military adventure. The king's attempt in April to enter Hull and remove the arms stored there, which was obstructed by parliament's emissary Sir John Hotham, was regarded as an outright provocation, and in May the parliament declared that Charles had made war on his people, justifying further military measures. But a 'peace party' emerging within the Commons still hoped to avoid conflict by securing some kind of accommodation with the king. Although many historians have regarded the Nineteen Propositions of early June as an ultimatum to the king which made some kind of appeal to arms inevitable, the response of the Commons to the king's rejection of the propositions was to debate them further and water down their most innovative demands. As late as July 1642, one member argued that the parliament had already achieved what in the past would have seemed 'a dream of happiness', and should not 'contend for such a hazardous unsafe security as may endanger the loss of what we have already' (Fletcher, 1981, pp. 272–81).

The paradox of 1642 is often said to be that it saw the outbreak of a war which nobody wanted. It is hard to say at what point civil war became inevitable, because apparently sincere attempts to reach agreement went on up to and even beyond the start of the fighting. Yet we must remember that royalists and parliamentarians were deeply engaged in a battle for public opinion. In order to mobilize the moderate support they would need if it came to war, each side tried to keep as much of the middle ground as possible, and especially to claim that the other side started the fighting. Parliamentarians were particularly aware of the likelihood that 'whoever was blamed for the outbreak of civil war would lose it' (Russell, 1991, p. 459). Parliament's military preparations were initially made in the name of national defence – indeed, in the name of the king himself – against the threat of Catholic attack. In the summer of 1642 it became ever clearer that if they were to fight anyone it would be the king, but the promoters of military preparedness were still arguing that 'if we receive a gracious message from the king ... then we shall quickly and easily undo that which we have done' (Fletcher, 1981, p. 274). They continued to hope for a victory without the use of military force, and expected the threat of force to deter the king.

It has been argued that the king was less reluctant to use force, and repeatedly raised the stakes in the process of escalation which led to the war (Russell, 1984a). If this is the case, then his main problem in early 1642 was lack of support. The nobility and gentry did not at first flock to join him at York, and it has been suggested that if he had started the civil war in May, he would have lost it without a battle (Russell, 1991, p. 496). Yet there were political pressures on Charles also to present his case as a moderate one and label the parliamentarians as extremists, and it must be remembered that he had by this time a significant body of support in the House of Commons, led by Edward Hyde (the future Earl of Clarendon and royalist historian) and others. The importance of this kind of 'constitutional royalist' support to Charles is shown in his reply to the Nineteen Propositions on 18 June, with its repudiation of absolute monarchy and charge of constitutional innovation against his opponents (Kenyon, 1986, pp. 18–20). At the same time he was trying to seize control of the militia for himself through the commissions of array, which were intended to override parliament's ordinance, and it was an ill-concealed secret that he had sent the queen abroad to raise money to finance an army. He was actually rather slow to raise a viable full army, however, and it has been a matter of debate whether this slowness was because he had less support than he expected, or because he was not really trying until late summer (Malcolm, 1978, 1983; Wanklyn and Young, 1981). Although both sides were threatening violence, both were, understandably, reluctant to bear responsibility for the horrors of a civil war, and the fact that they did so in the end has to be attributed to their having exhausted the alternatives. It had proved impossible for either the king or the parliamentarians to win a bloodless victory by force of argument, or to arrive at a viable political compromise. The protagonists eventually recognized that a peaceful solution was not going to happen, and each side acquired a party that was prepared to fight. To explain how this happened, however, it is not enough to look at events in parliament; we shall have to examine the ways in which the wider nation responded to the political conflict.

A Nation Divided

Many historians believe there was a wide gulf between the political leaders and the rest of the nation. For one, the war appeared in the localities as a 'most surprising and unintended catastrophe'; for another, it was a struggle between the partisans of both sides and the bulk of the population who did not want war (Fletcher, 1983, p. 174; Hutton, 1982, p. 51). Another holds that it was 'the force of religion that drove minorities to fight, and forced majorities to make reluctant choices'(Morrill, 1993, p. 47). For a time, the consensus among historians tended towards the view that sides were chosen on the basis of local issues, including the political commitments and internecine rivalries of county magnates who drew in the gentry as their clients and supporters (Everitt, 1969b). Few would now deny, however, that broad layers of the population were aware of national issues, even if their knowledge came in a somewhat distorted form through news and gossip, or through the ballads which commented on events such as the elections of 1640 (Cust, 1989; Sharpe, 1992, p. 856).

The argument that those who took up arms in 1642 did so mainly for religious motives might seem to relegate other divisions and allegiances to a minor place (Morrill, 1993, pp. 45–89). Local panics about Catholic plots or invasions throughout the country did play a part in heightening tension in 1642, and Charles's commissioning of Catholic officers in his army did not help his cause. Royalist propaganda appealed to opposite fears about 'anabaptists and atheists', who were allegedly threatening the established church. Yet many royalists were anti-Catholic and many parliamentarians were opposed to all religious sects outside the Church of England, so that the religious dividing line is as hard to draw as the political one. Puritan preachers seem to have been less reluctant than most people to contemplate the violence of civil war, but if one looks carefully at a recent account of Puritan pamphleteering in the 1640s, it does seem that they were anxious to avoid an overt call to armed resistance before war had actually broken out (Baskerville, 1993). Sermons such as Stephen Marshall's exposition of God's curse on Meroz (who failed to fight for the Lord's cause) in April 1642, in which he stated that 'if this work be to revenge God's church against Babylon, he is a blessed man that takes and dashes the little ones against the stones'(Hunt, 1983, p. 296), may horrify us now, but the religious language of the time often included such violent metaphors. The

Old Testament is full of them (Hill, 1993). Besides, Marshall's warlike images in his Meroz sermon were provisional: 'It may be', he said, 'that some of you may be called, as soldiers, to spend your blood in the church's cause' (ibid., p. 89). Perhaps the biggest difficulty, however, is distinguishing between religion as an independent motive and religion as a legitimation for political conflict. Both parties to the civil war, inevitably in a society where religion and politics were closely interconnected, claimed to have God on their side, and it would have been hard for most men to take up arms if they had not believed this. Before deciding on this issue, religious motivations must be placed in the context of the social and political issues in seventeenth-century England, which will be examined in later chapters.

Between 1640 and 1642 more people than ever before in England became aware of national political issues and involved in some kind of political action. From early 1640 local petitions were organized, urging the parliament to remedy popular grievances and supporting members who went up with a commitment to reforms (Sharpe, 1992, pp. 858–60). By early 1642 organized petitioning involved ordinary villagers as well as county gentry, and ensured that a wide range of people were kept informed about political matters. The petitions show 'that the hunger for news so evident at this time represented a real involvement in political affairs and a sensitivity to national issues' (Fletcher, 1981, p. 223). Petitions and other forms of popular participation in the crisis of 1640–2 must be taken into account in any explanation of the civil war, which was the first conflict of its kind to involve more than a tiny minority of the population in national issues. This is what made it different from the baronial wars of the late Middle Ages.

There were several waves of petitioning, beginning with the demand for the abolition of bishops in the early months of 1641. Though these petitions were clearly organized by groups of Puritan activists, they were often supported by more moderate opinion, since they included positive proposals for moral and social reform and implied that the laity should have more control over the church. Religious polarization in the counties did not become evident until the autumn of 1641, when county petitions were organized to defend the bishops and the prayer book against the alleged extremism of the Puritans (Fletcher, 1981, pp. 91–6, 283–91). The many petitions drawing attention to local difficulties caused by the decline of trade and manufacture in the uncertain political situation between January and March 1642 showed that localism – defending primarily the interests of one's own county or town – was also a powerful motivation for political involvement, alongside national issues and religious partisanship (ibid., pp. 223, 379–80).

The organization of national support for parliament's political perspective in 1641–2, however, involved a new feature: deliberate campaigning among layers of the population not normally involved in political activity. The House of Commons took the lead in seeking political support among the population at large with the Protestation of May 1641, an oath of allegiance to defend Protestantism, the king, parliament and 'the lawful rights and liberties of the subject'. The printing of the Grand Remonstrance in December was also an innovatory and controversial appeal to a wider audience. Their supporters in the localities effectively launched the first major grassroots campaign in early 1642, when they sought the 'general subscriptions of the multitude' for petitions supporting continued opposition to arbitrary government and defence of the country against the Catholic threat. These local efforts to mobilize popular opinion combined the respectability of institutional backing, such as grand juries and county meetings, with the impact of numbers. The actual numbers of county subscriptions, including those of 'villagers who could only manage a crabbed hand, a scrawl or an ungainly mark', ranged from 560 in Rutland to 30,000 in Essex (ibid., pp. 191–9). The petitions did not show support for civil war but an intense desire to avoid it, and the historian who has examined them feels that they do not exhibit the intense and irrational mistrust of the king which he sees in the opposition leaders at Westminster (ibid., pp. 406–19).

The politics of petitioning may be read in other ways, however. The flood of petitions addressed to parliament in early 1642 unambiguously adopted the opposition leaders' perspective on the defence of Protestantism and the subjects' liberties, and congratulated the parliament on its achievements in remedying the people's grievances so far. On the other hand, the petitions in which seventeen counties called for accommodation, or compromise, between March and November 1642 were almost all addressed to the king (ibid., pp. 268–70). Both campaigns show a strong desire to avoid war, but it is parliament which is urged on to a peaceful victory and the king who is warned that his actions, especially in leaving London and threatening further military force, are a danger to peace. The success these petitioning campaigns achieved by adopting a tone of moderation and the language of consensus surely also helps to explain the cautious attitudes of the parliamentary leaders in 1642. Though not exactly opinion polls, the petitions seemed to demonstrate, in the form of fat parchment rolls physically dumped in front of the Commons, the enormous size of the middle ground whose support they would need if it came to war (ibid., p. 195).

Many of those who would eventually fight in the civil war on one side or the other were reluctant to take up arms. Local élites in many counties and towns at some point made agreements not to raise forces for either side, to try to keep armies raised elsewhere out of their area and to petition both sides for peace; and in a few places this was occurring as late as the end of 1642, when the war was well under way. There has been much debate about the meaning of this wave of 'neutralism', but few historians would now identify it with apathy. It has been argued that it reflects deep-rooted provincialism, lack of understanding of constitutional issues and remoteness from national politics (Everitt, 1969b; Morrill, 1980). But a desire to protect local trade and property, to keep tenants and labourers where they were as both sides began recruiting during the harvest period, or to keep the county's stock of arms from being taken elsewhere, need not be identified with lack of commitment to the principles of either side (Fletcher, 1981, pp. 379–90). Some local neutrality pacts may have been a stratagem by those who felt they were at a disadvantage, to gain time or to prevent the other side from mobilizing (Hughes, 1989, p. 237). It was later alleged, for example, that the Yorkshire royalists who signed a county peace treaty in September 1642 were at the same time appealing for outside help from the Earl of Newcastle's army (ibid.; Malcolm, 1983, pp.

60–2). The most successful neutrality pacts appear to have been those in Staffordshire and Lincolnshire, but both collapsed before the end of the year, and it is doubtful whether they can really be regarded as a 'third force' offering an alternative to royalists and parliamentarians (Fletcher, 1981, pp. 385–7).

It was often difficult to choose sides in 1642, especially for people who had been accustomed to believe that loyalty to the king and to parliament were inseparable. When faced with conflicting orders from the very bodies which were supposed to maintain balance and harmony in the constitution, men and women accustomed to leadership in their communities agonized. 'Both sides promise so fair, that I cannot see what it is they should fight for', wrote Lady Sussex, while one gentleman attempted 'to steer the bark of state betwixt Scylla and Charybdis' and the Devonshire justices described their anguish 'whilst a twofold obedience, like twins in the womb, strives to be born to both' (Morrill, 1980, pp. 35, 162). Humbler people also, like the tenants of a Cheshire royalist landlord, stressed this dual allegiance: 'We would not for the world harbour a disloyal thought against his majesty', they assured him, 'yet we dare not lift up our hands against the honourable assembly of parliament'. Some of these tenants soon joined the parliamentarian forces, but it is very likely that the decision was as difficult for them as for their social superiors (Manning, 1991, pp. 268–9).

Although the choice was difficult, however, it was not arbitrary. The propertied classes on both sides had in common the fear that a breakdown of order was imminent in 1642, as outbreaks of rioting, hedge levelling, mass poaching and attacks on the houses of Catholic nobles and gentry spread (Morrill, 1980, pp. 34–5; Fletcher, 1981, pp. 374–5; Manning, 1991, pp. 242–318). But these fears did not necessarily produce neutrality. The king appealed to them in his answer to the Nineteen Propositions, foretelling 'a dark, equal chaos of confusion' and the end of nobility and social distinctions if royal authority were not maintained (Kenyon, 1986, p. 20). On the other hand, parliamentarians claimed that property was in danger, and that Charles's claims would 'pull up the very foundation of the liberty, property and interest of every subject in particular' (ibid., p. 221). There came a point at which many people of property and influence felt that the social order they wanted could be preserved only by a victory for one side or the other, and had to make up their minds which was the greater threat: popular violence or royal tyranny. This was a political choice, which depended on their understanding of their own social position and how it was related to power and authority, in their own communities as well as nationally. In some counties, the pattern of politics among the gentry had long been dominated by a few noble families whose supporters among the gentry followed them into the civil war. But such solid allegiances had in some cases, such as the county of Essex, been maintained by overt political and religious commitments rather than by simple deference and tradition (Hunt, 1983). In other counties a series of disputed elections, or a more open and competitive power structure, meant that political divisions already existed before 1640, while in some local areas the existence of Puritan enclaves had polarized opinion around the issues of religious authority and freedom (Fletcher, 1983). The influence of local magnates seems to have been less important than the complex of social relationships within each community, and there can be little doubt that pre-existing divisions and allegiances within English society played an important part in facilitating civil war once all attempts at political compromise had failed. Part of our enquiry into the causes of the civil war must be concerned with why the structures of power within English society proved so unstable when the fatal political breakdown occurred at the centre.

Attempts to explain allegiances in the civil war on the basis of differences in economic and social development must begin with Christopher Hill's contrast between the 'economically backward areas of the north and west' which were royalist, and 'the economically advanced south and east' which were parliamentarian (Hill, 1961, pp. 121–2). This was never a simple division, for most regions were divided internally, and the counties where urban cloth manufacturers and rural gentry were most sharply opposed were Yorkshire and Lancashire in the 'royalist' north. For a time, historians gave most weight to the composition of the gentry in each county, suggesting major differences between counties where the élite were of relatively recent and external origin and those where gentry families were older, more local and inward-looking (Everitt, 1969b, pp. 18–42). It came to be seen, however, that an analysis of the county gentry alone was too narrow a basis for distinguishing patterns of allegiance (Holmes, 1980; Hughes, 1989). Freeholders and even tenants did not necessarily follow the lead of the local gentry, and in some areas such as Somerset and Lancashire there seems to have been widespread popular opposition to royalist landlords. Where the gentry of a county were divided, it might even be that in effect 'the people were choosing between one set of rulers and another' (Manning, 1991, pp. 262–70).

A ground-breaking analysis of western England has suggested that royalist and parliamentarian sympathizers tended to come from two different regional cultures, characterized on the one hand by arable farming which was dominated by the landlord and traditional culture, and on the other by pasture farming, extensive woodlands, more rural industries and a more individualistic culture (Underdown, 1987). Each of these regional cultures produced a distinctive pattern of religious and political allegiance, reflecting a long-term divergence of 'two opposed political, economic and ecological systems' (Underdown, 1996, p. 48). But even within particular counties, there were many variations in the local economy and society in the seventeenth century, so that any close analysis produces a patchwork picture of great complexity. Local patterns of allegiance in 1642 make most sense when each county is seen as 'a unique combination or configuration of various elements ... present in all counties', the most important of these features being 'the geographical, economic and social divisions within them; the degree of cohesion amongst the social elite; and the nature of ideological, especially religious divisions' (Hughes, 1989, pp. 231–2). Recent explorations of local divisions and allegiances do have the merit of recognizing that popular royalism existed and has to be explained, as well as popular parliamentarianism. Economic and social 'backwardness', or the alleged passivity of tenants and labourers in the more remote areas, can no longer be regarded as sufficient explanation. Derbyshire lead miners, who had protested for many years against the tithe they had to pay to the church, supported the king in 1642 because they succeeded in bargaining with him, and agreed to provide recruits for his army only when he promised to abolish the hated tithe. This can hardly be described as passive or traditional behaviour (Wood, 1997, pp. 32–3).

As well as examining the ways in which the country divided in response to the conflict between king and parliament, we also need to look at the influence that divisions in the country may have had on the breakdown of relations at the centre. Several historians believe that intervention by the masses in national politics during 1640–2 decisively shaped the course of events (Manning, 1991; Lindley, 1997). London is especially important, for the impact of its citizens through petitions, demonstrations and the granting or refusing of financial support was immediate at several important points in the developments of 1640–2. In refusing to lend more money without the security of parliamentary taxation in 1639, and in demanding guarantees that the Long Parliament would not be dissolved by the king as the Short Parliament had been, the London merchant community had an important influence on constitutional developments from the start, though most of the ruling group who took the lead in 1639–40 were to choose the king's side in the war (Pearl, 1961).

The well-organized petitions demanding radical religious reform, which bore thousands of signatures and were presented by leading London citizens arriving in their coaches and wearing their best clothes, had, as we have seen, a vital influence on the opponents of episcopacy in parliament, who showed signs of being prepared to compromise had it not been for this pressure. The opening of the trial of Strafford saw similar petitions and demonstrations, led by 'men of good rank and quality' including several captains of the city militia. More spontaneous demonstrations were inspired around the same time by panics about real and imagined threats: the king's attempt to seize control of the Tower of London, and a rumour that the houses of parliament had been set on fire, apparently set off by an unfortunate description of heated debates as 'hot work and a great fire within' (Lindley, 1997, pp. 21–5). Control of the Tower was again an issue in December 1641, when merchants withdrew their bullion from the mint there in protest at Lunsford's appointment. The large demonstrations on this issue became a decisive outside intervention in parliamentary decision-making, effectively securing the exclusion of bishops from the House of Lords by preventing some of the bishops and their supporters from attending. Crowds of demonstrators became involved in violent clashes with Lunsford and his swordsmen in Westminster Hall, with the guards surrounding the royal palace of Whitehall, and with the archbishop of York's men at Westminster Abbey (ibid., pp. 103–13). At the London elections in late 1641, the city's government was taken over by men sympathetic to parliament, and their support was crucial in the early days of 1642, when the Commons took refuge in the London Guildhall after Charles's attempted coup. The spontaneous mobilization of the city militia on the night of 5–6 January – with over 100,000 men on the streets, women boiling water to throw on invaders and barricades of household furniture erected in the streets – gave Charles little choice but to leave his capital (ibid., pp. 4–35, 91–157).

Royalist historians always assumed that the London mobs were organized by the opposition leaders in parliament, and a modern one believes that there were men who 'could pour a mob into Westminster easily and on demand as a bar maid pours ale into a mug' (Hexter, 1941, p. 95). But such explanations seem to the latest historian of London radicalism 'highly improbable and almost certainly unnecessary' (Lindley, 1997, p. 32). The 1640–2 demonstrations were organized by groups of London religious and political radicals whose existence is well documented, from the pro-parliamentarian merchants who took control of the city in the 1641 elections to the Puritan activists, separatists and others who were to influence the revolution of the late 1640s (Brenner, 1993, pp. 199–315; Lindley, 1997). London was, moreover, a divided city, with significant groupings of support for the king and opposition to religious radicalism throughout the civil war, though these never mobilized mass political support on the scale of the pro-parliamentarian demonstrations.

Moderates in parliament were horrified by the London demonstrations, even the most respectable such as those which presented the 'root and branch' petition of December 1640. One MP was 'scandalized that such a great number came', and when the petition was debated later another appealed to his fellow members 'not to be led on by passion to popular and vulgar errors'. Another future royalist warned that this mass demand for 'an equality in things ecclesiastical' would inevitably lead to 'the like equality in things temporal' and to the dreaded *lex agraria* or agrarian law, a reference to the undermining of landed property in ancient Rome which sprang to many moderate minds whenever a crowd appeared (Fletcher, 1981, p. 123). They expressed the same fears about the rural rioting of 1640–2, most of which was certainly less overtly political than the London demonstrations (see chapter 5).

The direct effects of the London crowds' intervention in parliamentary politics were significant, but the indirect effects of this and other popular actions in 1640–2 were greater. Demonstrations of popular discontent divided the members of parliament and the ruling élite throughout the country into those who saw them as manifestations of justified dissatisfaction with the rule of Charles I which could be stopped only by removing the causes of their discontent, and those who saw them as a threat to the existing order which could be averted only by the reassertion of royal authority. The 'popularity' of parliamentarians such as Pym, who opposed a move to ban petitioning, saying 'God forbid that the House of Commons should proceed in any way to dishearten people to obtain their just desires in such a way', stood in stark contrast to the traditional élitism of a future royalist like Digby, who thought it wrong 'to give countenance to irregular, and tumultuous assemblies of people, be it for never so good an end' (Lindley, 1997, pp. 109, 17). Both were concerned to maintain property and order, but for Pym the respectable 'middling sort' were an essential, active part of the constitution which alone could guarantee property and order, while for Digby they were simply there to be ruled (Manning, 1991, pp. 102–30). In this way, the relationship between the ruling élite and other layers of society, in all its regional and local variety, was intimately linked to the political issues which had divided the nation and precipitated the outbreak of civil war.

3

Religious Conflicts

We have seen that religion played an important part in the conflicts involving Scotland and Ireland in the years immediately preceding the civil war, and that it holds a significant place among the issues which divided the Long Parliament and the nation in England. Many historians have not hesitated to claim that religious differences were the chief cause of the civil war in England itself. It has even been suggested that the conflict ought to be renamed 'England's wars of religion', and that England in the 1640s experienced a delayed Reformation crisis such as other European countries had gone through in the sixteenth century, rather than the first modern revolution (Morrill, 1993, pp. 33–44). The main problems with this interpretation would seem to be, first, that England had already experienced upheavals at the time of the Reformation, from the 1530s to the 1550s; and second, that the mid-seventeenth century conflict was unique among early modern wars of religion in that it was not between Protestants and Catholics but between two kinds of Protestants.

It can hardly be denied that religious differences played a prominent part in the situation which led to civil war in England, that religious ideas were important in seventeenth-century society, and that almost no one could take up the sword in such a traumatic internal conflict without believing in some religious legitimation for it. Opposition to Charles's religious policies may even have mobilized some to fight him who had no major objections to other aspects of his rule. It is important to take this religious context seriously, and above all to avoid dismissing religious language as a mere cover for other motives or interests. The vast majority of literate and articulate people in mid-seventeenth century Britain had a religious viewpoint of some kind, which was not only a focus for intense feelings but a major influence on their thoughts and actions. Religious language was a prominent feature of English culture at the time, and the Bible was a reference point for discussion on a huge range of subjects – literally, from astronomy to zoology. As Christopher Hill (1993) has shown, it was not just a case of biblical metaphors being handy and widely understood; whole visions of the world were imagined in biblical language. Humble villagers as well as university-educated clergy believed in the reality of religion, and could share to a greater or lesser extent in this common culture. There were of course sceptics and scoffers, among both the educated and popular layers of society: it simply is not true that 'all our ancestors were literal believers, all of the time'(Laslett, 1983, p. 71). But the culture, the institutions, and the language in which people communicated with one another, took it for granted that religious belief and commitment were normal for that society, as modern Western culture takes for granted a certain level of literacy.

As soon as we move beyond these generalizations, however, we have to examine what we mean by religion. It is a concept whose meaning changes over time, as well as differing between cultures and societies. There is, moreover, a certain danger of subjectivity entering the discussion. While modern historians may still occasionally betray their own Catholic or Protestant biases, for example, on what kind of religion is spiritually satisfying (Morrill, 1993, p. 89; Hill, 1986, pp. 98–100), agnostics, atheists and followers of religions other than Christianity may perhaps regard the religious issues that preoccupied seventeenth-century English people as unworthy of serious analysis because they are too irrational. In the modern Western world, religion is almost universally regarded as a private, personal matter. Its major concerns are the worship of God and the salvation of the individual soul. In early modern Europe, however, Christianity was not only a matter of individual belief and personal commitment. It has been said that the sixteenth-century French wars of religion were about religion 'as defined in contemporary terms: as a body of believers rather than the more modern definition of a body of beliefs' (Holt, 1995, p. 2).

Religion was also about authority and subjection. When Sir John Eliot (who died in prison in 1632 after clashing with royal authority in parliament) wrote that 'religion is that which keeps the subject in obedience', he was stressing the importance of getting religion right, not belittling or challenging it (Doran and Durston, 1991, p. 175). Religion was about the community as a whole, not just the individual, and if the community was not in good spiritual health, it was feared that God would show his displeasure by visiting disaster upon it. An Essex magistrate in 1629 advised that the best way to avoid a poor harvest was to punish the sin of drunkenness, and urged that if other magistrates did the same, 'we should then have less drunkards and less judgements' (Walter and Wrightson, 1976, p. 29). The aim of most serious Christians at the time was not only to practise true religion themselves, but to make sure that others around them also practised it. Religious division in this period, it has been said, 'derived its explosive force from the belief that religion ought to be enforced' rather than from theological doctrines (Russell, 1990a, p. 214).

The concept of a church was also very different from the modern one. For everyone except a very few separatists, there could be only one church in England, to which everyone born in England belonged, or ought to belong: the Church of England. Between 1560 and 1640, the vast majority of critics of the Church of England wanted to change it, not to leave it. When in the 1630s Archbishop Laud and his supporters tried to impose a more rigid conformity on all its members, some dissenters left England altogether, but many of those who stayed joined 'gathered' congregations which did not wholly conform but still considered themselves a legitimate part of the national church, congregations sometimes referred to by historians as semi-separatist (Tolmie, 1977, pp. 28–34). After the war, when there were efforts to replace the old ecclesiastical regime with some kind of new one, the preference for a comprehensive church which would unite the whole of English society remained important even to groups which were to have a future as separate denominations (Hill,

1986, pp. 3–10). The idea of a church as a private association of individuals exercising choice between different modes of worship and routes to salvation was almost non-existent in England before the civil war, and was still rare until the end of the seventeenth century. The most significant alternative view to emerge in the years following the civil war was that of an exclusive church of the true saints of God exercising their right to separate from the ungodly majority, arguing for religious liberty though not for reasons which we would recognize as liberal.

The church in seventeenth-century England, like the Catholic church in medieval Europe, was a multi-functional institution in a society which had not completely compartmentalized religion as a separate area of life and experience. The parish was a very ancient ecclesiastical unit, centred on the village or urban neighbourhood church and its churchyard, but it was also, from 1597, responsible for levying poor rates and administering poor relief under the supervision of the local magistrates. It was therefore both a religious and a secular institution. Yet the boundary between religious and secular matters was not absent, nor something indifferent: it was being contested all the time. The church courts dealt with many matters, such as marital separation and maintenance, or disposal of property by will, which modern societies would consider secular ones – as did some of the outstanding legal specialists of the early seventeenth century like Sir Edward Coke, who spearheaded a lawyers' struggle to remove cases from the church courts to the common law courts (Solt, 1990, pp. 153–8).

It is important, therefore, to situate any discussion of religious divisions in early seventeenth-century England in their contemporary context, and to relate them to what the people of the time meant by religion. This is not to treat religion as 'a sublimation of something else' (Clark, 1986, p. 108), nor to confuse religious beliefs with social relationships (Spufford, 1985). It is also important to be wary of twentieth-century interpretations of religious divisions in terms of modern values – such as liberty and authority, conservatism and radicalism, rationality and spirituality – which were not exactly aligned with opposing religious views at the time. Many revisionist historians make great play of this, pointedly dwelling on the conservatism of the alleged radicals, or the authoritarianism of supposed liberals (Collinson, 1982, pp. 141–88; Lamont, 1996, pp. 55–193). This is useful and necessary up to a point, but it may obscure the real differences that existed between opposing points of view which, when judged by modern standards, seem very similar.

Puritanism: Reform or Reaction?

From Thomas Carlyle to R. H. Tawney and William Haller, Puritanism was seen as the fundamental 'cause' for which the civil war was fought, a movement which in and of itself brought about an ideological polarization of lasting significance. To Carlyle, Puritanism was 'the last of all our Heroisms', to Samuel Gardiner it was a 'struggle onwards and upwards', and according to Tawney, 'it is from its struggle that an England which is unmistakably modern emerges' (Finlayson, 1983, pp. 62–3; Tawney, 1936, pp. 198–9). Haller (1957, p. 5) claimed that it was 'something old, deep-seated, and English' which in the seventeenth century nevertheless 'led to the revolutionizing of English society'.

Since the late 1960s these assumptions about the nature, the significance and even the existence of Puritanism have frequently been questioned. Historians have not generally followed the suggestion that the term should be abandoned as a misleading abstraction (George, 1968). It was used at the time, as early as William Bradshaw's *Puritanisme* in 1605, and its appearance demands some explanation. Nevertheless, many historians have argued that there was no body of ideas or activists that could be identified as a Puritan opposition movement within the Church of England between the 1590s and the 1630s. Puritanism as a movement, they claim, was created by the innovations of Charles and Laud, and the outlook of this Puritan backlash was conservative, defending the consensus of the Elizabethan and Jacobean church against change (Tyacke, 1973). The view that there was a consensus in the English church from the reign of Elizabeth to the accession of Charles I in 1625 has been powerfully supported by the work of Patrick Collinson, who has explored the many things (including sabbatarianism, for example) that those called Puritans had in common with others who were not so called (Collinson, 1982). From this perspective, Charles I and Laud appear as 'revolutionaries' who disrupted the church with sweeping changes, while their opponents were conservatives trying to preserve the church as they and their parents and grandparents had known it. One historian goes so far as to claim that mid-seventeenth century Puritans were 'the legatees, not of a continuous revolutionary tradition, but of a continuous *counter-revolutionary* one' (Lamont 1996, p. 57). We must remember, however, that these 'counter-revolutionaries' were struggling to defend the sixteenth-century Protestant Reformation, an innovatory movement which brought radical changes to Christian doctrine, worship and church organization over much of Western Europe. What the Puritan 'conservatives' opposed was an attempt to turn back the clock and re-emphasize the English church's continuity with the pre-Reformation past (Solt, 1990, p. 178). There is, therefore, a need to re-examine the question of what distinguished Puritans from other members of the Church of England, whether those who were called Puritans can be regarded as a movement before 1625, and whether what bound them together was basically conservative.

What seems to have driven most Puritans in the late sixteenth and early seventeenth centuries was the aim of further reformation. Although few who pursued this aim would have accepted the name 'Puritan' before the 1630s, they were recognized by themselves and one another as 'the godly', 'the well affected' or true 'professors' of the Protestant religion; they were, in Collinson's well-known phrase, 'the hotter sort of Protestants'. But to understand why a commitment to religious reform was not simply a question of being more of a churchgoer than one's neighbours in early seventeenth-century England, it is necessary to understand the nature of the English Reformation and the Elizabethan religious settlement. Although the initial break with the church of Rome had occurred in the 1530s under Henry VIII, England had been a Protestant nation continuously only since 1559, and most historians are agreed that even at that date

Protestants were still in a minority (Doran and Durston, 1991, pp. 190–2). The work of grassroots conversion to Protestantism was long and slow, and although Catholicism had been reduced to a few tens of thousands of followers by 1600, there were still (according to the reformers) far larger numbers who had yet to be touched by a positive commitment to Protestantism. In this sense, the Reformation could be regarded as an ongoing project, not a process completed in 1559.

The Elizabethan settlement had placed England firmly in the Protestant camp within a divided Western Europe, and this was made clear by its adoption of Protestant doctrines. On questions such as the sacraments, the denial of the real presence of Christ in communion, salvation by faith rather than works, and God's choice of the 'elect'alone to be saved, the English position leaned towards the Swiss Reformed churches, including Calvin's Geneva, rather than Lutheranism (Doran and Durston, 1991, pp. 17–22). In terms of worship, however, the 1559 *Book of Common Prayer* preserved the structure of the medieval Catholic Mass, removing the elements most objectionable to Protestant doctrine, such as the displaying of the consecrated bread for worship. The rubrics in this prayer book – the 'stage directions' between the words to be spoken – prescribed the traditional ceremonial clothing, and many medieval rituals were included. To admirers of the Swiss and German Reformed churches, the English church was only half reformed in ceremonies despite the acceptability of its doctrinal beliefs. As far as the structure of church government was concerned, the medieval church was preserved almost entire in England: not only bishops and archbishops, but all the administrative and ceremonial offices such as deans, archdeacons, the diocesan courts with their functionaries and procedures, formal visitations of parishes by representatives of the bishops, and so on, survived intact.

From the European perspective, therefore, the church in England was a unique combination of traditional and reformed elements, and to many Protestants, especially Calvinists, the Reformation had still to be completed. In the reign of Elizabeth, many ministers had resisted the prescribed dress and ceremonies, and a well-organized movement had campaigned to have bishops replaced by a presbyterian system of government. But this first Puritan movement had failed, and had been effectively suppressed by Elizabeth from 1590 onwards (Doran and Durston, 1991, pp. 102–4). Elizabeth had never hesitated to demonstrate that the monarch was the supreme governor of the English church in practice as well as in law, and this was accepted even by the Puritan opposition in her reign. Sixteenth-century English Calvinist ministers never confronted the state with the bitter demarcation disputes over godly authority that broke out in sixteenth-century Scotland, Holland, France and Geneva itself. The explosive confrontation which did come in 1640 was between king and parliament, in Calvinist terms the 'greater' and 'lesser' magistrates, not between magistracy and ministry.

James I's determination to maintain both the royal supremacy and the bishops was equal to Elizabeth's. More than two decades before, he had fought and won victory on both these points in Scotland against a stronger Calvinist faction than England had yet seen. Presbyterian hopes for a change in English church government were dashed; but at the same time James made it clear that he shared the Puritans' view of reformation as an ongoing process, and was sympathetic to both their theology and their preaching mission (Solt, 1990, pp. 130–9). Some ministers were expelled from their posts before 1610, for refusal to use the *Book of Common Prayer* or wear a surplice, and lay people were disciplined for outright refusal to attend their parish church (an offence committed by Catholics more than Puritans). But the main emphasis in the Jacobean church was on reconciliation and working together, and some bishops were celebrated for their success in achieving unity (Collinson, 1982, pp. 39–91). There were undoubtedly non-conformist individuals among both ministers and laity in the reign of James I, though no one seems to be agreed on their numbers, and there were even quietly non-conformist congregations (Collinson, 1983, pp. 1–17). But there were very few 'Nonconformists' as later centuries knew them, that is, separatists who left the main body of the church altogether. Separatist sects had disappeared from England in the repression of the 1580s, and did not reappear until 1616. Though the number of separatist and semi-separatist congregations grew slowly from then on, and their adherents increased especially in the 1630s when Charles and Laud were attempting to impose uniformity on the official church, it has been estimated that even in 1640 truly separatist congregations in England totalled no more than a thousand members (Tolmie, 1977, pp. 7–27).

English Puritanism did not disappear in the reign of James I, but was transformed into an evangelical revival movement which had to some extent the official blessing of the church authorities. Energies which had in the late sixteenth century been directed into Puritan politics were in the early seventeenth channelled into preaching, teaching and writing, and many Puritan activists from the reign of Elizabeth (and their pupils) were involved in this 'hearts and minds' campaign aimed at the manor houses and parish congregations of England (Haller, 1957, pp. 3–82). Most accepted that there was no immediate prospect of changing the church government, and even that the right kind of bishops could be useful to the work of reformation. The most characteristic face of Jacobean Puritanism was its evangelical missionary zeal: the emphasis on bringing the word of God to the believers who were to be saved, the internalization of the Christian message, the traumatic experiences of repentance and regeneration, and the encouragement of 'professors' of Christianity to stand firm in a hostile world. 'Painful preaching' – a favourite phrase which referred both to the care taken by the preacher and the soul-searching that it produced in the audience – was the typical Puritan practice (Hunt, 1983, pp. 113–29; Baskerville, 1993, pp. 49–95).

Informal networks of ministers and lay people sustained this effort of grassroots reform. Puritan gentry supported like-minded ministers through their right of appointing ministers to parish churches (livings) on their estates, and often sheltered those banned from holding a living (Cliffe, 1984, pp. 169–92). Godly members of town oligarchies encouraged Puritan ministers and lecturers to provide sermons on weekdays as well as twice or more on Sundays, to reach people from the surrounding villages coming to market as well as the townspeople. This movement did not include lay preaching: the pastoral role of the trained and ordained minister was still central for Puritans. But it was a cause which sympathetic lay men and women could promote by patronage, by contributions towards the endowment of lectureships, and above all by attending sermons. That lay people were often enthusiastic and keen to hear sermons is shown by frequent complaints about those who 'gadded'to churches outside their own parish to hear preachers. The aim of Puritan reformers was not only to convert individuals to a realization of their own salvation and a more godly way of life, however; it was also to reform each local community by a system of 'godly discipline'. They believed that they saw around them a society dominated by all kinds of wickedness: drinking, gambling, swearing, illicit sex and general looseness of life, which they had a God-given duty to reform for the spiritual health of the community. They called for a more effective repression of such public evils by village leaders, local magistrates and town councils; and since they also believed that these evils caused poverty, they campaigned for more effective policies towards the poor, directing and re-educating them into more godly ways of life (Wrightson and Levine, 1979; Hunt, 1983). Because Puritans were determined to interfere with traditional sociability and popular culture in their fight against loose living, and to confront both individuals and communities with vivid and vehement denunciations of their alleged sinfulness, some historians (like some contemporaries) have seen their activities as fundamentally divisive. To the Puritans themselves, it was bound to be so: because the elect, chosen by God to be saved, were an embattled minority in a hostile world, they would inevitably encounter resistance. The struggle might be divisive, and failure still more so, but to succeed in achieving godly discipline – the orderliness of a 'city on a hill' such as Dorchester or Gloucester in the 1620s and 1630s – was above all to reunify the community under the leadership of the saints (Underdown, 1992; Clark, 1979). To some extent, the Puritans' aim of a godly, disciplined society was shared by the official leadership of the early seventeenth-century church. The bishops' courts punished sexual misdemeanours and enforced sabbath observance too, and Puritans tended to complain about their ineffectiveness rather than their aims, at least before the 1630s (Collinson, 1982; Parker, 1988). It is not so much their aims as their interventionist, activist, participatory methods that distinguish Puritans from other concerned Protestants. Their behaviour cannot have been a conservative force, even if their moral aims differed little from those professed by the mainstream in the Jacobean church.

There has been much argument among historians about whether Puritans had a theological position distinct from that of the Jacobean Anglican mainstream. Puritans were Calvinists – but so, it has been claimed, were most English Protestants who had any grasp of theology from the 1550s to the 1620s (Tyacke, 1973; Doran and Durston, 1991, pp. 194–5). Peter White (1992) and others have shown that there were some exceptions even in the Elizabethan church, but the dominant position, as loosely defined by the Thirty-Nine Articles of 1563 and all official glosses on them, does seem to have stood firmly in the Calvinist tradition. Some historians find useful the distinction between 'credal Calvinists', who accepted Calvin's theology as a set of articles of faith but did not draw from it any activist conclusions, and 'experiential Calvinists' for whom these beliefs implied the necessity of an aggressive, interventionist programme to unite the godly in joint activity in the world (Kendall, 1979; Lake, 1987). To appreciate these distinctions it is necessary to understand something of the Calvinist doctrine of predestination, which is often a stumbling block for modern students since it is based on assumptions which are not even shared by the vast majority of modern Christians. We must try to understand this, however, because the confrontation between Puritans and the church authorities in the reign of Charles I was partly over this issue, and the whole conflict is often presented as basically a theological one, between Calvinism and Arminianism.

From Luther onwards, Protestant reformers had attacked the medieval Christian theology of salvation by individual merit or good works. Since the fall of Adam, they argued, human nature was so corrupted by sin that human beings were incapable of merit in the eyes of God – only Christ's death could atone for such sinfulness, and only God's free gift of faith could enable any of them to be saved. The human will, by its own efforts, could do nothing but sin; only God by his choice could save any soul from eternal damnation. Those chosen by God were the 'elect', and only God knew who they were or why he had chosen them. It was quite explicit in Calvinist theology that God had not chosen them because he foresaw that they would live good lives; the elect were only able to live less sinful lives than the rest of humanity because God had chosen them. It seems paradoxical that people who held these beliefs, denying human beings free will, should in practice have such a voluntarist outlook, in which action was always urgent and inaction disastrous. Statements such as Herbert Palmer's, that there were 'thousands and millions gone to hell, out of this kingdom ... for want of good laws and through wicked magistrates, civil and ecclesiastical, and wicked ministers and neighbours' (Baskerville, 1993, p. 84), seem to suggest that human action, or inaction, could frustrate the will of God. But the Puritan emphasis was on the belief that those who did take action in the godly cause were God's instruments, and this could sustain them through all confrontations with their opponents and doubts in their own minds. For them, it was God's providence and not their own human contribution which determined the outcome. Although Puritan preaching has often been seen as fostering self-doubt and anxiety by its stress on innate human wickedness and the need to feel guilt and repentance, for the preachers these tactics were a means to an end, the personal assurance of one's own salvation, which would enable the believer to act with confidence (ibid., pp. 2–8, 96–116; Hunt, 1983, pp. 118–22). Statements of belief such as the preambles of wills frequently stressed the assurance of salvation for the elect, and the idea that any member of the elect might fall from grace was understood by educated lay Calvinists to be a threat to all they believed in.

For those called 'credal' Calvinists by some historians, it was enough to know that believers would be saved by God's will. Further theological exposition might be dangerous, because it could be misunderstood as meaning that people's conduct was irrelevant to their salvation, and the whole question was so difficult that it was unwise to elaborate on it too much, except among an audience of scholars. Despite their shared belief in Calvin's theology, therefore, credal and experiential Calvinists were heading for confrontation already in the late sixteenth century, when a group of churchmen drew up the Lambeth Articles (1595) restating the Calvinist position. These articles included such contentious matters as God's double decree (his positively choosing the damned as well as the saved) and the impossibility of the elect ever falling permanently from grace. The 1595 articles were rejected by Queen Elizabeth and were never adopted by the English church, but the defeat rankled with the harder Calvinists.

For all Protestants, those chosen by God to be saved constituted the real, invisible church within the outward, visible church that included the whole nation. English Puritanism aimed to mobilize the elect as a force for change – change to a more orderly, disciplined society in which the wicked would be restrained by the law's punishment and the good enabled to reach salvation. In theory and in practice, they constituted a church within a church, a society secret to human beings but known to God, of the spiritual élite whose mission was to change the world. Such a vision was in some ways authoritarian, but it was not necessarily conservative (Collinson, 1982, pp. 140–88). Indeed, historians have in the past argued that English Puritanism was an inherently radical movement. Weber's contribution was to construct from early modern history an ideal type of the 'Protestant ethic', exemplified in English Puritanism, which prepared the way for the 'spirit of capitalism' which has since come to dominate the modern world (Weber, 1930). For Marxists this connection was simpler: Puritanism was an ideology produced by the early rise of capitalism. The Puritan outlook, with its stress on work and profits, embodied the ideals and aspirations of the 'industrious sort of people' at the time: yeomen farmers and self-employed artisans, critical both of aristocratic values and of the ungodliness of the idle poor (Hill, 1969, pp. 121–211).

The most obvious and justified criticism of this view is that Puritanism in seventeenth-century England cut across all classes: there were Puritan peers like the Earl of Warwick, Puritan gentry who played a very active part in the godly cause, and indeed Puritan labourers, as well as many of the industrious middle sort (Hunt, 1983, pp. 163–5; Spufford, 1974, pp. 319–50). In some respects, Puritanism acted as a bond of common interest across classes, especially in political crises in the 1620s and early 1640s.

Puritans were not a majority in any class: the suggestion that the network of godly gentry constituted a 'class within a class' (Cliffe, 1984, p. 45) could also be applied to godly artisans and labourers. But it is highly unlikely that Puritans made up the same proportion in every class: they were certainly a small minority among the peers and a larger one among artisans. Statistical evidence sufficient to settle the argument numerically is unlikely ever to be available. It is also clear that seventeenth-century English Puritanism did not consistently support 'capitalist values' such as moneylending at interest, the pursuit of profit, or the view that worldly success reflected godliness, as Weber and his followers have suggested. Puritan preachers frequently condemned all interest on loans as sinful usury, and many of their gentry supporters had doubts about charging (or paying) interest on loans. While they regarded employment for the poor as one of the charitable obligations of the wealthy, there are plenty of Puritan texts in which excessive exploitation is fiercely denounced as 'grinding the faces of the poor'; and Puritan preachers frequently condemned the belief that worldly success means anything in the eyes of God (Hunt, 1983, pp. 127–8; Cliffe, 1984, pp. 104–24; Baskerville, 1993, pp. 58–63, 116–18).

It is perhaps more useful to regard Puritanism as being, among other things, a language in which social consciousness could be expressed, rather than as having a fixed content 'reflecting' the interests of one class. Many Puritan nobles and gentlemen resented the fact that the bishops appointed by Charles I were from what they regarded as inferior social classes, and they found the view that these nobodies had direct authority from God offensive (Kenyon, 1966, p. 151). By contrast, the poor Puritan's attraction to the idea of an invisible godly élite included the implication that this could turn the existing social hierarchy upside down (Baskerville, 1993, pp. 116–18). Meanwhile, the godly artisan valued hard work and honest dealing, but was suspicious of riches acquired by exploiting others (Seaver, 1980). There are, however, some central features of Puritan language which point to a higher level of approval for the values of the middling sort than of those of other layers of society: the condemnation of idleness in the rich as well as in the poor, the spiritual value placed on work and on setting others to work, the challenge that the invisible classification of the elect and the damned posed to existing hierarchies based on birth and rank. These things cannot have been, as was stressed in chapter 1, an anticipation of the values of a future 'middle class' in modern industrial society, but they can certainly be related to the growing concern of village élites to maintain order in society through labour discipline and waged employment, improving waste lands, bringing to an end the old village regime of common rights, and distancing themselves from the traditional popular culture that sanctioned 'idleness'. In ways such as these, the language of Puritan godliness could promote change while stressing stability and order (Sharp, 1988).

English Puritanism can, moreover, be regarded as radical in its promotion of social and political activism, of positive intervention by even humble individuals in the hope of improving things or resisting evil (Walzer, 1966; Hughes, 1991, pp. 101–3; Baskerville, 1993, pp. 1–48). Puritans advocated political and social action, but the opportunities for such action were provided by the English political and administrative system, which received an additional boost from experiential Calvinist ideology. The identification of Puritanism with a drive for social control – the project of disciplining the poor, setting them to work and regulating their sexuality – has been doubted because a similar drive to discipline and control the poor can be seen in the manorial records of the late thirteenth and early fourteenth centuries, caused not by a religious revival but by an economic and demographic crisis (Spufford, 1985). Nevertheless, if it was not Puritanism which created the impulse to control the poor, it may have been the struggle for authority in local communities which made Puritanism attractive to village leaders, at a time when the proliferation of poor landless people posed a threat to order but the manor court and the social authority of the landlord were in decline (Hunt, 1983, p. 144). The radicalism of Puritanism would seem to lie, therefore, not in its autonomous 'religious' characteristics (if such there can be), but in its function as a shared language or culture of activism and reform in the community. We could conclude either that a religious movement was diverted by material motives into a drive for social control and political participation, or that these secular concerns were hijacked by Puritan activists into their religious movement. There may not, in the end, be a great deal of difference between these two conclusions.

Anti-Puritanism: The Polarization of Opinion

Whatever its social and political potential, Puritanism was politicized and mobilized in the decades before the civil war by the polarization of Puritan and distinctly anti-Puritan views. Mainstream historical opinion has come to blame this polarization on the rise of Arminianism (Tyacke, 1987; Doran and Durston, 1991, pp. 195–6; Hughes, 1991, pp. 108–14). This was a specific theological position named after Jacob Arminius or Hermandzoon, a Dutch scholar who opposed the developments in the theology of predestination since Calvin's death. He feared that some Calvinists appeared to blame God for the sins of the damned, but was accused in turn of giving human beings some credit for their own salvation and casting doubt on the permanent assurance of salvation for the elect (White, 1992, pp. 22–38). His ideas split the Protestant church in the Dutch republic into two parties, who confronted each other at the Synod of Dort in 1618. The British delegation to Dort supported the Calvinist party (though not its most extreme positions), and this was uncontroversial at the time (Tyacke, 1987, pp. 87–105; Solt, 1990, pp. 158–63).

It was not until 1624 that public controversy over Arminian theology broke out in England, with the furore over Richard Montagu's book, *A New Gag for an Old Goose*. Montagu claimed that in the English church only Puritans, and not the mainstream, were Calvinists. This certainly politicized the issue, leading to resolutions and angry scenes in the House of Commons, and to royal injunctions banning public discussion of such contentious theological points (Tyacke, 1987, pp. 125–63). Opinions polarized, as the royal favourite, the Duke of Buckingham, and King Charles I (who succeeded his father in 1625) patronized Arminian clergymen and raised them to positions of power in the church, and the exponents of hard Calvinist views felt that they alone had been silenced.

William Laud, who was raised to the bishopric of London in 1628 and became Archbishop of Canterbury in 1633, has been seen as the leader of this Arminian faction which gained power in the English church within a few years of the accession of Charles. It is hard to establish what Laud's own position on these theological issues was (Tyacke, 1987, pp. 266–70). But to attribute the politicization of religion in the 1620s and 1630s to Arminianism alone is to amalgamate several issues into one, and perhaps to obscure the situation. It has recently been argued that although the dispute over Arminian theology was politically important in 1628–9, it was far less so in 1640 (Davies, 1992, pp. 87–125). Putting the theological issue in perspective could help us to understand the other major issues often equated with Arminianism. These were the Laudian view of the nature and history of the Church of England, Charles I's use of the royal supremacy, the stress on the authority of the clergy, and the imposition of a strict conformity in terms of ritual.

Distinguishing Arminian theology from other motives for anti-Puritanism would also help to explain the political significance of hostility to Puritanism in the early 1620s, before the Arminian controversy became a major issue in England (Cogswell, 1989). James I's 'Directions concerning Preaching' in 1622 were motivated by political rather than theological concerns, centring on foreign policy and his plans to marry his son Charles to a Catholic princess. The outbreak of war in central Europe between the Catholic Austrian emperor and the Protestant German princes, the negotiations for a marriage treaty with Catholic Spain, and James's suspension of the penal laws against Catholics had brought political and religious issues together at this time. There was a surge of preaching against royal policies, and James responded by ordering the preachers not to discuss 'matters of state'. But his Directions included general restrictions on preaching that seriously threatened the Puritan evangelical enterprise. All except bishops and deans were to avoid difficult theological questions, and 'indecent railing speeches' against Catholics were forbidden. Ministers were to preach only on obedience, faith and the good life; and Sunday afternoons were to be used for readings from the official *Book of Homilies*, or examining children on their catechism (ibid., p. 32). As well as politicizing the Puritans' sense of preaching mission, the royal decree showed the potential of royal authority in the English church. Charles I was to use this authority on a scale which has put James's Directions of 1622 in the shade, but their significance in turning apparent consensus into open conflict should not be overlooked. At the time, however, the resolution of the political conflict by the abandonment of the Spanish marriage and moves towards war against Spain and Austria moderated the religious polarization.

The Laudian view of the Church of England had little or nothing to do with Arminianism originally, but was developed by late Elizabethan and Jacobean thinkers such as Richard Hooker. These stressed the continuity of the English church over the centuries, and the underlying common identity of Christians, whatever their immediate differences. Bishops were the essential link with the primitive church of the apostles, through the laying on of hands from generation to generation, and despite the errors of Rome the Christian church was still essentially 'Catholic' (i.e. comprehensive or all-inclusive) and members of the Roman Catholic church were part of the body of Christ's people (Davies, 1992, pp. 53–5; Doran and Durston, 1991, pp. 23–4, 67–9). This contrasted sharply with the dominant Protestant view of the Catholic church, that it was the Antichrist foretold in the Book of Revelation, not just anti-Christian but the opposite, the utter negation, of Christianity (Hill, 1990, pp. 1–40). These differences, which had existed without arousing acute controversy in England for most of James's reign, became divisive in the reign of Charles, for it was the king's commitment to the doctrine of continuity through the divinely ordained institution of bishops which brought him into confrontation with the Presbyterian party in Scotland as well as antagonizing mainstream Calvinists in England. Although Presbyterianism had virtually disappeared in England soon after James's accession, the Laudian insistence on *iure divino* episcopacy – the institution of bishops by God rather than human convenience – was more than many Puritans could stomach, and led to a new questioning of the institution.

Charles seems to have put his own God-given responsibility for the church in England at the centre of his perspective. Henry VIII, in the 1530s, had taken the title Supreme Head (under Christ) of the church in England and had acted very much like a national pope, but Elizabeth and James seem to have regarded their position as Supreme Governor as mainly having to do with jurisdiction, rather than spiritual matters. Charles I, however, took a more spiritualized view of his own role in the church, as head of the clerical hierarchy above the bishops, a view amounting in the opinion of one historian to 'sacramental kingship'(Davies, 1992, pp. 18–24, 299). At times, he seems to have been trying to elevate the status of royal decrees above that of the canons of the church made by the clergy in convocation (ibid., pp. 25–6). Charles's view was not unanimously accepted by the bishops themselves, and even Laud was to say when pressed that the authority of God might sometimes have to be preferred over that of the king (ibid., pp. 24–45; Solt, 1990, p. 188).

Whatever their differences on the ultimate source of authority in the church, the reinforcement of the clerical hierarchy and episcopal control was very important to both Laud and Charles. Laudians did not hesitate to use the term 'priest', which implied a mystical and sacramental role for the clergy and had long been avoided by most Protestants in favour of the functional term 'minister'. Laud campaigned to restore the material endowments of the clergy, which had suffered since the Reformation, but above all the efforts of the king and the archbishop were directed towards imposing uniformity on the church by controlling and disciplining the ministry. The collaboration of the active Protestant laity which had been crucial to the post-Reformation church (and in some views, crucial to the whole Protestant Reformation) seemed to be pushed aside in favour of a regime which harked back to the medieval clerical establishment. Laud's efforts to increase church revenues, the favour shown by Charles to the immunities of cathedrals and colleges, and the appointment of bishops to high offices in the state, all contributed to an anti-clerical reaction, which came to be increasingly identified with Puritanism in the 1630s (Sharpe, 1992, pp. 392–401). This does not necessarily mean that theology did not matter to English lay people, but the social and political elevation of the clergy was an additional factor polarizing opinion in the 1630s.

The Laudian stress on the priestly function was linked to a greater emphasis on the sacraments and rituals of the church. Preachers, whose numbers and activities had proliferated under the impetus of Puritan evangelism, were to be strictly controlled and limited. Only ministers with cure of souls (i.e. parish rectors, vicars or curates) were to be allowed to preach, sermons had to be preceded by a Prayer Book service, and all preachers appointed to lecture were to conduct Prayer Book services also. Laudian bishops were to a greater or lesser degree suspicious of preaching, though far from being totally against it; and their severity in suppressing lectures and unlicensed preachers varied greatly between dioceses, with Laud himself as Bishop of London and Archbishop of Canterbury being less repressive than others such as Bishop Wren of Norwich (Davies, 1992, pp. 136–71).

The Laudian emphasis on the sacraments of baptism and the eucharist was in the mainstream Protestant tradition, though the Arminian theology of grace gave them a more prominent role. It was not just the sacraments, but the insistence on enforcing the ceremonies laid down in the Prayer Book of 1559 and the Canons of 1604, such as the sign of the cross in baptism and kneeling to receive the eucharist, that proved most controversial. The policy of restoring the communion table permanently to the east end of the church and railing it around like a medieval altar was particularly contentious. Together with allowing (though not enforcing) the practice of bowing towards the altar, this approach seemed to favour the doctrine of the real presence of Christ in the sacrament, which was anathema to the Calvinist and other Reformed churches. Perhaps, in view of the recent tendency to describe Puritans as splitters and disturbers of their communities, it needs to be stressed that denying communion to parishioners who refused to kneel at the altar rails to receive it, as some of the Laudian clergy did, amounted to a public humiliation of those who could not in conscience conform (Davies, 1992, pp. 205–50). Few things are more serious for a Christian than being refused the sacrament, and Laudianism too divided communities.

Laud believed that many Protestants, in England and on the

Continent, had gone too far in stripping the church of visual appeal and dignified services. In a well-known statement, he wrote that 'the want of uniform and decent order in too many churches' was driving people back to the Catholic church. He believed that both Roman Catholicism and Puritanism were extremist, and that the Church of England ought to preserve a middle way between the two (White, 1993; Solt, 1990, p. 198). The laws of the church were on his side: though some bishops pushed further, Laud was basically enforcing the Canons of 1604, which had confirmed the Elizabethan rules on ceremonies and discipline (Davies, 1992, pp. 62–4). Mobilizing the full force of authority in church and state, the king, Laud and the bishops set out to win by punishing their opponents as well as by the slower and far less successful method of persuasion, but 'show trials' such as that of William Prynne (who had his ears cropped for publishing an attack on the Laudian church) backfired by giving the Puritan cause – as more and more now recognized it – martyrs to identify with (Lamont, 1996, pp. 15–25).

Both Laudians and Puritans saw their opponents as innovators, trying to change the nature of the Church of England as it had been established in the reign of Elizabeth, and both could easily find justifications in a selective reading of the past. The church under Elizabeth and James had accommodated different views of Christian history and Protestant theology, and a variety of devotional and evangelical practices. Charles and Laud made the most determined and (temporarily) successful attempt since the Reformation to force consistency and uniformity on the English church. It polarized under the strain, not into two churches but into a national church deeply divided by partisanship and mutual antagonism. By 1640, each side firmly believed that the other was involved in a dangerous conspiracy to undermine true religion and legitimate authority.

Was the Laudian polarization of opinion purely about 'religious' matters such as worship and theology? Most historians would argue that it was also about authority in the church and state. Religion and politics could not be kept apart when James and Charles tried deliberately to use the pulpit as a medium of propaganda for royal authority, ordering preachers to defend the

Spanish marriage or the forced loan (Solt, 1990, pp. 173–4). The Arminian clergymen Montagu, Manwaring and Sibthorpe aroused a storm of criticism with their views on royal authority, but these views did not arise out of the theology of free will; indeed, the politics of Arminianism in England have been described as 'remarkably illiberal' considering the intellectual content and different history of Arminianism in the Netherlands (Reeve, 1989, pp. 68–70). The Laudian politics of hierarchy (in both the ecclesiastical and the secular sense) were specific to the situation in England, and although Laud's supporters may indeed have formed a party around a fairly coherent programme which included freedom to express Arminian views, they did not owe all their ideas and outlook to the Dutch theologian (Foster, 1989).

It has been suggested that Laudianism and Puritanism had different social and cultural locations in seventeenth-century England. Laudian policies were popular, and Puritanism unpopular, in traditional communities of the open-field, corn-growing and sheep-rearing type, where manorial authority was still a presence and the population kept stable by restricting immigration. The periodic revels of these communities such as feast-days, processions, May games and church-ales (traditional parish fundraisers) were prime targets of the Puritan attack on ungodliness, but supported by the Laudian clergy as harmless diversions which maintained parish solidarity (Underdown, 1987, pp. 9–105). Undoubtedly, there is a social and cultural geography of Laudianism and Puritanism to be further explored by historians in all regions of England, which may help to elucidate yet another dimension of the religious and political polarization which took place.

Anti-Catholicism

The polarization of opinion into two religious parties disputing the nature of one English church in the 1630s may have been multi-dimensional, but it produced two powerful, over-simplified images: the Laudian one of Puritans as dangerous subversives bent on destroying legitimate authority in church and state, and the Puritan one of Laudians as a secret Romish faction trying to reverse the Protestant Reformation in England. In fact, the Laudians were far from considering a return to Roman Catholicism. Laud himself, whatever his views on the Catholicity of the international Christian church, said he saw Roman Catholics as the most dangerous of the king's subjects (Solt, 1990, pp. 197–8). Despite both having Catholic mothers and wives, James I and Charles I were little inclined to convert to their religion, and both interestingly upheld the value of Protestant wet-nurses (in an age when royal mothers rarely fed their own babies) in avoiding the religious contamination of Stuart infants (Marshall, 1984, p. 45; Mack, 1992, p. 36). Charles clearly had a preference for elaborate religious ceremonies and baroque art, which to many of his subjects were the obvious visible signs of Roman Catholic ideas; but since he never adopted crucial Roman doctrines such as the authority of the pope, or transubstantiation in the sacrament of communion, he did not consider that he had broken with Protestantism and sometimes seems to have been angered because many of his subjects thought he had. Both Charles and Laud were well known to argue against Catholic doctrines, and expressed disapproval of the public conversion of courtiers to Rome, especially of the missionary activities of Buckingham's female relatives after his death. Catholic courtiers, including the brother of the Earl of Manchester, were banished from time to time, and the regular prosecution of Catholic recusants recommenced in the 1630s (Hibbard, 1983, pp. 36, 55; Donald, 1990a, p. 182; Sharpe, 1992, pp. 301–8).

Why, then, were Puritans so afraid of Roman Catholicism that some historians have argued that this fear, rather than any theological or ceremonial position, is what distinguishes Puritans from other Protestants in early seventeenth-century England (Finlayson, 1983)? It is all too easy for us to dismiss it as irrational, and it is unwise to describe it in such terms as ' pathological hatred', 'ugly religious hatreds' or 'paranoia' (Doran and Durston, 1991, p. 66; Young, 1997, p. 178; Underdown, 1996, p. 29). From a modern perspective, Charles I's tolerance of Catholics may seem more humane than Pym's hatred of them, but to attribute the latter to 'the imaginative poverty of the seven-

teenth century'(Fletcher, 1981, p. 408) is to miss the vital importance of meaning and context in dealing with ideas in history.
'The historian ignores at his peril a body of ideas which at one
time aroused intense passion and controversy. He must try to find
out what lies behind ideological concepts which have lost their
significance for him', Christopher Hill wrote in an influential
passage on the idea of Antichrist (Hill 1990, p. 2).

Hill and others have shown that the Puritans' fear of
Catholicism can be a vital clue to their system of religious and
political priorities. Among the meanings that Catholicism held for
them they included idolatry supplanting the worship of God and
displacing Christ from the centre of Christianity, blind devotion
rather than intellectual conviction, external practice rather than
internal conversion, and fleshly versus spiritual values. Perhaps
most fundamental of all was the Catholic implication of optimism
about the potential of fallen human nature, as opposed to the
Puritan conviction of human sinfulness which was supposed to
lead to absolute trust in God alone. It was not just wrong: it was
a total inversion of the values of Christianity as Puritans saw it
(Clifton, 1973; Lake, 1989). The Laudians did not share the
Puritans'total opposition to Catholic religious values, such as the
association of holiness with beauty. They regarded the appeal of
ritual and ceremony to the common people in traditional communities as a positive feature of the Christian tradition, and the
Reformed and Calvinist reaction against ceremonies as harmfully
extreme. That beauty and emotion should play a larger part in
religion than reason and education seemed to them to fulfil a
human need which to Puritans was not a need but a weakness, dis-
tracting the soul from a proper understanding of sin and salvation.

Fear and distrust of Catholicism must also be seen in the
context of the European war of 1618–48, in which the forces of
Catholic reaction made considerable gains by the bloodiest
methods. It is easy for us to see that continental Protestantism
would survive the Thirty Years' War, but to many at the time it
looked distinctly possible that it would not. Catholic France, it is
true, entered the war on the Protestant side in 1635, but the
Protestant minority in France itself suffered heavy defeats. When
John Pym said that Catholic pleas for leniency were not to be

trusted because, 'having gotten favour they will expect a toleration, after toleration they will look for equality, after equality for superiority, and having superiority they will seek the subversion of that religion which is contrary to theirs'(Solt, 1992, p. 164), he surely had in mind the current erosion in France of the provisions for the toleration of Protestantism in the Edict of Nantes. Real toleration of religious diversity was still rare in the early seventeenth century, the dominant trend being towards the 'confessional state' adhering to a specific faith. The exceptions were to be found where compromise was the only practical way of coping with diversity, rather than being signs of commitment to liberal principles (Grell, 1996).

For the people of the 1620s and 1630s, the Reformation itself was not a distant historical event. The infamous St Bartholomew massacre of Protestants in France was, at the time of the English alarm over the Spanish marriage negotiations in 1622, more recent than the Nazi Holocaust at the time I am writing this book. Sir Edward Coke, still sitting in the House of Commons in 1628, was born before the Catholic Mary Tudor became queen, and her burning of English Protestants was to his generation a childhood memory as well as a tradition embodied in Foxe's influential *Book of Martyrs*. Recent work on the sixteenth century has stressed the lengthiness of the process of creating a Protestant nation in England. If the survival of Catholicism was even half as substantial as some historians have argued, it was not unrealistic for English Protestants to feel insecure about the permanence of their Reformation (Doran and Durston, 1991, pp. 111–12). For James I and Charles I to dream of a Christendom reunited by peaceful diplomacy was less realistic in the circumstances than for Puritans to fear the continued advance of the Counter-Reformation, at least up to the closing years of the Thirty Years' War in the late 1640s.

The English Puritans' more immediate fears were not imaginary, either. The increasing visibility of Catholics during the 1620s and 1630s at court and in London, where they took advantage of the queen's chapel to attend Mass openly, and the always newsworthy conversion of a trickle of English and Scottish courtiers to the Roman faith, aggravated such fears throughout

Charles I's reign. Puritans rightly suspected that Charles had promised the French in his marriage treaty that he would relax the recusancy laws against English Catholics, though he was no better at keeping these promises than any others (Carlton, 1995, p. 66). An official emissary from the pope was openly received at court in 1636, and Spanish diplomats spread rumours that he came to receive Charles's conversion. There is more than enough evidence to show that the Puritan fears of a 'popish plot', which had such a substantial influence on the events of 1640–2, had their roots in the 1630s and were credible even though they were not wholly accurate (Hibbard, 1983). Charles's raising of an army in Ireland officered by Catholics was a disastrous move from the point of view of public relations, and even Wentworth, his loyal deputy, advised him against it at first (Fitzpatrick, 1988, pp. 82–3). Fear of Catholic assassination plots in London in the early 1640s seemed justified when a justice drawing up lists of Catholic recusants was stabbed to death in Westminster Hall (Lindley, 1997, p. 13).

That there was also an irrational and superstitious element in Puritan anti-Catholicism cannot be denied. Discussing the violent destruction of images in Essex on the eve of the civil war, William Hunt suggests that Puritans had a 'subliminal dread' of religious objects. The Catholic belief in the spiritual power of physical objects was an invitation to Protestants to a kind of inversion, imbuing the same objects with a malign or diabolical power (Hunt, 1983, p. 308). Priests, as persons credited with special powers by the Catholics, also elicited a special kind of fear, associated in the Puritan mind with blasphemy, and the contrast between the toleration with which the gentry treated their Catholic neighbours and their frequent demands in parliament that no mercy be shown to Catholic priests may be significant (Russell, 1979, p. 120). Underdown relates a chilling account of the execution of a Catholic priest at Dorchester in 1639, at which a local clergyman screamed for the blood of the 'blasphemer' and the crowd played football with his severed head (Underdown 1993, pp. 197–9). Bizarrely, convicted criminals on Newgate prison's death row in 1641 rioted in support of the Commons' demand that seven Catholic priests who were their fellow prisoners be executed immediately, as it was feared the king intended to reprieve them (Lindley, 1997, p. 78). We have to place such evidence of a mentality which may be shocking to us in the context of a changing and insecure society, literally a witch-hunting society, in which the old certainties of 'church magic' had been withdrawn but the spread of confidence in science still lay in the future (Thomas, 1971). It would be wrong, however, to look only to these subconscious mentalities for the meaning of anti-Catholicism among English Puritans. It also embodied very concrete and explicit fears in the turbulent world of seventeenth-century war and politics, which were reasonable (though biased) in the circumstances of the time, and helped define Puritan religious values by identifying their opposites.

While it is true that Arminians and Laudians were more tolerant of Catholics, they were intolerant of Puritans, and used whatever power they acquired to harass and punish those whom they saw as dangerous religious and political extremists (Reeve, 1989, pp. 68–70). While Puritans were terrified by the spectre of Catholic triumph, Laudians saw themselves as struggling for survival against a powerful and dangerous Calvinist conspiracy which threatened the destruction of the state as well as the church of England. Like the Puritan fear of Catholicism, these attitudes, if read carefully, can show us the nature of the 'competing sets of social and political, as well as religious, priorities and values' which were in conflict in seventeenth-century England and played an important part, as we have seen, in the outbreak of war in 1642 (Lake, 1989, p. 97).

4

Political Tensions

From the mid-nineteenth century until the 1960s, the dominant explanation of the English civil war portrayed it as a struggle between opposing principles of government, inherent in English politics since the accession of James I. This 'struggle for the constitution' could be seen either as a conflict of ideologies, absolutism versus constitutionalism, or as a struggle for power between rival institutions, monarchy and parliament, competing for the position of ultimate authority in the English state. In this interpretation, 'parliament' almost invariably meant the House of Commons, and the ultimate outcome was seen as a triumph for principles of liberty and as an early achievement of the movement towards parliamentary reform which was adopted by the Whig party in the 1830s and 1840s. For this reason, and its more general association with belief in history as the story of progress, it has come to be known as the Whig interpretation (Richardson, 1988, pp. 72–3, 95–7).

This view has come under major attack since the mid-1970s from revisionist historians, who believe that the constitutional interpretation is anachronistic, and condemn it as teleological – deriving the causes of events from their eventual outcome. For Geoffrey Elton (1966), there was no 'high road to civil war' running from the Commons' Apology of 1604 to the Grand Remonstrance, while for Conrad Russell (1976) the problem is that the Whig historians saw the parliamentary history of 1603–29 out of perspective because they treated the conflict of the 1640s as its inevitable outcome. Another revisionist found Gardiner's classic nineteenth-century history of the political conflict so unsatisfactory that he called for 'a return to the drawing-board, rather than another repair of the old canvas'(Sharpe, 1978, p. v).

The alternative picture which emerges from revisionist work on parliament is one in which there was before 1640 an ideological consensus shared by monarchs and parliamentarians, and co-operation between the two was the principal aim of all those involved in politics. The most intense parliamentary rows of the 1620s are said to have been caused by rivalries among the nobles of the king's council, foreshadowing in this interpretation the 'baronial war' of the 1640s. According to Russell, the long-term strains and tensions between kings and the House of Commons that did exist were due to a stubborn and short-sighted refusal by MPs to deliver the goods expected of them – extra revenue for the king and helpful legislation for their constituents – rather than to a contest for power. However, Russell considers the immediate problems of the 1620s as 'a war decade'more important than any long-term tensions in explaining the troubled relations between king and parliament, and sees a close correspondence between the tensions caused by continental wars in the 1620s and those set up by the British wars of 1639–42 (Russell, 1979, pp. 35–8, 48–51).

It is alleged that the breakdown in relations between Charles I and his parliament in 1628–9, which was followed by eleven years without parliaments, arose out of mistrust and misunderstanding , or a 'crisis of counsel' in which the dominance of the Duke of Buckingham, who was assassinated in 1628, had produced the direst effects. The misjudgement or bad behaviour of a few individuals, especially at the end of the 1629 session, is made to carry some of the blame (Kenyon, 1986, p. 54; Sharpe, 1978, p. 42). The eleven years from 1629 to 1640 are described as a protracted cooling-off period, which saw harmony restored to the political nation by peaceful reform, and co-operation between central government and the gentry who ran the counties. The period once known to historians as the 'eleven years' tyranny' is said to have been harmonious, and rather than being on the point of breaking down, Charles I's government in 1639 was in good working order. According to this view, only the Scottish rebellion and its consequences broke the political calm (Sharpe, 1992, pp. 603–730; Russell, 1990b).

An immense amount of research has been poured into the revisionist effort, and it has opened up many previously neglected topics
and original sources to lively historical discussion, but it has not
convinced everyone that ideological and constitutional conflicts in
the decades before the civil war were figments of the imagination of
Whig historians. Some have stressed the importance of absolutist
theories of monarchy as a major cause of political divisions
(Sommerville, 1986; Wootton, 1986). Historians of parliament have
reassessed the importance of episodes such as the dispute over war
finance in 1624–6 and the challenging of the king's collection of
tonnage and poundage in 1629, in a way that restores to them some
of the significance denied by revisionist historians (Young, 1989;
Popofsky, 1990; Thompson, 1986). Above all, the parliamentary
events of 1628–9 are beginning to resume their place as a serious
crisis whose nature may help us to understand the breakdown in
relations between king and parliament in 1640–2 (Reeve, 1989).

The main reason why many historians still deny that relations
between the early Stuarts and their parliaments reflect real ideological divisions before 1640 is that the early Stuart kings, their
advisers and courtiers, lawyers, members of parliament and articulate subjects often appear, to a modern eye, to have made inconsistent statements about theoretical and political issues. Attempts
to divide them neatly into royalists and parliamentarians, absolutists and constitutionalists, upholders of the prerogative and
defenders of liberty, inevitably run into the problem of individuals and groups who seem to fall into both camps, share ideas with
their opponents, or say different things on different occasions.
When faced with such evidence we should not say, as historians
sometimes did in the past, that the people of the time were confused, or discussed the problems of authority in government
'without understanding the essential nature of these issues'
(Judson, 1949, p. 8). Historians of ideas have taught us to
acknowledge that it is probably we who have not understood what
the people of the time were talking about, and that the closer
reading of texts and the study of their contexts are necessary to
understanding them.

We also need to be cautious about contemporary statements,
made at the height of political conflicts, in which people imputed

long-term aims or ideological motives to their opponents. In 1629 Charles I accused the House of Commons of having 'of late years endeavoured to extend their privileges, by setting up general committees ... a course never heard of until late'. In fact, general committees were not a recent innovation in 1629, and the Commons regarded themselves as defending, not seeking to extend, their privileges (Reeve, 1989, p. 105). Similarly, the Grand Remonstrance's charge that the cause of conflict between Charles I and his parliaments was 'a malignant and pernicious design of subverting the fundamental laws and principles of government', going back to the beginning of his reign, needs to be treated with caution (Burgess, 1996, pp. 18–28). The distortions induced by hindsight did not begin with the nineteenth-century Whigs, they appear even before the civil war itself.

Monarchy

The Whig historian Macaulay firmly laid the blame for constitutional conflict on James I, whose claims for royal authority 'took a monstrous form which would have disgusted the proudest and most arbitrary of those who had preceded him' and who constantly 'enraged and alarmed his parliament' by repeating such claims (Macaulay, 1913, vol. 1, p. 62). Macaulay lumped together the divine right of kings, absolute monarchy and the question of the royal prerogative as one 'monstrous form' of monarchical theory, but recent discussions of politics and ideology in early Stuart England suggest that it would be useful to differentiate these three ideas and examine them one by one.

Most educated people in early seventeenth-century England did not consider the divine right of kings an offensive claim. James I's subjects were familiar with biblical quotations and theories of natural law which stressed that the power of earthly rulers was God-given and analogous to the authority of fathers in their families (Ashton, 1978, pp. 3–15; Russell, 1993b). Invocations of divine authority for the rule of kings depended very much on the context and the audience a speaker or writer was addressing. The more general the context and the wider the audience, the more likely it was that the power of the English monarchy would be derived directly from God: this was, for example, a common theme of sermons on the virtue of obedience (Burgess, 1992, p. 133). The theory probably became more acceptable, rather than less, in early seventeenth-century England because of the fear of Catholicism. Although divine right had its roots in the Middle Ages, it was given a new lease of life in early modern Europe as a Protestant weapon against the papacy. Popes claimed the right to depose rulers (including Elizabeth of England) for heresy, and Catholics in the early seventeenth century defended and practised political assassination, or 'tyrannicide'. In James I's lifetime the Dutch leader William of Orange, the French king Henri III, and several members of the Scottish royal family had been assassinated; he narrowly escaped assassination himself with discovery of the Gunpowder Plot in 1605, but the murder of Henri IV of France by a Catholic fanatic in 1610 reminded everyone of the clear and present danger. In this climate, claims that the king was God's anointed, and that violence against him was sacrilegious, were not considered outrageous by educated and propertied English people (Burgess, 1992, pp. 129–33; Wootton, 1986, p. 30).

Radical Protestant doctrines that advocated resistance to tyrannical rulers were also unwelcome in early seventeenth-century England, though they may eventually have played an important part in rallying support for parliament in the civil war. Although there is immense debate among historians as to how far Calvinist doctrine permitted resistance and rebellion, Calvinist writings in support of the sixteenth-century Reformation in Scotland, which had led to the deposition of James's mother Mary Stuart, were regarded in England as proof of the connection. In the reign of Charles I, when Laudians insistently equated Puritan opposition in the church with rebellion in the state, English Puritans may have become especially keen to repudiate this association. In 1632, for example, a leading Puritan minister in Dorchester, who later supported parliament in the civil war, preached that 'magistrates are gods' and that disobedience to the ruling authorities was 'not a trespass against men, but a sin against God himself' (Burgess, 1992, pp. 17–62, 116, 133).

Belief that the king was divinely appointed and could not be resisted was, however, compatible with differing views on the extent of his powers. The view that the authority of the English ruler, while derived from God, was at the same time defined and limited by the 'ancient constitution', was widespread. This constitution was not a single written document, but a tradition believed to be embodied in the common law, a body of precedents and interpretations built up over the previous 500 years. The chief exponents of the common law in the early seventeenth century, such as Sir Edward Coke, made very high claims for it, believing that it represented not only the immemorial customs of the English people, but also the laws of God and nature. Such claims may seem irrational and unhistorical to a modern mind, but they reflected the belief of most educated people that their political and social world was designed by God just as much as the natural world. To believe that the king was appointed by God to rule within the common law of England was mainstream thinking, and was compatible with a theory of mutual obligations between monarch and people, or even with theories of government by consent (Burgess, 1992, pp. 1–105; Sommerville, 1986, pp. 22–7, 86–111).

Divine right was also compatible with the view that kings were limited by law, and James I repeatedly stated that he recognized this limitation. He usually said this in such a way, however, that he reserved his position in theory that kings were not originally limited by laws, although in 'settled states' such as England they were (e.g. Kenyon, 1986, pp. 11–13). Were such arguments a manifestation of consensus or of deep ideological division; of James I's goodwill towards his English subjects and their constitution, or of his pigheaded insistence on having his own pedantic way with theory? Historians have argued both cases, but the question must in the end be judged in the political context of James's reign. It does seem, however, that the polarization of opinions on divine right was greater in Charles I's reign, above all in the context of his attempts to raise money by a forced loan in 1627. Two clergymen of Arminian leanings, Robert Sibthorpe and Roger Manwaring, aroused widespread controversy by preaching and publishing their view that subjects had a God-given duty to pay any tax or contribution demanded by the king, and that the laws of the land could not override this obligation. It has been argued that these views were not new, so much as their application to this controversial issue. It may be true that the divine right of kings was 'an uncontroversial theory, and was not seen as threatening to customary legal and political theory or practice, provided that it was used within certain tacitly recognised boundaries,' but Sibthorpe and Manwaring's sermons, compared with others printed at the time, notably transgressed these boundaries (Sommerville, 1986, pp. 127–31; Burgess, 1992, pp. 173–8, 118).

Some historians argue that if the basic principle of divine right was not in itself considered threatening, it became unacceptable in the early seventeenth century because it was associated with the idea of absolute monarchy; that it was 'divine right absolutism' which polarized English political thinking (Wootton, 1986, p. 30; Sommerville, 1986, pp. 9–56.). It is important to remember that contemporaries did not use our word 'absolutism', but they frequently described kingly power as 'absolute', and this was not always contentious. The word became more controversial in the forty years before the civil war, and there was a distinct shift from the positive use of the term to distinguish the English monarch from elective or temporary heads of state, to a more negative sense, in which absolute monarchy was identified with unlimited royal power, as it was by many members of the Long Parliament (Daly, 1978). Yet there was a time when even Sir Edward Coke, the leading common lawyer, could say 'that the kingdom of England is an absolute monarchy, and that the king is the only supreme governor' (Sommerville, 1986, p. 107). Sir Walter Raleigh in 1619 was quite willing to describe the English monarchy as absolute, whereas by 1642 even Charles I denied that it was (Wootton, 1986, pp. 22, 34).

For some time, or in some circumstances, in the early seventeenth century, to state that the English monarchy was 'absolute' was not incompatible with believing that it was limited. The view that the English monarchy was limited, not only by the laws in general, but by specific institutional arrangements including parliament, was familiar from the fifteenth- and sixteenth-century writers Fortescue and Smith. Fortescue had described the English constitution as a mixed one combining features of monarchy and 'political' (i.e. republican) government, while Sir Thomas Smith had stated that absolute power resided in parliament, which included the king as well as the Lords and Commons. Members of parliament were familiar with these theories, and can be found citing Fortescue in debates (Sommerville, 1986, pp. 88, 154, 166; Elton, 1960, pp. 234–5; Russell, 1976, p. 9). That Charles I adopted the theory of mixed government in his reply to the Nineteen Propositions in June 1642 suggests that it was widely known and popular enough for the king and some of the royalist party to feel that it was their best defence (Kenyon, 1986, p. 18). This does not mean that the king had not espoused absolutist theories earlier in his reign.

One of the problems about Charles I, however, is that unlike his father he was not an intellectual, well versed in the subtleties of early modern scholastic political theory. Simple concepts such as the honour of the king and the obedience of the subject meant more to him than theoretical discourse, and he was ill equipped to negotiate his way across this minefield of educated political beliefs (Carlton, 1995; Young, 1997). Glenn Burgess concludes that 'Charles spoke the political languages of his day' but spoke them 'unidiomatically' (Burgess 1992, p. 200). Charles's impatience with theory helps to explain the contrast between his father's handling of arguments about the king's powers and his own.

Early in James's reign, a dispute arose over impositions, which were new customs duties on trade. When their legality was tested in Bate's case (1606), the judges of the exchequer bent over backwards to argue that impositions were a matter of foreign policy rather than property rights, even suggesting that Bate's shipment of currants still belonged to the Venetians from whom they had been purchased at the time the duty was charged. This may seem tortuous to us, but it suggests that they were determined to remain within the existing consensus about the king's powers (Burgess, 1992, pp. 140–4). Nevertheless, the House of Commons took the position that the judgement in Bate's case implied a serious threat, tending 'even to the utter ruin of the ancient liberty of this kingdom, and of your subjects' right of propriety [property] of their lands and goods'. This would seem to indicate that despite their intentions the king and the judges had not succeeded in staying within the consensus, though they had tried (Sommerville, 1986, p. 153).

Another incident which may reveal much about James I's political realism as well as his intellectual background is his reaction to the outcry over *The Interpreter* (1610), a legal textbook by the civil lawyer Robert Cowell. (Civil lawyers practised in the church courts and were trained in Roman imperial law.) Cowell claimed that the king was 'above the law by his absolute power' and that 'to bind the prince to or by these laws, were repugnant to the nature and constitution of an absolute monarchy'. James agreed to ban the book and argued against Cowell's work himself, declaring that 'every just king in a settled kingdom is bound to observe that paction made to his people by his laws' (Sommerville, 1986, pp. 117–27; Burgess, 1992, pp. 149–53). Yet despite this nod in the direction of a theory of contract between king and people, James had his own way over impositions (on imports, if not on exports), and continued to refer to the laws as 'his'. This did not satisfy everyone, but neither did it lead to a serious political crisis. Charles I's treatment of Sibthorpe and Manwaring was rather different. When the 1628 parliament impeached Manwaring, Charles agreed to ban the circulation of the offending sermon, but stated that 'the grounds thereof were rightly laid', and soon after rewarded him with a rich parish, and later with a bishopric (Sommerville, 1986, pp. 130–1; Burgess, 1992, p. 177).

The theoretical point at issue in both Bate's case and the controversial Five Knights' case of 1627 was not divine right or absolute monarchy as such, but the royal prerogative, or discretionary executive powers. None of the king's critics denied that the monarch had some discretionary power to take necessary action for the public good without reference to parliament or the law courts, not only in emergencies such as war, but in normal circumstances in matters such as the coinage. Controversy about these powers was first aroused by the statement of one of the judges in Bate's case, which distinguished between the king's normal rule and his exercise of these prerogative powers. 'The king's power is double, ordinary and absolute', he said, asserting that the 'absolute' kind of power was not constrained by the common law, and that the area covered by this power, which had to do with the public good rather than private citizens, 'is most properly named policy and government' (Kenyon, 1986, pp. 54–5). Defenders of this view argued that there was an area of potential royal action in which 'reason of state' ought to prevail over strictly legal limitations. Burgess has claimed that this judge's view of a 'duplex' royal prerogative was widely held at the time, but at the next meeting of parliament (1610) a fear was expressed that however small the area in which the king's power was absolute, it could be 'extended much further, even to the utter ruin of the ancient liberty of this kingdom'. The poet John Donne compared the king's prerogative to God's ability to suspend the laws of nature by miracles: 'Miracle is not like the prerogative in anything more than this, that no body can tell what it is'. Exceptions that could not be defined were problematic: some members of parliament wanted a definition, but others thought the lack of definition a protection (Sommerville, 1986, pp. 153, 166).

The lawfulness of his discretionary power to act for the public good in emergencies was Charles's chief argument for the forced loan of 1627. He had a fleet and an army to supply, and parliament had not granted him enough money (before he dissolved it in anger at an attempt to impeach his favourite Buckingham); therefore, he argued, he had the power to raise money to meet these urgent needs. He then went on to aggravate the controversy by arguing that his prerogative also extended to imprisoning loan refusers without stating his reasons, and insisting that the common law courts recognize this in the case of five knights who had been arrested for refusing to pay. The effect of these actions was to turn the opinion of the 76-year-old Sir Edward Coke against his own previous views. Although as a judge Coke himself had recognized the king's power to imprison people without revealing the cause, he told the 1628 parliament that he now realized he had been reading the wrong legal textbook (White, 1979, pp. 233–6).

Russell has suggested that the parliament of 1628 was futilely attempting to 'debate civil liberties in wartime'(1979, p. 343), but this is both anachronistic and misleading. Seventeenth-century war situations were not 'total' like twentieth-century world wars, and Charles was imprisoning not pro-Spanish conspirators or spies, but leading subjects who refused to hand over money on a matter of principle. (If any modern British analogy were appropriate, it might be as if the Prevention of Terrorism Act had been used against poll tax refusers during the Gulf War.) Most historians agree that in 1626–8 Charles I was playing on ambiguities and using loopholes so as to maximize his 'absolute' prerogative in areas normally covered by the common law. He also appears to have interfered with due legal process, ordering the record of the Five Knights' bail hearing to be altered to turn a negative statement into a positive one in his own favour (Burgess, 1992, p. 279, n. 72).

The implications of the dispute over the forced loan fostered a fear of 'arbitrary government'which, as we have seen, was acutely felt in the Long Parliament. Without rules and systematic structures, there would be no rationality, no laws, no regular government and no political discourse – a state such as Europeans believed the Turkish empire to be. Whereas Raleigh had written in 1619 that Philip II of Spain 'attempted to make himself, not only an absolute monarch ... but Turk-like to tread under his feet all [the Netherlanders'] natural and fundamental laws, privileges and ancient rights', in 1628 a member of the English parliament could claim, 'We now little differ from the course in Turkey' (Wootton, 1986, p. 35). 'Absolute monarchy' came to be identified as a threatening alternative to the ancient constitution and the rule of law. In the 1628 parliament John Pym described monarchies 'not regulated by laws or contracts between the king and his people' as absolute, and Sir John Eliot in 1630 believed Charles I aimed 'to make monarchy unlimited, an absoluteness of government without rule' (ibid.; Sommerville, 1986, p. 158).

The debates over the king's discretionary powers also spread anxiety about the scope of the common law, since it appeared that the king might have powers the law could not limit (Russell, 1979, pp. 350–1; Burgess, 1992, pp. 179–80, 212–31). This was not just a matter of lawyers defending their own professional credibility, for belief in the power of common law was shared by the propertied classes of early modern England in general. Ahigh proportion of the gentry had at least a smattering of legal education through attendance at the Inns of Court (the London law schools), but belief in the law as a 'science' that could resolve human problems objectively was an educated assumption comparable to confidence in natural science in the nineteenth century or economics in the twentieth. Not only the greater gentry who filled the benches as Justices of the Peace in the provinces, but the lesser gentry and yeomanry who served on juries and inquests, were involved in the administration of justice throughout the country (Herrup, 1983; Hughes, 1991, pp. 69–70). For them, the rule of law was more than a slogan; it was what gave them standing in their communities and authority over the 'lower sorts'of people.

David Wootton has argued that the Five Knights' case made constitutional change inevitable, and when the solution arrived at in 1628, the Petition of Right, proved inadequate, it was an open question whether absolutism or constitutionalism would triumph (Wootton, 1986, p. 35). While it would probably be wrong to project this polarization of ideologies back into the 1610s or even the early 1620s, it may not be so inaccurate with regard to 1628–9. Though the distinctions between divine right, absolute monarchy and the royal prerogative may help us understand the early Stuart period better, they come close to disappearing in the political situation of 1628. The alarm aroused by Charles I's use of his 'absolute' prerogative helped to make absolute monarchy a suspect term, while Sibthorpe and Manwaring put divine right in a sinister light by associating it with the view that the king was not limited by law. If, as many recent historians have convincingly argued, these concepts were part of separate and manageable discourses before 1628, their amalgamation under pressure made this political crisis especially traumatic. Though it seems difficult to justify the view that an ideological conflict between absolutism and constitutionalism dated back to 1603, it seems hard to disagree that such a conflict had appeared on the scene by 1629.

It is, as will be shown below, hard to tell how the electorate viewed the political situation during the 'cooling-off period'of the personal rule when no parliaments were summoned. But it may be significant that in one case where – through the chance survival of private records – we do have evidence of discussion of Charles I's levying of Ship Money among the Kentish gentry, some said 'that this being declared law made the king more absolute than either France or the great duke of Tuscany (held in their own dominions the most potent of any princes for the power at their wills of raising money).' Sir Roger Twysden, who recorded this discussion, believed 'that the whole discourse of Fortescue ... was to show the king had not an absolute power'. The belief that absolute royal power endangered the English constitution may have penetrated quite deeply into the political nation by 1637, for there is no reason to believe that this circle of Kentish gentry was in any way exceptional or untypical (Fincham, 1984, pp. 233–6).

Parliament

In the Whig view of history outlined above, parliament played a heroic role in the 'struggle for the constitution'. From 1604 onwards, the House of Commons determinedly opposed the absolutist tendencies of the Stuart monarchs, defended the principles of liberty and property which were the essence of the ancient constitution, and increased its own power. In this unfolding plot, every constitutional question, from the commons' insistence on validating their own members' credentials in 1604 to the events of the Long Parliament, became part of a cumulative contest for sovereignty between monarchy and parliament. The persuasiveness of the revisionist charge that this was a distorted reading of seventeenth-century political history can be shown by looking at Tanner's *English Constitutional Conflicts of the Seventeenth Century*, a textbook which has been almost constantly in print since 1928. There, we find unashamed hindsight: the reign of James I was 'only the Prologue of the same great play' as the Glorious Revolution of 1688 (p. 1), and the obscure preoccupations of lawyers such as Coke in the early 1600s are given equal weight with major events such as the 1628 Petition of Right.

Elton and Russell have led the attack on this 'high road to civil war'. There were conflicts and tensions between kings and parliaments, they argue, but these were essentially discontinuous, and if any threads connected them, they were not constitutional issues, but the problems of war, finance and the intervention of court factions in the affairs of both houses. Russell especially denies any continuity between the issues and divisions in the parliaments of

1604–29 and those of 1640. His detailed study of the parliaments of the 1620s seemed to confirm this perspective (Russell 1979), and a number of other historians contributed to the revisionist parliamentary history project from the late 1970s on.

More recently, however, parliamentary historians have suggested that the revisionist view is itself distorted. Seeking to compensate for the old Whig bias, it has built in new biases – against debates on constitutional issues, the expression of ideological views, or consideration of the political nation outside parliament before 1640. This is despite the immensely valuable detailed work which revisionists have done and the more serious standards of scholarship which they have injected into parliamentary history. Much potential ammunition for the anti-revisionist comeback can be found in the rich details of Russell's own *Parliaments and English Politics*; but more, it seems, can be added from evidence which he has omitted (Thompson, 1989, 1986; Young, 1989).

Revisionists are right to stress that parliament in the early seventeenth century was a very different institution from the one we know in Britain today, despite an undeniable hereditary resemblance and the continuity of rituals (rituals of course designed to convey a particular view of past constitutional issues). Parliaments did not sit continuously, nor for long, before 1640, and we strictly cannot speak of what 'parliament' was doing or thinking when it was not in session. Russell (1983) has insisted that parliament was not an institution but an event: contemporaries spoke of parliaments in the plural. Nevertheless, they did generalize about the institution. When Charles I in 1626 said, 'Parliaments are altogether in my power, for the calling, sitting and continuance of them', he was not taken to be referring simply to his right to call and dissolve each meeting (Russell, 1979, pp. 391–2). Members of parliament did show concern for the survival of parliaments in general, and therefore may be said to have considered parliament an institution which was an essential part of the constitution.

Parliaments were called in the seventeenth century 'to do the king's business' in making laws, granting taxes, and being consulted on affairs of state; but in giving their consent in these matters the House of Commons also represented his subjects, the people of England (Russell, 1990a, pp. 6–7). The Commons' claim to represent the people has been regarded with scepticism by revisionist historians. In sociological terms, they represented a small minority, for the members were overwhelmingly landed gentlemen. It has been argued that members were not 'elected' as we understand the term, but 'selected'by other local gentlemen whose main aim was to avoid degrading election contests, in which, as one complained, 'fellows without shirts' had equal votes with themselves (Kishlansky, 1986, p. 61). They aimed to present an unopposed candidate through negotiation among themselves, and patronage played a major part in this process. In this view the ruling élite tried, paradoxically, to keep politics out of elections – or at least behind closed doors among themselves.

A major study of the contested elections that did take place in this period finds that the number of contests increased from 13 in 1604 to 40 in 1624, and to an unprecedented 60 in the spring and 80 in the autumn of 1640. It also shows that when contests took place, they were usually in larger constituencies, counties or boroughs with thousands of electors; and they may have been more frequent in areas undergoing rapid economic change (Hirst, 1975; Cust, 1989, p. 160). Contested elections might still be battles between rival patrons for local influence, but the admission into the political process of the 40-shilling freeholders in the counties, and the shopkeepers and artisans who voted in some larger boroughs, could provide the middling sort with opportunities for genuine political self-expression (Hirst, 1975, pp. 109–31). An uncontested election, moreover, might signify the prevalence rather than the absence of popular political feeling, as in the widespread unopposed return of candidates known to be against the forced loan in 1628 (Cust, 1987, pp. 307–8).

There was a definite relationship between members of parliament and their constituents, though Russell argues that the need for representatives to justify their voting of taxes to the electors more or less paralysed the Commons politically, leaving them in the position of 'embarrassed pig-in-the-middle' between the crown and the taxpayer (Russell 1983, p. 19). Others see the relationship as more active and political, pointing to the appearance in the 1620s of widespread interest in politics among the electorate and the emergence of a concept of 'the country' as a set of political principles opposed to those of 'the court' (Zagorin, 1969; Cust, 1989). In the debates surrounding foreign policy in the early 1620s, there is evidence of popular support for the 'patriots'in parliament and at court who agitated for war with Spain; and a detailed study of Essex in these years has shown the interaction of these issues with local affairs (Cust, 1989; Hunt, 1983). There existed long before the civil war 'a comparatively large, well-informed, experienced, "public", capable of political action and influence', which was part of the context of parliamentary politics just as much as factions at court or patronage in local society (Hughes, 1991, pp. 69–72).

A comparison of the rival narratives offered by the Whig interpretation, the revisionist account and recent 'post-revisionist' work, though necessarily condensed, may help us to judge the significance of relations between king and parliament in the period 1604–29. According to the traditional Whig account, relations between king and parliament worsened from the start of James I's first parliament (1604–10). The Commons defended their right to adjudicate disputed election results, rejected James's proposed union of England and Scotland, and drew up an 'Apology and Satisfaction' (1604) asserting that 'our privileges and liberties are our right and due inheritance, no less than our very lands and goods' (Smith, 1984, p. 394). In the 1610 session, the argument about the impositions on trade led them to express fears for 'the ancient liberty of this kingdom and your subjects' right of propriety of their lands and goods' (Sommerville, 1986, p. 153). The 'Addled Parliament' of 1614, in which the Commons reacted angrily to royal attempts to influence the elections, and refused to grant the king any money unless their grievances over impositions were redressed, showed parliament's ability to use its control over the royal purse strings, though this led to an angry dissolution and a period of seven years without parliaments.

When James summoned another parliament in 1621, the Whig account continues, it was dominated by bitter arguments over free speech in the area of foreign policy, and the revival of the medieval practice of impeaching the king's ministers. The commons' protestation at the end of this parliament appealed to the nation, asserting that 'the liberties, franchises, privileges and jurisdictions of parliament are the ancient and undoubted birthright and inheritance of the subjects of England' (Kenyon, 1986, p. 42). James's last parliament, in 1624, succeeded in getting the policy of war with Spain which the patriotic Protestant Commons demanded, largely because of the helpful support of the royal favourite, Buckingham, and the king's heir, Charles.

The 1625 parliament, Charles's first as king, showed its continued desire to limit the king's actions by controlling his revenue in refusing him the customary lifetime grant of tonnage and poundage (the traditional customs revenues). Dissatisfaction with the corruption and military incompetence of Buckingham led the parliament of 1626 to attempt to remove him from power by impeaching him. Charles's attempt to mitigate the loss of money which he sustained in dissolving the parliament to save Buckingham, by raising a forced loan, led to the culmination of these constitutional conflicts in his next parliament with the Petition of Right (1628), which according to this view was intended to alter the balance of the constitution by limiting the monarch's prerogative. Charles managed to avoid the consequences only by disregarding the Petition of Right, quickly dissolving the 1629 session when the Commons protested, and ruling without parliament for eleven years. The thread of constitutional struggle which parliament was forced to drop in 1629 was taken up by the parliaments of 1640, which moved on to victory against absolutism by abolishing the institutions that most directly embodied the royal prerogative.

The alternative revisionist narrative emphasizes the basic desire to co-operate repeatedly expressed by James and his first parliament (1604–10), and argues that the failure of the Commons to extract any significant concessions on the matter of impositions by withholding supply in 1614 shows that with this 'weapon' they could only shoot themselves in the foot, for impositions continued to bring James £70,000 per year and he had no need to recall them until 1621 (Russell, 1976). The Commons' wrangling over their own 'liberties and privileges' has also been seen by revisionists as narrow self-interest, for it now seems incredible that concern for the freedom of members' servants from arrest during sessions, or the right to disbar for ever a parliamentary candidate who got on the wrong side of a patronage dispute, was anything more than 'the barking of dogs-in-mangers', or that such privileges could ever really have been identified with the common good (Morrill, 1996). On the 1620s, revisionist narratives contrast sharply with Whiggish ones. The 1621 parliament is distinguished by its eagerness to restore good relations with the king and grant supplies, while its attacks on corrupt royal servants and unpopular monopolists did not antagonize the king, and the issue of free speech became a conflict only at the very end of the parliament, when advice about foreign policy inadvertently trespassed on the more sensitive ground of Prince Charles's marriage (Russell, 1979, pp. 85–144). Harmony and co-operation were again the keynotes of the 1624 parliament, in which Buckingham and Charles – by now committed to war with Spain – skilfully managed the Commons and obtained their support in the face of opposition from the king and the pro-Spanish faction at court, though they did not succeed in obtaining fully adequate supplies for this war (ibid., pp. 145–203). Charles's first parliament, in 1625, was disrupted by plague rather than by political conflict, and its failure to grant the king tonnage and poundage at all was the unintended result of attempts to secure a rewriting of the traditional grant with explicit reference to impositions. Though the Commons in 1625 showed anxiety about the royal favour shown to Arminian clerics, it is alleged that there were no other major disputes in this parliament (ibid., pp. 204–59).

The parliament of 1626 was a disaster by all accounts. The two houses co-operated in an attempt to impeach Buckingham, and Charles eventually dissolved them without receiving the money he needed. But revisionists lay the blame for this disaster on privy councillors rather than members of parliament, as Buckingham's opponents on the council intruded their power struggle into the two houses; and the impeachment of Buckingham cut Charles to the quick not because of its constitutional implications but because it included a charge of having hastened James I's death by unauthorized medical intervention (Russell, 1979, pp. 204–59). The patronage system which had allegedly secured harmony in the parliaments of 1621–5 blew up in the faces of Buckingham and Charles in 1626, though Russell expresses some discomfort at the 'mystery' that some of Buckingham's 'clients' in previous parliaments turned against him in 1626 and 1628 (ibid., pp. 243–4, 381).

There can be little disagreement about the seriousness of the issues confronted by the 1628–9 parliament in the aftermath of the forced loan and the Five Knights' case. But Russell insists this was a new departure, an 'intellectual watershed' in which parliamentarians first developed fears for the constitution; this was 'the first parliament of the decade'that 'came to Westminster with the conscious and deliberate aim of vindicating English liberties'(ibid., p. 344). Nevertheless, the Petition of Right was essentially a conservative document, which reasserted what parliamentarians believed to be the law rather than breaking new constitutional ground. Though the assassination of Buckingham removed one of the major issues (and apparently quieted the House of Lords) before they met again in January 1629, the Commons attacked customs officials for collecting the tonnage and poundage which they had declared illegal. When briefly reconvened in March, they brought the issues of religion and taxation to a crisis by attempting to pass resolutions condemning innovations in government and religion. Russell considers that in 1629 the Commons once again fatally weakened their own constitutional position. Despite getting themselves recognized as the representative of the people, they were on a route to extinction rather than civil war, because they alienated Charles I and secured not their own sovereignty but their own eleven-year absence, which might well have become permanent had it not been for the Scottish war in 1639 (Russell, 1976; 1979, pp. 323–416).

Both these narratives describe a pattern of two cycles in the relations between king and parliament, the first ending in the constitutional crisis of 1614 and the second in that of 1629, each followed by a period without parliaments. Most historians seem to agree that the 1621 and 1624 parliaments showed some concern to restore harmony, for example by underplaying the contentious issue of impositions. The rapid escalation of war in Europe also made both king and parliament anxious to show unity in the face of external danger. A potentially serious breach over James's policy of diplomatic and dynastic alliance with Spain was averted by Charles and Buckingham's dramatic conversion to an anti-

Spanish stance in 1623, a turn of events which was hailed in parliament and the country as a 'blessed revolution'(Cogswell, 1989).

There is much more argument over the parliaments of 1624–6, especially in relation to the question of war. Since Russell has identified 'the strains of wartime' as the major cause of political tension in the late 1620s – an explanation which he insists invalidates the alternative of constitutional conflict – it is vital to ask why there was war. Russell himself appears inconsistent on this question: while he has accused the House of Commons of clamouring for intervention in the Catholic–Protestant struggle and then refusing to grant adequate supplies, thus demonstrating their political immaturity, he has at the same time argued that they showed little enthusiasm for war, being 'almost as reluctant partners in the enterprise as King James himself' in 1624 (Russell, 1973, pp. 101–5; 1979, pp. 78, 164–5, 172–3, 190).

Michael Young has argued that it was Charles and Buckingham who made the decision to embark on war, and 'orchestrated the proceedings of the 1624 parliament toward that end'. In 1625 they tried to force the Commons into financing commitments they had not made, to a war which had not yet been declared, against an enemy who had not yet been identified, as many members pointed out at the time. When they turned on Buckingham in 1626 for his military and diplomatic failures, there was explicit reluctance to throw money into an apparently bottomless pit (Thompson, 1989; Young, 1997, pp. 37–47). Evidence for widespread popular concern about the threat to continental Protestants in 1622–4 and parliamentary enthusiasm for a militant stance against Spain does not seem to fit with this (Cogswell, 1989). But there was a difference between the kind of war which Charles and Buckingham wanted, which was an intervention on the European mainland, and the naval war against Spain which the Commons wanted. The latter was an unrealistic expectation according to Russell but less so according to others (Reeve, 1989, pp. 229–30). It might also be helpful to distinguish between defensive and aggressive policies, since Russell uses the term 'defence budget'in its ambiguous modern sense. The Commons in 1621–4 seem to have been most committed to a defensive war against Spain, which they feared might follow the breaking off of diplomatic relations. Russell takes it for granted that England's involvement in the European conflict was only a matter of time, while Young describes powerful policy-makers playing war games behind the backs of a hesitant but loyal assembly, perhaps revealing a difference between a British historian who remembers Hitler and an American one who remembers Vietnam. War was not a simple, 'external' factor in the politics of the 1620s. War involved constitutional tensions even before the forced loan. The Commons pursued their opposition to continental military intervention by obtaining the right to supervise the spending of the 1624 subsidies, which was regarded as astonishing at the time and clearly encroached upon the royal prerogative (Young, 1989, pp. 18–22). They demanded accounts in 1625, and attempted to link the question of further supplies for the war, which still had not started, to reformation in government as well as to action against Catholics at home (Thompson, 1989). They pursued the matter in 1626 so far as to question members of the Council of War about which of them were responsible for advising support for Count Mansfeld's unsuccessful campaign in Germany, the kind of military adventure they had explicitly tried to rule out in 1624 (Young, 1989). Closer examination of the parliamentary sources actually leads some historians to conclude that constitutional conflict did not come out of the blue in 1628, and that the old Whig interpretation stands up better than the revisionist one (Young, 1997, pp. 34–71; Thompson, 1989).

If new perspectives on war can restore constitutional conflict to the narrative of the second cycle of relations between the early Stuarts and their parliaments, the thread that could restore a link with the first cycle is property. In the conflicts over both impositions in 1610 and 1614 and the forced loan in 1628, there was an outcry about property rights in danger. Members of parliament claimed that English subjects had property rights which 'may not without their consent be altered and charged'; that if the subjects' lands or goods could be taken from them by the king's absolute power, they were 'little better than the king's bondmen'. They protested that Manwaring's divine right sermon 'robs the subjects of the propriety of their goods', and that 'the ancient and undoubted right of every free man is that he hath a full and absolute property in his goods and estates'(Sommerville, 1986, pp. 153–8; 1989, pp.

57–8). The same arguments were repeated in public and private discussions of Ship Money in the 1630s and in the Short and Long Parliaments in the 1640s. This thread therefore links the first and second cycles of seventeenth-century parliamentary history to the crisis of the early 1640s (Sommerville, 1986, pp. 57–8; 1989, pp. 159–60; Kenyon, 1966, pp. 109–12; Salt, 1994, p. 258).

The concern to defend property was common to ruling classes throughout early modern Western Europe; but in England there were complications. The Commons took refuge in general arguments because, despite searching ancient records in 1610, they could not find the principle they were looking for in the common law, and in 1628 they feared that the legal ideology in which they had such confidence might fail them (Judson, 1949, pp. 230, 242). Some common law texts seemed to agree with the controversial Cowell, who asserted in 1610 that only the king possessed absolute property in land, because all landed property in England was supposedly held from him 'in fee'– that is, by what we would now call a feudal tenure (Aylmer, 1980). But leading common lawyers such as Coke nevertheless held that ordinary subjects had absolute property in their lands, and had had for centuries (Pocock, 1974, pp. 56–69). This ambiguity could not be resolved without a fundamental challenge to the legal rights of the crown, and the lawyers' definitions changed only in the years after the execution of Charles I (Aylmer, 1980, pp. 92–3).

Parliament's claim to be defending property rights had widespread popular appeal, given the importance of landed property and the profits to be derived from it in seventeenth-century England. Not only the gentry, but freeholders, customary tenants and urban landlords depended on the common law to resolve their property rights, and they were very litigious people. Some historians doubt that the middling and lower sorts could identify with the gentry in their opposition to prerogative taxation, because as a class the gentry were notoriously under-assessed for parliamentary taxation, and because they were as landlords and employers exploiting those beneath them (Russell, 1979, p. 257; Young, 1997, p. 105). But there is abundant evidence in the records of resistance to the forced loan that ordinary taxpayers did believe that taxation 'in a parliamentary way' was in their own best interests (Cust, 1987, pp. 185, 284–306).

Fear about the insecurity of parliament as an institution also runs through both cycles of early Stuart parliaments. In 1614 one member saw the end of the Addled Parliament as 'a dissolution not of this, but of all parliaments' (Russell, 1976, p. 9), and similar fears were voiced in the counties in 1614 and 1622 when James attempted to raise money by benevolences, which were free but assessed gifts (Cust, 1987, pp. 152–8). In 1621, when it was proposed to revive the 1604 Apology defending the commons' privileges, one member urged that 'we shall never sit here again if they be not maintained'(Sommerville, 1986, p. 181). Those who urged co-operation with the monarchy in the early 1620s suggested a positive need 'to secure from his majesty the love and frequency of parliaments' (Russell, 1976, pp. 6–7). Comparisons with the decline of representative institutions on the Continent were regular: 'We are the last monarchy in Christendom that retain our original rights and constitutions', one member said in 1625 (Judson, 1949, p. 221). Ominously, it was a close adviser of Charles I who pointed out in 1626 that parliaments 'were in use anciently' in most kingdoms, but as a result of their 'turbulent spirit' other monarchs had got rid of them (Kenyon, 1986, p. 45).

Some historians have regarded these fears as irrational, arguing that neither James I nor Charles I ever seriously thought of doing away with parliament as an institution. Others suggest that they exaggerated the decline of representation abroad. They could not know that the 1614 meeting of the French estates-general was the last before 1789; but they did know that it was the first full assembly since 1588 (Richet, 1973, p. 96). Russell maintains that the parliamentarians' anxiety stemmed from an uncomfortable realization that they were not delivering the goods the Stuarts needed to make them worth the effort of calling, though Charles I was a 'prince bred in parliaments' who did his best to get on with them and only reluctantly adopted 'new counsels' when they made this impossible (Russell, 1979).

It is not certain whether Charles I did contemplate the permanent abolition of parliaments. Some historians maintain that he never intended ruling without parliaments until 1629, though others see him as being impatient with them from the start and casting them aside after the experiences of the late 1620s (Sharpe,

1992; Young, 1997). What makes this question difficult is that Charles was capable of saying one thing and doing another, and that it was not his beliefs so much as his actions that produced conflict. The proclamation which he issued after the dissolution of 1629 said that he intended to call parliament again, when feelings had cooled and harmony between the king and his subjects was restored. But there is evidence that the king's first draft suggested an end to all parliaments, and he was persuaded to alter it by some of his advisers (Reeve, 1989, p. 111). Rumours about the king's intentions abounded for the next couple of years, and foreign ambassadors were as eager to second-guess him as historians have been to repeat their speculations.

While some historians believe that Charles would never have called another parliament had it not been for his defeat in the first Bishops' War, most of his advisers as well as his politically aware subjects seem to have expected that one day he would do so (Cope, 1987; Sharpe, 1992, pp. 702–5). We have already seen what happened when he did call another: the Commons in the Short Parliament of 1640 immediately took up the main grievances of 1629 from where they had left off, and protested about the treatment of members imprisoned after the last session. Though the personal rule is regarded by some as 'an experiment not allowed to run its full course'because it was interrupted by the Scottish war, it is hard to imagine what length of time or achievements of royal government would have induced Charles's more politically conscious subjects to forget the grievances and conflicts of the late 1620s. Moreover, as 'the intermission of parliaments'for eleven years was itself presented as a grievance in 1640, it is hard to believe that an intermission of, say, twenty years would not have been a cause of complaint (Young, 1997, pp. 115, 133–4). As it happened, the events of 1628–9 and the eleven-year absence of parliaments contributed substantially to the political crisis of 1640–2.

Local Government and the Personal Rule

The dissolution of parliament in 1629 was followed by over two years of instability, including bad harvests, industrial stagnation, outbreaks of plague, and rioting in London and parts of southern England (Reeve, 1989, pp. 116–32). Though the refusal of merchants to pay tonnage and poundage by stopping trade lasted only a few months, it caused the customs receipts to fall from £500 to £1 or £2 per day and the monarchy was virtually bankrupt (Sharpe, 1992, pp. 124–6). But order did not break down. Talk of future parliaments was forbidden by royal proclamation, and Charles shamelessly manipulated legal procedures to keep in prison those members arrested for their part in resisting the dissolution; but protests were muted and acceptance of the need for a strong royal hand may have been widespread among the gentry, at least in the short term (Cope, 1987, pp. 11–33). It must be said that in many ways Charles's strategy was successful: merchants were soon reconciled with the monarchy, trade recovered when he ended his wars with France and Spain, and since many of the grievances which had led to conflict in the parliaments of the late 1620s had been related to the war situation, peace did allow the political temperature to drop and normal relations between central and local government to be restored.

Though this period was labelled by Whig historians 'the eleven years' tyranny', it was not unconstitutional for the king to rule without parliament. Indeed, it was normal, considering that parliament met irregularly and for only short periods. The eleven years from 1629 to 1640 were to be the longest period without a meeting in the history of parliament, but the record was not broken until 1636. The normal functioning of English government depended on the co-operation of the classes that provided and elected members of parliament, but in their own localities rather than at Westminster. That co-operation was not withdrawn, and many men who had opposed the king as members of the 1628–9 parliament were willing to serve him locally in the 1630s (Russell, 1979, pp. 83, 423–4).

Co-operation between central and local government did not necessarily mean that all was well. The personal rule has been seen as intensifying a growing polarization between the interests of the court and those of the country, in which a fundamental tension between centralism and localism caused relations between the monarchy and local government to deteriorate and eventually to break down, producing a 'revolt of the provinces' against central-ization (Zagorin, 1969; Ashton, 1978; Morrill, 1980). But it has proved difficult to distinguish separate court and country interest groups among the ruling élite, since the Justices of the Peace who ran local government in the counties were often the same men who served the king more directly as local and national officials, and sought friends and influence at court whenever they had the oppor-tunity (Morrill, 1980, pp. 14–16). It has often been said that the conflict between court and country interests lay within the breasts of the gentry themselves, rather than between them and a narrow élite of courtiers.

Whether Charles's approach to the counties during the personal rule amounts to a new departure in centralization is debatable. He did indeed set out to secure a more efficient and uniform function-ing of local government under the supervision of the privy council, but the strategy he adopted was a traditional one. 'Books of Orders' had been issued to the Justices of the Peace in previous reigns, and the 1631 version was, like them, stimulated by economic and social crisis and the fear of disorder which poverty and hunger could bring (Sharp, 1980, pp. 43–81). The council's orders essentially demanded that the Justices control and oversee the grain trade, and implement the poor laws for the relief of distress. They also required a uniform pattern of meetings, with regular petty sessions in each part of every county, and regular reporting back to the council. Evidence suggests that Justices shared the council's belief in control of the grain trade at times of crisis, but they often had dif-ferent ideas about the relief of poverty, and resented the imposition of a common system of priorities and methods, especially the privy council's attempts to maintain employment and minimum wage levels in conditions of industrial depression (Walter and Wrightson, 1976; Fletcher, 1986, pp. 43–60; Sharp, 1980, pp. 53–61). A major study of local government in the seventeenth century has concluded that Charles I's Book of Orders 'highlighted rather than solved ... the problem of tension between the centre and the localities' (Fletcher, 1986, p. 59).

The privy council attacked the local Justices for negligence whenever economic crisis led to outbreaks of disorder, but had no effective power to change their ways. There was little overt resistance and no confrontation between the council and the Justices, but a widespread tendency to ignore the orders, or to adopt 'a bland and uninformative approach', and the privy council did not have the time, personnel or local knowledge to enforce its will (Sharp, 1980, pp. 66–7, 435–46). The assize judges' visits on their twice-yearly circuits were used to instruct and supervise the Justices, but their effectiveness declined in this period, partly because of low attendance at the assizes, and the unpopularity of the judges due to their 'haughtiness, petulance and failure to regard local sensibilities' (Fletcher, 1986, pp. 56–7; Herrup, 1983). Studies of local government in the 1630s appear to confirm Gardiner's view that this was 'a government not of fierce tyranny but of petty annoyance' (Young, 1997, p. 98). Yet there was one kind of punitive action Charles could and did take against members of the local élite which cut far deeper than petty annoyance among the class of gentlemen addicted to honour, reputation and public service: he could humiliate and downgrade them by removing them from the Justices' bench (Fletcher, 1986). The fact that he did so repeatedly for political reasons, removing enemies of Buckingham in 1626–7, opponents of the forced loan in 1628–9 and of Ship Money in the late 1630s, and supporters of parliament in a final purge in 1642 on the eve of the outbreak of civil war, is probably an underrated contribution to the hostility that many of the gentry felt towards Charles (Fletcher, 1986, pp. 10–13; Cust, 1987, pp. 186–252).

Had the Stuarts by 1639 'lost a critical battle in their relations with the people who did their governing for them', a battle for control over local government (Fletcher, 1986, p. 60)? If so, the reason was possibly that the power of local governors in practice depended more on the collaboration of lesser men in local society than on royal authority. The county court, quarter sessions and petty sessions depended on the presence and participation of freeholders, juries, parish constables, sureties and witnesses. Men of this kind also assessed and collected subsidies, attended parliamentary elections, and provided grand juries at the assizes. It has been suggested that during the personal rule 'participatory situations' of this kind became fewer, as no elections took place, no subsidies were granted, and attendance at the assizes in some places declined (Herrup, 1983). It was perhaps not excessive centralization but failure to maintain contact and influence in local government which weakened the monarchy during the personal rule. At the same time, a study of Ship Money collection in Cheshire has shown the way in which this bypassed the usual hierarchies of county government and involved the sheriff (whose office had long been a largely honorary one) directly imposing royal authority on relatively humble people such as village constables. In the end, some of these 'most local of local officials' could be faced, if they were reluctant or ineffective in collecting the levy, by a direct order from the privy council, an unusually direct and authoritarian relationship between the centre and the localities (Lake, 1981, pp. 56–61).

Though revisionist historians see the personal rule as evidence that Charles I was an innovative and modernizing king, resisted by a backward-looking gentry and nobility (Morrill, 1993, p. 13), he made no structural changes and created no new institutions of government. The only real threat to the local power of the Justices of the Peace in the seventeenth century, the granting of letters patent to private individuals to enforce particular laws in James I's reign, was stopped by the 1624 parliament (Ashton, 1978, pp. 45–9). Charles's outlook was explicitly traditional rather than modernizing, looking back to 'an idealized past of social order, harmony, community and respect for authority and law'with the king at the centre (Sharpe, 1992, pp. 195–6). He even considered at one point reviving the feudal ceremony of homage and fealty to bind the landowning class more closely in personal obedience to him. His proclamations ordering the gentry and nobility to leave London and 'keep their habitations and hospitality' in the country suggest perhaps that he wished to reverse, or was unaware of, the long-term decline in the political importance of the noble household and the landlord's manor court (ibid., pp. 414, 421–2; Morrill, 1993, pp. 184–6). Many of his ways of raising money, from fining landowners who had not applied to be knighted at his coronation, to fully exploiting his feudal rights to wardship and purveyance, may have irritated the ruling élite of the counties because they harked back to a past society which had changed in ways that they themselves had not fully come to terms with.

The confusion surrounding the legal status of the militia in early Stuart England made military matters a bone of constant contention between the government and the localities, aggravating the crisis of the late 1620s and continuing during the personal rule. Charles's view that only the nobility, in the role of lords lieutenants, should have any authority over musters and training was often regarded by Justices of the Peace as an interference with their authority, though resistance mainly took the form of endless quibbling about raising money and paying muster masters (Ashton, 1978, pp. 54–9; Cope, 1987, pp. 94–106). By 1639 Charles had fallen far behind the military revolution in weaponry and organization which had swept the rest of Europe, and this contributed significantly to his failure in war against the Scots in 1639 and 1640 (Russell, 1993a, pp. 39–44; Sharpe, 1992, pp. 799–800).

Though he did without an army in the 1630s, Charles wanted a more effective navy to secure English control over the surrounding seas and demonstrate that he was still a player in the European power game (Sharpe, 1992, pp. 545–52; Young, 1997, pp. 100–3). Although by the mid-1630s his ordinary revenues had increased greatly, largely because of the revival of trade, he could not afford to equip the fleet he wanted without a substantial extra contribution from his subjects. A levy of ships and money on port towns in 1634 was insufficient, and in 1635 Ship Money was demanded from the whole country. Since inland counties could not supply ships as some ports did, it was in effect a direct money tax on property like the parliamentary subsidy, but rated and collected by the sheriff. Charles made a great point of finding precedents and keeping within the law as he saw it, but as a national and annual levy Ship Money was unprecedented. When its legality was tested in Hampden's case in 1637, the judges decided in Charles's favour, but on a narrow majority and on mostly technical grounds. Despite these problems, however, Ship Money was a success in financial terms: from 1635 to 1639, 90 per cent of what was demanded was paid. Widespread refusal occurred only in 1639 and 1640, when people were also being asked to pay coat and conduct money for the militia (Lake, 1981; Clifford, 1982). This has led some historians to describe Ship Money as an indication of support for the personal rule up to 1639, despite the protests against it in the Short and Long Parliaments (Sharpe, 1992, p. 585; Morrill, 1980, p. 24). Most historians think, however, that there was significant opposition to Ship Money, but that its nature shows some of the problems of assessing relations between central and local government during the personal rule. There is evidence that the issue was widely discussed, especially during Hampden's case, and that the constitutional implications were recognized. Resistance to paying took the form of innumerable petty disputes about rating, jurisdiction and procedures rather than protests about the principle, but private criticism might go further than public resistance. Behind outward compliance could lie principled disagreement, as we know from a few private archives which happen to have survived (Salt, 1994; Fincham, 1984; Cope, 1987, pp. 117, 120–1). The knowledge that even a few people concealed principled disagreement behind outward compliance casts doubt on Ship Money payments as an indication of support for the regime. We have to remember 'that it was dangerous to express hostility to the crown, and there were more prudent ways of dealing with objectionable policies than strident protest' (Young, 1997, p. 105). Most people who disagreed with Ship Money or other royal policies 'elected to grumble rather than to take more daring action … they had no wish to cause disorder or incur punishment'(Cope, 1987, p. 212). These circumstances make it difficult to judge the state of public opinion during the personal rule.

Public opinion did exist in the 1630s, quite broad layers of people being informed by news and involved in discussion about events such as Hampden's case. Media which had first appeared in the 1620s, such as manuscript newsletters sent out from London and recopied as they passed from hand to hand, and printed 'separates' or one-off publications, continued to circulate in the 1630s, and unpublished political tracts circulated in manuscript. Diaries and letters show gentry and professional men taking an interest in the latest news or gossip about the kingdom's affairs, and news also reached literate farmers and artisans. Offering an alternative to official media which stressed harmony and obedience, news often dramatized conflict and tended to present polarized opinions. Since news highlighted cases of repression such as the imprisonment of the leaders of the disturbance in parliament in 1629 or the corporal punishment of Puritan dissidents, people were also informed of the dangers of criticizing the regime (Cust, 1986).

There is a growing consensus among historians that beneath the surface calm during the personal rule there was an accumulation of bitterness and suppressed conflict. The suspension of parliaments closed down an important channel of communication between the monarchy and those who ruled the localities, and this caused English society to become 'politically unstable and distinctly vulnerable to crisis'(Reeve, 1989, p. 293). 'The troubles in Scotland wrecked the personal rule in England because of the depth of alienation that existed anyway', claims one historian, while another argues that 'the true impact of the personal rule may be best measured by what happened afterwards' (Hughes, 1991, p. 165; Young, 1997, p. 111). It is clear that active resistance to Charles's policies, such as refusal to pay Ship Money, increased once he had taken the decision to call a parliament in 1640. As in 1628, 'the prospects for a parliament crucially influenced the balance of power and range of options, both nationally and locally' (Cust, 1987, p. 317). Petitions of grievances were drawn up in many counties in early 1640, showing even to revisionist historians 'that, for all the surface calm, resentment had built up in the localities and that a parliament was now expected to redress them' (Sharpe, 1992, pp. 858–60). It was the calling of a parliament in England, rather than the troubles in Scotland as such, which aroused the expression of grievances that led to confrontation in 1640, and it is quite conceivable that this would have happened whatever Charles's reason for calling his next parliament. An intense and broadly based 'backlash against the personal rule', and a harking back to the political conflicts and grievances of the late 1620s, were essential components of the political confrontation of 1640 (Young, 1997, pp. 132–5). Many of the developments which followed, which have been traced in chapter 2 above, can be said to have sprung to a large extent from that backlash, rather than from a reaction to the Scottish war alone.

5

Economic and Social Change

One of the most fundamental disagreements among historians about the causes of the English civil war is whether economic and social changes in sixteenth- and early seventeenth-century England were significant factors. Dissatisfaction with Marxist accounts of causation led Conrad Russell in 1973 to assert that 'for the time being ... social change explanations of the English Civil War must be regarded as having broken down' (Russell, 1973, p. 8), and his major recent analysis of the causes of the conflict simply ignores social change altogether (Russell, 1990a). Many revisionist historians point out that social change explanations of the war are unproven, though in reality this does not make them different from any other suggested causes. It has become quite common for student textbooks on the civil war simply to ignore the question, or to make sweeping statements while avoiding causal implications, such as the bald assertion that 'England in 1637 was well on the road to modernization' (Bennett, 1997, p. 16). But the question of modernization has deeply divided recent historians of early seventeenth-century England, whether or not they have been concerned with the causes of the civil war as such. John Morrill has stated that the 'revisionist revolt' in the 1970s was chiefly inspired by a conviction that descriptions of early seventeenth-century England as a modernizing society by Lawrence Stone and others were fundamentally anachronistic (Morrill, 1993, pp. 4 n., 34–5). By the early 1980s some historians were arguing that the English economy had not grown, that there had been no significant social change, and that there was no clear break with the medieval outlook in the century before the civil war (Coward, 1980, pp. 1–80). Later works by Wrightson (1982) and Coward (1988) usefully tried to strike a balance between aspects of English society which did change significantly and those which remained traditional, but a volume of essays in honour of Lawrence Stone in 1989 was defiantly entitled *The First Modern Society* (Beier et al., 1989). An assessment of this problem is vital to any consideration of recent debates on the causes of the civil war, since it is still a central tenet of revisionism that any explanation of the causes of the civil war must be 'appropriate to a stable, aristocratic *ancien régime* society' rather than to a modernizing one (Burgess, 1990, p. 612).

The place of Marxist theory in this debate will be discussed in chapter 6, but the present chapter aims to provide a survey of economic and social change and continuity in the century before the civil war. It is essential, moreover, to have some picture of the social context of religious and political divisions in a culture which is at least half-alien to us in the late twentieth century. On the whole, economic historians have been more inclined to conclude that the period did see significant changes than social historians, and for this reason the analysis will be divided into economic and social topics. Economic history may be defined as primarily having to do with production, distribution and exchange, and with matters such as agriculture, trade and prices. Social history is harder to define, because there has been much discussion about its nature and purpose (Wilson, 1993). It will be taken here as having to do above all with social groups and how they were perceived at the time.

The final section of this chapter will bring these different strands of economic and social history together by examining the problem of disorder in the period before the civil war. There has been much disagreement about this. Some historians have seen the period as one of mounting disorder due to the intensification of social conflicts (Manning, 1991, 1996), while others have argued that England before the civil war experienced a relatively low level of disorder, especially when compared with continental Europe (Morrill and Walter, 1985). Many observers at the time, however, perceived the situation as one of increasing disorder, and this perception, as we have seen, was an important factor in the political choices they made in 1640–2.

The English Economy: Progress or Backwardness?

Any discussion of the English economy in the sixteenth and seventeenth centuries must begin with agriculture, since it was overwhelmingly the largest and most important productive activity. The
vast majority of the population lived in the countryside and made
all or part of their living from agriculture. Though rural occupations
could be surprisingly varied, many rural inhabitants practising
crafts or trade also worked their own plots of land (Coward, 1994,
p. 9). From about 1500 there was more and more pressure on the
land to feed a growing population. We have no reliable statistics
from the period, but most historians agree that the population rose
from about two million in 1500 to five million by 1630, and that the
general rise in prices by about 400 per cent over roughly the same
period was chiefly caused by pressure on food supplies (Clay,
1984). In a modern economy we tend to take for granted the market
relationship in which a rise in demand stimulates an increased
supply. In 1500, however, much of the food grown in England was
not produced for the market, but for consumption by the peasant
families who produced it. In some areas of Western Europe where
peasant farming for direct consumption remained dominant, and
the land was divided into smaller plots to accommodate the rising
population in the sixteenth century, the amount of surplus coming
on to the market may actually have decreased at the very time when
fewer and fewer people were able to produce enough for themselves, and this could lead to the classic 'Malthusian crisis' of
famine and disease imposing a drastic check on population growth.
  Most historians are agreed that this kind of crisis was avoided in
England because what happened was a shift towards farming for
the market rather than for family consumption. Larger farmers
who increased their holdings could farm with an eye to the profits
to be made from rising prices rather than the balance between
hands to labour and mouths to feed which was paramount in the
traditional peasant household. The larger farmer's outlook and
mode of operation therefore could produce more of a market
supply than the meagre surplus of hard-pressed peasant families.
Although some historians have pointed out that farming for the
market had been known in England since at least the thirteenth

century (Coward, 1980, pp. 6–7), it does appear to have declined in the late Middle Ages when the population fell and there were fewer markets. According to a standard work on the economic history of this period, English agriculture was still dominated by peasant farming at the beginning of the sixteenth century, but the next century and a half saw a significant increase in markets and commercial farming (Clay, 1984, vol. 1, pp. 56–72). The actual acreage required to support a household, and the size of farm which could produce a market profit, varied according to the type of soil and the kind of crops grown.

There is evidence from many parts of England that larger farms were increasing in number and in their overall share of the land in the sixteenth and seventeenth centuries, while the middle-sized holdings which supported whole households at a subsistence level declined. In the lowland areas of England, the traditional pattern of farming had been on scattered strips in huge open fields, and it was here that the consolidation and enclosure of larger farms and the introduction of improvements, such as flooding water-meadows or alternating arable farming with pasture for a few years at a time, contributed to the growth of commercial agriculture and the prosperity of a section of the agricultural population (Clay, 1984, vol. 1). It seems that in the south midlands, however, the survival of peasant family farms was accompanied by a substantial increase in crop yields, suggesting that improved methods that increased the marketable surplus were not impossible within the more traditional structure. But even in this region about a third of the cultivated area included in a recent study was held in farms of more than 100 acres, although the proportion of the farming population who held these larger farms was much smaller (Allen, 1992, pp. 73–4).

If rising food prices provided opportunities for some farmers, these were certainly only a minority of the rural population. As peasant farmers producing for household subsistence were being squeezed out in many areas, the number of small peasants with holdings too small for subsistence grew everywhere, and so did the number of landless agricultural labourers dependent on what they could earn from waged work. Some regions, particularly in the north of England, did not experience the rise of larger farms and commercial farming, but still saw the size of peasant holdings shrink and the number of underemployed labourers grow as the population swelled. Perhaps parts of the north of England did come close to suffering a Malthusian type of crisis in the late sixteenth century (Appleby, 1975). Even in those regions where there was a growth of larger farms and we have some evidence of improved farming methods being adopted, it has been suggested that the number of very small holdings being farmed less efficiently by peasants without capital to improve may have prevented the productivity of agriculture from increasing overall (Outhwaite, 1986). This is hard to judge, because we have little evidence for the smallholders' farming methods, or whether they mostly grew grain, kept animals or practised market gardening.

Most historians incline to the view that the productivity of agriculture did increase substantially over this period. It appears that, except in years of acute harvest failure, English grain supplies were feeding the increased population by the early seventeenth century, and the rise in grain prices was slowing down by 1620. A significant increase in the market product of English agriculture could have been achieved by the diversion of produce from peasant consumption to the market, an increase in the cultivated area by fen and forest clearance, and some investment in improved methods, though not on the scale of that of later centuries (Clay, 1984, vol. 1, pp. 102–16). This was no easy progress: there were years in the late sixteenth century in which people died of starvation, and the situation of smallholders and agricultural labourers appears to have been precarious as they were less able to produce their own food and more dependent on wages from agricultural work.

Because of the nature of the larger farmers' demand for hired labour – a few live-in servants who were mostly young people, plus a very variable demand for casual and seasonal workers – the agricultural labour force was chronically underemployed, and wage labour alone could not provide a reliable living for poor rural households. What the more pessimistic historians of early modern English agriculture ignore, however, is that in many areas the rural population had other employment, in the cottage industries which spread especially in areas of woodland and pasture where stock rearing, wool growing and dairy farming predominated over arable. The cottage economy in these areas was a multi-occupational compound of household production, part-time wage earning and the use of common rights (Levine, 1987, pp. 19–61). The prevalence of this cottage economy among the poor in some regions was part of a pattern of regional differentiation in both agriculture and manufacture that was developing in this period, for example areas of dairy or arable farming, heavy woollen cloth production or the lighter 'new draperies'. Perhaps these patterns did provide the conditions for the later agricultural revolution in the arable areas and industrial revolution in the pastoral ones, but these more substantial economic changes were still far in the future (Thirsk, 1984, pp. 182–216).

On a national scale, the largest and most significant of the cottage-based manufactures were those which produced various kinds of woollen textiles, from the traditional heavy woollen broadcloth of the west to the new draperies of East Anglia. These included goods for export which presumably helped England to import the extra food supplies needed in years of poor harvests. But export industries were also vulnerable to the trading crises of the sixteenth and early seventeenth centuries which could leave the poor of whole regions temporarily without the manufacturing work they had come to depend on (Supple, 1959). It may be that these crises, together with dislocation caused by changes in the textile manufactures, meant that total production for export did not increase between about 1550 and 1640 (Coward, 1980, p. 21). But the plentiful evidence for the spread of cheaper textiles and other manufactures for the home markct rather than overseas ones makes it pretty certain that overall manufacturing production did increase, mainly based on the cheap part-time labour of poor people (especially women, children and old people) whose families may have had small plots of land and other casual wage-earning opportunities (Thirsk, 1978; Clay, 1984, vol. 2, pp. 1–43).

There were many small-scale rural manufactures, supplying mainly the home market for cheaper products, which provided labouring people with at least part of their livelihood in areas where most agricultural holdings were small, common lands extensive, and the opportunities for agricultural wage labour limited. In addition to the better-known textiles, these included pin-making, stocking-knitting and starch-making, together with a host of minor wood and leather crafts in areas where these raw materials were close at hand (Thirsk, 1978). It is important to realize that there was in early seventeenth-century England almost no modern industry as we know it. Not all manufacture, it is true, took place in the countryside: some towns were the focus of specialized manufactures, such as particular types of cloth or metal wares (Jack, 1996, pp. 55–60). The mining and metallurgical industries expanded considerably, from a very tiny base at the beginning of the period (Clay, 1984, vol. 2, pp. 43–64). But nothing like the urban-based industrial revolution of the late eighteenth century yet existed.

Most non-agricultural production took place either in people's homes or in small workshops, on a scale similar to that of peasant farming. Most manufacturers were independent small producers working at home with their families, one or two apprentices, and possibly a couple of skilled journeymen or lower-paid unskilled servants. In some areas, small-scale manufacture came under the control of merchants who 'put out'raw materials or partly finished products to households where they were manufactured into finished products. Workers in these industries were less independent, but the merchant employers needed very little starting capital and most of their assets consisted of raw materials or goods. The importance of the tools and equipment which cottage workers owned themselves is preserved for us in the word 'heirloom': a loom was perhaps the most valuable piece of moveable property that a working person could inherit. The spread of these small-scale industries, which was important for the economy as a whole and for the livelihood of the poor, is sometimes called 'proto-industrialization'. Economic historians have argued about the usefulness of this term (Clarkson, 1985), but it does serve to remind us that the English economy in the early seventeenth century was undergoing change and development. It is important, however, not to equate this early development of manufacturing with industry in a modern economy where fixed capital and specialized, full-time wage earning are the norm and most industry is urban.

Trade was also a significant part of the early modern English economy, but again it is the less quantifiable aspect, internal trade, which was probably most important at the time, especially as it facilitated regional specialization in agriculture and industry.

Overseas trade was still largely concentrated on exchanges with nearby Western Europe, but the development of more long-distance trades – to the Baltic, the Mediterranean, the Far East, Africa and the Americas – was the beginning of a trend which was to become much more important after 1660 and really significant after 1700 (Clay, 1984, vol. 2, p. 163). The quest for luxury imports, especially from the Far East, Atlantic and Mediterranean, was what mainly drove English merchants to invest in long voyages to distant parts of the world, rather than a deliberate drive to export more English products (Brenner, 1993, pp. 3–50). The seventeenth century saw recurrent crises in English cloth exports to Europe, and the response of merchants and manufacturers was to try to get diversification and improvement in the manufacture of textiles from wool (such as the new draperies aimed at Southern European markets) in the belief that their trade could be revived by such measures, although European wars and Dutch commercial competition were probably more to blame than the quality of English cloth (Supple, 1959).

The new long-distance trades were generally not organized in a more modern, competitive way, but were restricted by company monopolies and high entrance fees because of the risks involved and the need for government protection (Brenner, 1993, pp. 51–91). The appearance of joint stock companies in some of these trades looks more like the appearance of a modern institution because organizations based on this principle later became important in modern industrial society; but in the context of the period before the civil war a joint stock arrangement was also one way of restricting trade to a wealthy minority with monopoly privileges and excluding others. Most overseas trade passed through London, reinforcing the dominance of the monopoly companies, despite the growing importance of Bristol to the Atlantic trade and south coast ports to the trade with France and Spain. Not all the new trades were controlled by monopolists, however. Trade with the new English colonies in the Caribbean, where Barbados and a few smaller island territories were acquired before 1640, and on the North American mainland, where Virginia was founded in 1607 and the New England colonies from 1620, developed in a less regulated way. There also seem to have been many interlopers willing to risk competing with the monopolists in the trades which were restricted (ibid., pp. 113–95).

London's domination of both overseas and internal trade was one of the reasons for the extraordinary size and influence of the capital. The growth of London between 1500 and 1640 was spectacular: from about 50,000 inhabitants to around 400,000 in the city and suburbs combined. This was twice as fast as the growth of the population in general, and meant that by 1650 about 7 per cent of the English population at any one time were living in the metropolis (Finlay and Shearer, 1986, pp. 37–8). Since many London residents were temporary – apprentices and servants, or gentry spending part of the year in the capital, for example – and many more spent time there on business, attending the law courts, or as part of the ramifications of the royal court, a far higher proportion of the population must have had some experience of London life. The impact of the metropolitan demand for food and other consumer products was substantial. London's network of grain suppliers reached ever outwards (especially in years of shortage) up the Thames Valley and the east coast, while cattle born in Scotland or Ireland and fattened in the midlands ended their lives at London's Smithfield market, and cheese from the Cheddar Gorge was already appearing on London tables. The importance of a market of this size and purchasing power to the development of commercial food production and regional specialization was, like the size of the metropolis itself, out of proportion to the scale of the rest of England's economy (Fisher, 1971). The proliferation of small-scale industries in the city itself and its crowded suburbs, breaking the bounds of the city's traditional guild controls despite the efforts of the authorities to implement them, also made London a major manufacturing centre (Beier, 1986, pp. 141–67).

Despite the size and importance of London, the overall proportion of the English population who lived in towns was small. Indeed, London may have contained about half the total urban population in the mid-seventeenth century. Most other towns were tiny by modern standards. About 600 market towns contained fewer than 1,000 people each, while the largest regional capitals such as York, Norwich and Exeter had between 10,000 and 20,000, and Bristol, the second most important port by 1640, about 15,000

(Barry, 1990, pp. 2–3). The gap between 'supercities' of over 50,000 and smaller towns was widening in continental Europe also, and England seems to present an early and extreme example of this pattern (De Vries, 1984).

There has been much disagreement among historians about urbanization in early modern England, related to wider debates about the role of towns in history (Jack, 1996, pp. 159–84; Clark, 1976b). Many historians and sociologists have dismissed the pre-industrial town as a much more parasitic and less dynamic institution than its modern, industrialized counterpart. In addition, some English historians have seen the century before the civil war as a period of urban crisis, in which many provincial towns suffered problems such as the loss of their traditional manufactures, periodic trading crises, outbreaks of bubonic plague, and poor migrants moving to towns especially at times of food shortage or unemployment (Clark and Slack, 1976). There is some dispute about when the recovery of English towns from this period of crisis began, and the fact that many towns suffered disruption and destruction during the civil war itself has led some historians to deny that there was any upward trend before 1650.

One of the problems is that the fortunes of individual towns varied so much. Some declined, and some rose (often at the expense of others, like Maidstone's development as a marketing centre causing problems for Rochester), while others suffered for a time but began to recover before the civil war. It is hard to define any general pattern, but the dominant view now seems to be that there was an overall increase in the urban population and a shift towards larger towns, while smaller towns stagnated up to and beyond the civil war (Jack, 1996, pp. 159–84). Provincial urban centres such as Coventry, Worcester, York, Ipswich and Colchester grew in the century before the civil war, though not uniformly or continuously (Corfield, 1976). Those towns which prospered were 'developing specialized functions in a range of areas including education, leisure activities, trade and manufacturing', and the greater growth of larger towns meant that 'town dwelling as a way of life was coming to mean the big town experience as opposed to the small town life' (Jack, 1996, pp. 182, 184). The significant urbanization which did take place in seventeenth-century England was urbanization in the context of a pre-industrial society, different in several ways from the urbanization that came later with industrialization.

One other feature of economic life in mid-seventeenth century England is important to the debate about modernization: its basic units were not firms but families. Most production as well as consumption took place in household units consisting of a married couple, their children, and servants if they could afford them. There is little sign, among working farmers, artisans and labourers, of the 'traditional' extended family as defined by nineteenth-century sociologists. The largest households were found among the gentry who could afford to keep extra non-producers around them. But the presence, in very many households, of servants whose roles included producing, selling or transporting the commodities central to the family's activity as well as domestic tasks, gave the early modern household something of the character of a firm as well as that of a family as we know it. In fact, the term 'family' was understood at the time to include the hired labour in the household. Peter Laslett has stressed the difference between the modern world of work and that of early modern household production, the 'world we have lost'. But whether the predominance of this multi-functional unit means that the workplace was more like a family as we know it, or that the family was more impersonal and the father more like an employer, has been the subject of endless debate among historians (Laslett, 1965; Stone, 1977). For some, there was no significant social or economic change and no modernization of English society as long as this traditional environment of the family/workplace did not change, and this view has had a substantial influence on revisionist historians of the English civil war. But to Stone (1977) and Macfarlane (1978) the predominance of the nuclear rather than extended family, of individual rather than kin-group ownership of the land, and of individual choice in personal decisions such as marriage and career, means that the family was already modern, or becoming modern, in mid-seventeenth century England.

The question of modernization in this period cannot be resolved by economic history alone, as the example of change in the family suggests, but economic historians have had a lot to say about it, perhaps because of the important place that industrialization holds for them. This may be a pitfall rather than an asset, because the temptation is to assess the seventeenth century chiefly in terms of 'steps towards' the agricultural and industrial revolutions of the eighteenth and nineteenth centuries. The growth of manufacturing activity can be seen as a move away from agriculture and hence towards industrialization, but the form in which it mainly grew – cottage industries where the producers were self-employed and the merchant capitalists had no control over the production process – was different from that of the late eighteenth-century industrial revolution. In a sense, industry at this time was growing in a different direction from that which it later took.

The significance and direction of changes in agriculture are also disputable. Most economic historians argue that the general trend in early seventeenth-century English agriculture was a rise of agrarian capitalism, since an increasing number of larger farmers employed hired labour and produced for the market, while the peasant family farm was beginning its long period of decline (Clay, 1984, vol. 1, pp. 53–72). But others doubt that agrarian capitalism was widespread outside a few areas of the south of England. They see the rise in rents in this period as being largely the product of 'fiscal seigneurialism' or 'rent exploitation'. What is meant by this is that landlords were simply taking advantage of population pressure on the land to extract higher rents, sometimes by creating more small holdings which were less efficient in market terms, rather than by encouraging improved production and marketing by larger farmers (Appleby, 1975; Manning, 1988). All agree that the period saw an increase in the number of small-holding and landless labourers, but the labour force available and seeking employment in agriculture was growing faster than the capacity of large farmers to employ it. There were certainly substantial and growing differences in regional responses to this situation. Individual landlords' behaviour also varied according to their status and resources, with a local resident squire holding a small or medium-sized estate being more likely to farm part of the land himself or encourage his larger tenants to improve, while a nobleman or rich gentleman with large and scattered estates would be more inclined simply to squeeze out more rent from all tenants and smallholders (Manning, 1988, pp. 153–4).

The questions of modernization, urbanization and agrarian capitalism have been particularly important to the general theories which offer economic explanations of the civil war. These will be discussed in chapter 6. But our more immediate perspective here is concerned with how much strain changes in the economy put on the social organization of seventeenth-century England, and whether this can in any way help to explain the polarization of allegiances which took place in 1640–2.

Social Groups: A Traditional Hierarchy?

In a well-known speech in 1654, Oliver Cromwell defended 'the ranks and orders of men, whereby England hath been known for hundreds of years', and went on to give an example of this traditional order: 'a nobleman, a gentleman, a yeoman'(Carlyle, 1888, vol. 3, p. 21). Many historians have emphasized the importance of this idea of a traditional hierarchy in early seventeenth-century England, and argued that the dominance of hierarchical ideals ruled out the possibility of significant social change. Whatever the measure of economic changes, they argue, England had a strong and resilient social system, based on status rather than wealth or class, which absorbed and neutralized such changes, maintaining the same people in power (Sharpe, 1987, pp. 160–6; Clark, 1986).

Upon closer examination, however, the status hierarchy of early modern England appears neither so ancient nor so changeless as its exponents (then and now) have assumed. The distinction between a nobleman and a gentleman was not a very old one. A nobleman in England was the owner of a title of nobility (baron, viscount, earl, marquis or duke) and the right to a seat in the House of Lords, but this parliamentary peerage had not become a fixed, hereditary group until the mid-fifteenth century, and until then there was no social distinction between a gentleman and a nobleman (Pugh, 1972, p. 96). Sixteenth- and seventeenth-century writers who considered the English social hierarchy as a whole were inclined to revert to using the term 'nobility'to include both the peerage and the lower ranks of knights, squires and gentlemen, distinguishing 'greater' from 'lesser' nobility or pointing out that in the rest of

Europe these normally constituted one order of society rather than two (Wrightson, 1982, pp. 18–23).

The peerage was, moreover, a group with a built-in tendency to rapid turnover. Since titles were inherited through males only, family lines were subject to the biological hazards not only of childlessness but of sonlessness, and from 1300 to 1500 they had died out at a normal rate of around 25 per cent every 25 years (McFarlane, 1973, pp. 146–9, 173–6). Monarchs could let the numbers decline, fill the gaps or increase the peerage by new creations, but without new blood the English nobility would have died out. There were some seventeenth-century noble families whose origins did go back to the thirteenth or fourteenth century, but they were very few, and they had been swamped by new creations in every generation since 1500 (ibid., p. 173).

Both Tawney and Stone have argued that the English nobility underwent a prolonged period of crisis in the century before the civil war. Tawney (1941) saw this as caused by their clinging to old feudal lifestyles and failing to improve their incomes from land as the gentry did. Stone (1965a) sees their problems as less purely economic in nature. The 'inflation of honours' by the creation of new peerages after 1603, especially when they were openly sold by the crown between 1615 and 1628, devalued the peerage as an institution and diminished the respect in which it was held by others and the confidence of those who possessed it. As the buying and selling of land intensified from the 1530s, peers as a group sold more than they purchased, and their spending power fell. At the same time, prices rose and the temptation to overspend increased. Though the practice of medieval rural hospitality – keeping open house for strangers and the poor as well as social equals – may have been less general and suffered less of a dramatic decline among the nobility than Tawney supposed (Heal, 1984), conspicuous consumption was more than ever a mark of status. The attractions of London pleasures, attendance at court, and the pomp that the holding of local office required, contributed to the shrinking of many noble fortunes. But Stone found that from about 1620 the incomes of many noble families recovered, as they turned their attention to raising rents and exploiting the commercial possibilities of their estates such as large-scale pasture or mining.

This upturn in the economic fortunes of the nobility was followed by a change in the crown's policy towards them. The 'orgy of indiscriminate honours' which had brought many courtiers and men with no local influence into the peerage since 1603 was severely curtailed from 1629, and the personal rule was a period of consolidation. In the 1630s, Charles I pursued a policy of sustaining and reinforcing the privileges and powers of the aristocracy, seeking to restore their 'ancient lustre' and inviting them to 'join in the management of the affairs of the commonwealth', as he put it in 1629. He promoted the Renaissance idea of an aristocracy of virtue and public service, while at the same time hankering after traditions of feudal loyalty and even considering a revival of the obsolete homage ceremony. In pursuit of an improved militia, he bypassed parliamentary authority (which had been the basis for the militia until 1604) and relied on the nobility as lord lieutenants to be directly responsible to him (Sharpe, 1992, pp. 417–22, 487–91). This was one of Charles's least successful policies, as was seen in 1639, which may indicate that the nobility no longer enjoyed sufficient influence in their county communities to make it work. On the other hand, parliament's Militia Ordinance of 1642 also assumed that nobles were the appropriate people to put in charge of armies, and their new lord lieutenants are said to have included twice as many peers whose titles went back before 1529 as those whom they replaced (Morrill, 1993, p. 11). This may indicate that the older noble houses were more likely to have found a *modus vivendi* with other layers in the changing society of early seventeenth-century England than the new nobles whose fragile credibility Charles was trying to reinforce from above.

Stone's thesis of the crisis of the aristocracy stressed the decline of noble military power in its traditional form of private armies. The ability of the peerage to raise and command armed forces was both necessary and dangerous to sixteenth-century monarchs, but as the result of a long, slow effort they tamed these powerful subjects, and together with the increasing wealth and independence of the gentry this shift transformed England from an aristocratic society into a modern one by the early seventeenth century (Stone, 1967, p. 12). His critics have argued that although the traditional military power of the nobility did decline, their influence did not.

Instead, it was manifested in the (mostly) non-violent form of a patronage system. This was a pattern of relationships in which the nobility provided members of the gentry, their social inferiors, with 'good lordship', favours through influence at court, and the local prestige of friendship with the great. In return these gentleman 'clients' provided their patrons with political and other forms of support, and with a flattering deference which can be read in surviving correspondence and memoirs (Farnell, 1977).

Most studies of the gentry agree, however, that this group became more independent both socially and politically in the sixteenth and seventeenth centuries. Gentlemen as a distinct social layer had emerged in the previous two hundred years (Cromwell was right, but only just), though the collective term 'gentry' first appears in the 1580s (Morrill, 1993, p. 195). Although some historians see the early modern gentry as simply the descendants of the lesser nobility of the Middle Ages, who were part of the feudal military and landowning class (Mingay, 1976, pp. 18–28), it could be argued that what had happened since about 1500 was more than a change of name. The numbers of landowners who claimed the status of gentlemen trebled between 1540 and 1640, from about 5,000 to 15,000, and there was an especially marked increase in the number of 'parish gentry' owning just one or two manors, leading in some areas to a dramatic increase in the proportion of villages which had a resident squire. This suggests a long-term change in the structure and role of the gentry (Stone, 1972, p. 72; Clay, 1984, vol. 1, pp. 156–7).

The growth in numbers, especially of the parish gentry, reflects in part the social mobility which was a marked feature of early modern English society. Sixteenth- and seventeenth-century writers such as William Harrison and Thomas Wilson recognized that despite the ideal of gentility as a hereditary quality, many men were becoming gentlemen because their wealth enabled them to adopt the lifestyle and manners of gentlemen (Wrightson, 1982, pp. 18–23). These new men could then defer to the old definition of the gentleman as armigerous ('bearing arms' in both the military and the heraldic sense) by paying the king's heralds to recognize a largely fictitious genealogy and a newly invented combination of traditional emblems as a coat of arms (Stone, 1967, pp. 38–9). There was also an increase during this period in the numbers of men calling themselves gentle-men without owning land, inventing genealogies or seeking to acquire coats of arms. These were often successful professionals: crown servants, lawyers, scholars and clergymen; or wealthy mer-chants who might own some land but had no desire to turn them-selves into country squires. Historians sometimes refer to these as the 'pseudo-gentry', or even 'urban pseudo-gentry'. But sixteenth-century writers were willing to recognize, however grudgingly, that the status of a gentleman could be acquired by wealth and excel-lence. William Harrison had even added to his various categories of gentlemen, 'they that are simply called gentlemen' (Heal and Holmes, 1994, pp. 6–9). The place of the gentry in the traditional social order was, therefore, much more fluid than Oliver Cromwell supposed, or than many twentieth-century historians have argued. Paradoxically, the dividing line between gentlemen and non-gentle-men, which some historians have seen as the most important social distinction in seventeenth-century English society (Coward, 1980, p. 40), was remarkably vague.

The men who crossed this line into the gentry most frequently were yeomen, or prosperous larger farmers. Again, this was rela-tively new terminology: Chaucer in 1400 had called such a person a franklin and a foot-soldier a yeoman. By the sixteenth century, yeomen farmers producing for the market might own their own land as freeholders, rent or lease it from a landlord, or combine these different forms of legal tenure. Studies of probate inventories (lists of the movable goods they had at the time of their death) confirm that what characterized the yeomen as a social group was a certain comfortable lifestyle, including consumer goods such as pewter pots and linen shirts, and a variety of furniture in the sub-stantial 'Tudor'farmhouses which have inspired so many bad imi-tations in modern suburbs. They owned or rented sufficient land to prosper by producing foodstuffs and raw materials in a seller's market, but they did not share the classical education and élite culture of the gentry. In many villages they constituted a local élite, drawing closer in economic and political interests to the gentry above them, further away from the subsistence peasant and labouring cottager. They were often employers of the local poor, and conscious of their own importance in the maintenance of order

(Wrightson, 1982, pp. 30–3; Sharpe, 1987, pp. 199–201). These were an important layer of the 'middling sort'whose co-operation, it has been suggested above, was crucial to the effectiveness of local government in England, and whose responses to the problem of a threatened breakdown of order in 1642 were central to the development of opposing parties and eventually of civil war.

Below the yeoman in the village hierarchy stood the husbandman, or family farmer. Though husbandmen are sometimes described by historians as subsistence farmers, because they produced food primarily to feed their own household and rarely if ever employed wage labour, they also had to produce a regular surplus in order to survive, since they had to pay rent to the landlord and tithes to the church. But in years of poor harvests they might be hard pressed to meet these obligations and have enough to eat, and local studies often show their holdings disappearing in periods of crisis such as the 1590s (Spufford, 1974). Those few who were successful acquired larger holdings and rose into the yeomanry, across another indistinct borderline. Those who could not keep their landholdings in a crisis had to survive wholly or partly by working as wage labourers for others. Nevertheless, there were regions where husbandmen survived in large numbers and prospered over the period as a whole, notably in the midlands (Allen, 1992), and they were still a long way from disappearing altogether in any region in the mid-seventeenth century.

Labourers were at the bottom of the social hierarchy in the countryside. They might have a little land, some claim on the commons for pasture and firewood, or nothing at all other than their capacity to labour for others. If they had no land at all, they were highly likely to depend on the local community for poor relief (raised since the late sixteenth century by a poor rate levied by the parish on property owners). The numbers of the labouring poor were increasing, and they were more than ever dependent on the property owners in their local communities – potential employers and ratepayers – and on retaining whatever rights they had in the local common lands (Sharp, 1988). A specialized study of agricultural labourers in this period concludes that the old customary social order of the village community which had provided them with some protection was breaking down, and that social divisions were growing between

labourers and farmers, as well as between the better-off labourers
who had some land and those who had none at all (Everitt, 1967).

The underemployment of the labouring masses was largely seen
by other social groups at the time as a problem of 'idleness' and
'masterless men'; to say nothing of masterless women with neither
a husband nor an employer, who were perceived as even more of a
danger (Underdown, 1987, pp. 36–7). The view that the poor needed
reforming rather than indiscriminate assistance, and the perception
that those among the poor who took to the roads in search of work
or subsistence were a threat to order in society, became dominant
among the propertied classes in the seventeenth century. The poor
were becoming more and more of a marginalized group in society,
but the vagrant poor were regarded as being outside the social order
altogether. Many of those labelled vagrants were migrants in search
of opportunities for survival, moving towards towns or woodland-
pasture communities with extensive common lands. The lowest
levels of society were the most geographically mobile, and examinations of vagrants in this period show that craftsmen and labourers
migrated twice as far, and servants three times as far, as gentlemen
or yeomen did if they moved at all (Beier, 1985).

Those who migrated to the towns found themselves at the
bottom of another stratified society, in which upward mobility was
far from easy, though wages might be higher than in the countryside (especially in London) if work could be found. The freemen
of towns, described by sixteenth-century writers as the social order
of citizens or burgesses, did not include the immigrant poor. The
social hierarchy in towns was becoming more varied, as professional groups such as lawyers, doctors, schoolmasters and clergy
joined merchants and the larger manufacturers in the top layer
(Jack, 1996, pp. 21–3). But in most towns of any size, merchants
still played the most important role, and this was especially true of
towns with significant regional or overseas trade, or manufactures
reaching wider than local markets. Local studies frequently
confirm the local power of the mercantile element. The aldermen
of York and Oxford, for example, were usually merchants, while
in Coventry the 'distinctively and self-consciously urban and mercantile élite' tended to come from the trades which controlled the
finishing and marketing of cloth, and in Bristol the merchant élite

were especially concerned to keep craftsmen and shopkeepers out of the lucrative business of overseas trade (Richardson, 1992). In wealth and social position, London merchants stood head and shoulders above those of provincial towns. Those who held the office of lord mayor or alderman were recognized as the social equals of the gentry, and the fortunes of the richest rivalled those of the wealthier peers (Heal and Holmes, 1994, p. 8; Clay, 1984, vol. 1, p. 201). Many of those who rose to the top of the London hierarchy had, however, come from gentry families, especially as younger sons who did not inherit the family land were sometimes apprenticed to London merchants.

Historians have often argued that successful merchants tended to buy country estates and join (or rejoin) the gentry. Though this does seem to have been a significant phenomenon in some counties close to London, it was almost non-existent in others, including Kent (Everitt, 1969b, pp. 37–8). Arecent study of the ownership of country houses in three counties argues that the movement of merchants into the landowning gentry in the period before the civil war has been much exaggerated (Stone and Stone, 1984). Yet gentry status seems to have been a strong attraction in the early seventeenth century to the merchants of Norwich, perhaps a typical 'provincial capital'; though the merchants of Coventry, a smaller urban centre, were more inclined to form semi-permanent urban dynasties (Evans, 1979; Hughes, 1992). Perhaps more work needs to be done on overall patterns of social mobility, aided by information technology which was not available to the historians of the rise of the gentry in the 1940s and 1950s, before we can draw conclusions about how interpermeable the social groups of gentry and merchants really were. But one thing is clear: it was in this period very rare indeed for a merchant, even an outstandingly wealthy one, to rise directly into the peerage. Only three merchants were ennobled between 1602 and 1641, though peerages were openly sold for much of that time (Stone, 1967, p. 89).

Below the merchants in urban society were usually the local food suppliers such as butchers and bakers, and the 'manufacturers' – a term which did not then mean large employers, but artisans producing goods in their households and employing only a small number of apprentices and journeymen. Though these small

masters were often organized in guilds, and valued the local standing such membership gave them, they were usually subject to the
power of the local élites. In many towns in the early seventeenth
century, the élite seem to have been increasing their grasp on local
power and excluding the rank and file of the freemen (Hirst, 1975,
pp. 44–50). But the freemen themselves were a privileged group
compared with the labouring poor and migrants from the countryside. Urban communities were very attached to the 'liberties'
which had exempted them from noble control in the Middle Ages,
and guarded these privileges against others, including recent
migrants. The term 'foreigner', found especially in urban records
in the early seventeenth century, meant someone from outside the
town, not necessarily from another country.

The labouring poor in the towns were increasingly dependent on
the property owners for work or assistance, as they were in the
countryside. There has been much debate among historians about
the extent of poverty in sixteenth- and early seventeenth-century
English towns. Tax assessments and local surveys of the poor have
led some to estimate that a very large proportion of the urban population – between a quarter and a half in some towns – lived on or
just above the level of destitution (Sharpe, 1987, p. 83). But
exemptions from taxation have been shown to be unreliable, some
individuals who were exempted turn out to have been quite well-
off; and surveys of the poor were usually undertaken only in
periods of acute crisis when those whose households would normally have been independent were forced by high food prices to
seek relief (Barry, 1990, pp. 18–20). But this very vulnerability of
the urban poor to such problems as bad harvests and trade depres-
sions meant that they featured prominently in the anxieties of those
who worried about the social order in early modern England.

There was widespread concern about the social order in the early
seventeenth century, and the fears frequently expressed that it would
break down under the pressure of economic and social change have
often been seen as a sign of deeply ingrained conservatism. The traditional ideology of a hierarchical society was still strong, and
changes in the structure of society, such as the appearance of new
classes, or in its balance, such as a growth in the numbers of masterless men, were seen as a threat to the order created by God and

nature. Nevertheless, ideas about society at the time were more adaptable and flexible than would appear at first sight. The traditional language of three 'estates', nobility, clergy and common people, was from the sixteenth century coupled with the more flexible concept of 'degrees' in society: this was still a hierarchical concept, but it could admit new levels and distinctions. A new language of 'sorts'was also coming into use: the better sort, poorer sort, and middling sort. It has been argued that this expressed a different perception of changing social reality, one that developed further to become the concept of social classes early in the eighteenth century. Because any hierarchical view of society is understandably considered conservative in our own society, historians may not have been sufficiently alive to the distinction between defending the old, medieval order and defending what was in many ways a new order in the 'complex and dynamic social reality' that was early seventeenth-century England (Wrightson, 1987).

Disorder and Social Protest

Some historians argue that despite economic pressures and demographic change, the hierarchical ideology of the time enforced traditional relationships of dominance and subjection, from inequality in marriage, through differences in social status, to the divine right of kings. Social relationships were marked by 'unquestioning subordination', and the deference shown to social superiors and political authority was a universal habit of mind learned in the family household by children and servants who would expect the same from others when they became householders themselves. If things began to change, they did so during and after the civil war, not as a cause but as a consequence of the conflict (Laslett, 1983, pp. 210–28). The very success of the English republic in the 1650s has even been attributed to the deep penetration of 'ideologies of acquiescence and order' in English society, which dictated obedience to the existing government (Morrill and Walter, 1985, p. 165). The editors of a volume on *Order and Disorder in Early Modern England* take the position that the mental world of the 'great chain of being' and the hierarchical social order changed only slowly over the longer period from 1500 to 1800 (Fletcher and Stevenson, 1985, p. 3). Others have been more sceptical about the reality of hierarchical relationships in the early seventeenth century, pointing out that most of our accounts of the social order come from members of the ruling élite. 'Ordinary men and women ... did not necessarily believe everything they were told', and 'we should not be star-struck by the self-congratulatory image of the early modern English hierarchy' (Reay, 1988, p. 61). 'The notion of the idyllically stable society', one historian suggests, 'was most poignantly celebrated when it was already losing touch with reality' (Underdown, 1987, pp. 11–12). Perhaps there was 'a more equivocal relationship between the people and their governors in early modern England' than the élite at the time believed (Walter, 1985, p. 143).

While on the one hand writings about society in this period sought to reassure their audience that the social order was as it had always been and always would be, on the other they convey a pervasive fear that that order was being threatened by widespread insubordination. The most famous work of hierarchical political theory, Sir Robert Filmer's *Patriarcha*, which based authority in the state on the authority of fathers in families, was written in 1632 when its author already felt that 'the unnatural liberty of the people' was a threat (Underdown, 1996, p. 44). Such worries were not confined to the élite: people of all classes feared chaos and disorder, and constantly expressed concern that young people, women, servants and the poor were acting in insubordinate ways (ibid., pp. 45–67). Historians have drawn attention to the plentiful misogynist writings of the period expressing male fears of women's insubordination, and point out that women were subjected to increasing repression, including outbreaks of witch-hunting and the development of the ducking stool as a punishment for scolding (Underdown, 1985; Kermode and Walker, 1994). But expressions of misogyny were not new in the seventeenth century, nor was criticism of women who competed for business with male crafts and trades (Bennet, 1991). Increased male anxiety about the position of women was hardly caused by a real increase in women's independence, for this was not an age of growing freedom or power for women; indeed, it was rather the reverse

(Fraser, 1984, pp. 1–6, 464–70). Women were beginning to find a voice, but they 'did not ask to govern, claim equality with their husbands or declare the family an irrelevant institution', and gender relations were not challenged explicitly. The problem seems to be rather with the 'stricter definition of order which became prevalent in the early seventeenth century' (Amussen, 1988, pp. 133, 176, 182). Male perceptions of women cannot be considered in isolation from other social and political concerns. This is not to say that the gender tensions in early modern society were not real. Indeed, it is a revealing indication of the reality of women's subordination in society that male thoughts turned to the repression of women when they feared for the wider social order (Underdown, 1996, pp. 45–67).

Was the whole phenomenon of anxiety about the social order, especially in the crisis of 1640–2, a mere 'moral panic' without any substantial foundation in social reality? Some historians would have us believe so: they identify the fears and 'fantasies' of the propertied classes as the main source of anxiety, claiming that the press of the early 1640s inflated public perceptions of the extent of disorder, and would have done so 'even if there had not been an increase' (Morrill and Walter, 1985, pp. 137–8). We are told that early seventeenth-century English society was 'surprisingly stable' (Fletcher and Stevenson, 1985, p. 38), and that outbreaks of rioting over food shortages were remarkably few (Walter and Wrightson, 1976, p. 42). On the other hand, David Underdown believes that the whole period from 1560 to 1640 saw an ongoing 'crisis of order' (1996, p. 61), and Brian Manning (1991) sees a rising tide of popular social protest as an essential component in the background to the crisis of 1640-42.

It is true that early seventeenth-century England did not experience disorders of the more spectacular kinds that occurred in contemporary France, especially noble rebellions and regional peasant risings in which royal officials were murdered, peasant armies organized and towns occupied (Mousnier, 1971). Though English historians may refer to the 'midland rising' of 1607 or the 'western rising' of 1626–32, these were a series of interconnected local riots, not organized insurrections on the continental model. Popular insurrection was not altogether unthinkable in early modern England: in 1596 a handful of Oxfordshire labourers planned and attempted to organize a general rising against the rich. Although many people had heard of their plan and some even admitted to saying that they would join in if others did, on the date set for the start of the rising only four turned up (Walter, 1985). There was a rather wide gap between the 'seditious words' in which individuals expressed their sense of oppression and voiced threats against the existing order, and the collective behaviour of crowds who organized their protests around more limited aims and specific occasions (Clark, 1976a; Walter and Wrightson, 1976).

There were scores and possibly hundreds of these local and limited disorders, which Roger Manning calls 'village revolts', in the century before the civil war. Manning distinguishes four issues in these revolts: enclosure, tenure disputes, 'festive disorders' and food prices. Enclosure is a complex issue, and the form it took in this period was different from the better-known enclosure movement of the eighteenth and early nineteenth centuries, when whole open-field villages were enclosed by act of parliament. In the sixteenth and seventeenth centuries, piecemeal enclosures of open fields, common pasture or village waste land were usually carried out by agreement between the landlord and the larger farmers, though it may be that such agreements 'often concealed both coercion by the lord and resistance on the part of his tenants' (Manning, 1988, p. 110). Even piecemeal enclosures usually left smaller tenants and cottagers deprived of resources to which they had previously had access, such as common pasture or woodland, and they frequently showed their discontent by destroying the enclosing hedges. The largest outbreak of hedge-levelling in the reign of James I was in the midlands in 1607, but it became endemic in several western counties in the late 1620s, when Charles I systematically leased out areas which had formerly been royal forest to courtiers and others, denying local communities their traditional common rights (Sharp, 1980, pp. 82–125). The issues were similar in the eastern fenlands, where large tracts of swamp land on which the local inhabitants depended for fishing and fowling were allocated for drainage schemes financed by nobles and courtiers (Lindley, 1982). Though sixteenth-century laws forbidding enclosure where it deprived people of a livelihood were still technically in force, they were rarely implemented by local magistrates whose sympathies were often with the enclosers. Charles I fined landlords for illegal enclosures in the 1630s, but the gap between the government's declared intentions and its actions in the forests and fens limited the effects of this stance.

There were also conflicts between landlords and tenants over rents and tenures in the early seventeenth century, as rents continued to rise and disputes over copyhold often came to a head. Copyhold was a manorial tenure which many landlords wanted to convert to less secure forms of tenancy, while tenants were inclined to claim (with some important legal opinions on their side) that inheritable copyholds were their absolute property. It has been suggested, however, that such disputes took place mainly on estates where the landlords were pursuing a policy of rent squeezing or 'fiscal seigneurialism' rather than the improvement of farming (Manning, 1988, pp. 132–54). This might explain why there were more clashes between landlords and tenants in the north, while landlords and their larger tenants in other regions had more of a common interest in improvement (Morrill and Walter, 1985, p. 153).

Much popular protest in early modern England was festive and ritualized, with the participants, often including a high proportion of women, marching to drums, singing, parading or burning effigies of their enemies, and celebrating with cakes and ale. Many historians have regarded these protests as non-political or pre-political, since they appealed to traditional ideals of popular justice and made a show of festive 'misrule' rather than proposing radical alternatives to existing society. Riots against enclosure, especially in the southwest of England, often took a form similar to the charivari or skimmington, which was a ritual shaming of people, usually women, who violated the sexual or gender norms of the community (Underdown, 1987, pp. 100–3). London apprentices regularly celebrated Shrove Tuesday by attacks on brothels in the decades before the civil war, sometimes going on to attack prisons in the city and attempting to release the prisoners (Manning, 1988, pp. 187–219). But festive forms do not rule out rational purpose or political involvement. Enclosure riots were often part of a longer-term strategy including legal action and the raising of common funds; and there is little doubt that some of the London disturbances of the 1620s had a clear political content, being directed against the royal favourite, the Duke of Buckingham (ibid., pp. 106–12, 187).

Riots protesting at the high price of food, or seeking to stop the transportation of grain at a time of shortage, were also a common form of disorder. It has been argued that food riots were part of a pattern which reinforced the values and structure of society rather than challenging them. 'Collective protests, as long as they were grounded in obvious grievances and obeyed certain conventions, might be half tolerated by local magistrates. In this way they confirmed rather than weakened the established order'(Clark, 1976a, p. 381). The poor petitioned the authorities to act to control prices and the food supply, or rioted if they took no action, but the usual pattern was for the authorities to respond to popular expectations and take action to regulate trade and prices, for 'government and governed alike subscribed to a common consensus on the proper ordering of the economy in the face of dearth' (Walter and Wrightson, 1976, p. 41). But while some historians present food riots almost as a kind of licensed protest, or an extreme form of petitioning (Sharp, 1980, p. 43), the authorities did not regard them as harmless. In 1622 a proclamation concerning food prices threatened protesters with severe punishment, on account of 'his majesty having … carefully provided for relief for his poor sort of subjects', and in 1630 the privy council condemned what it regarded as lenient treatment of some Berkshire food rioters because 'they are no less unthankful than undutiful to his majesty, whose princely care of provision for the poor in this time of scarcity is manifestly known to all his loving subjects' (Sharp, 1980, pp. 50, 69). The leaders of two grain riots at Maldon in Essex in 1629, including a woman, Ann Carter, were hanged, though this seems to have been a uniquely savage punishment reflecting the insecurity the central government felt in the first two years of the personal rule (Walter and Wrightson, 1976, pp. 35–7).

Another feature of food riots which alarmed the authorities was that the participants were predominantly not peasants but artisans and wage earners, especially in areas of rural industry which were often hit by unemployment at the same time as high food prices. It has been said that 'the connection between landlessness, rural industrialism and direct action can hardly have been accidental' (Sharp, 1980, p. 7). While there were several measures that the authorities could take to regulate the supply and price of grain, there was much less they could do about a shortage of work in rural industry. Ordering merchants to buy cloth which they could not sell, or to employ cottagers when there was not a market for their products, could not and did not succeed. It may be true that 'the roots of social tension in the instability of a pre-industrial economy and the propertylessness of wage-earning artisans were beyond the reach of any government' (ibid., p. 79), and that this made it difficult for the authorities to deal with.

There is a growing consensus among historians that the main reason why popular disorders were limited and (relatively) infrequent in early seventeenth-century England was that the leaders of village society, the yeomen and more prosperous husbandmen, had a stake in the existing order, since they benefited from the development of agrarian capitalism, and feared the propertyless poor as much as the gentry and government did (Fletcher and Stevenson, 1985, p. 4; Morrill and Walter, 1985, p. 152; Sharp, 1988, p. 105; Manning, 1988, pp. 310, 316). Without the leadership of disaffected village notables and minor nobles found in French popular revolts (it is alleged) popular protest could not seriously threaten the social or political order. Yet in the case of the one series of widespread disorders in which substantial husbandmen, yeomen and gentry did participate, the protests against fen drainage schemes in the 1630s, it has been claimed that the participation of yeomen and minor gentlemen only reinforced the 'defensiveness, conservatism and restraint' of the rioters and the non-political nature of the protests (Lindley, 1982, pp. 57–64).

Not all historians agree that popular protests were non-ideological and non-political, for a coherent rationale or political language has been seen behind the riots, based on the defence of traditional rights and customs (Reay, 1988). The disorders of the west and southwest in the early seventeenth century have been seen as evidence for the emergence of popular politics based on the defence of the local community, politics which were polarized around 'two opposed political, economic and ecological systems', broadly speaking the open-field and the woodland-pasture areas, which led to different allegiances in the civil war (Underdown, 1987, pp. 106–45; 1996, p. 48). The commitment of protesters in the fenlands to self-governing village communities has also been seen as radical, and related to their commitment to parliament in national politics (Holmes, 1985). Even the neutralist protests of the peasant 'clubmen' who opposed both royalist and parliamentarian armies in the mid-1640s were self-organized, suggesting that 'these were not the deferential reflexes of people who could do nothing without gentry leadership' (Underdown, 1987, p. 157). While to some historians the predominance of the belief in traditional rights is essentially a sign of conservatism, of protesters 'vainly attempting to restore a lost world which may never have existed' (Manning, 1988, p. 320), this conclusion is ambiguous. A social order which had never existed in the past would be a new one, and to be or become an independent, self-governing community ordinary villagers would be both denying the manorial past and resisting the authority claimed by the Stuart state.

It is an open question, therefore, whether the alliance of small property owners with the local ruling élites in maintaining order against the tumults of land-hungry labourers and masterless men and women was a conservative factor in the English crisis of 1637–42. It has been argued that changes in the economic, social and cultural structures of English society in the century before the civil war did not make a breakdown of order probable, let alone necessary (Morrill, 1993, p. 283). But these changes had brought about a situation in which the maintenance of peace in the community depended on the new alliance, forged in the process of economic and social developments since 1500, more than on the authority of central government or royal power. Changes in English society therefore made not only civil war, but the possibility of an independent political order without the king and even without the nobility, sustainable in a way which would have been unimaginable a hundred years before, let alone two hundred years before, when nobles had waged civil war with armies based on their private power over lands and men.

It would be wrong to suppose that a background of social protest in recent decades necessarily produced parliamentarian or radical allegiances in the civil war, though some towns or areas with a recurrent history of political and religious dissent, such as Newbury in Berkshire or the northern Chilterns, may indeed have had a radical tradition long before the 1640s (Durston, 1992; Hindle, 1998, p. 77). But in the arable downland areas of the west of England, the clubmen of the mid-1640s mobilized the tradition of defending community rights to resist both royalist and parliamentarian armies. Derbyshire lead miners, as we have seen, supported the king in 1642 because they succeeded in bargaining and winning concessions from him (Wood, 1997, pp. 32–3). Patterns of popular allegiance in the war may have depended largely on the allegiance of the local élite, and whether their relations with those beneath them in the social hierarchy were good or bad. As one historian has recently suggested, 'it is the shifting configurations of interest within the social order that are crucial' to understanding the significance of outbreaks of disorder and their relationship to national politics in the decades before the civil war (Hindle, 1998, pp. 76–8). In 1642 England was a nation divided at its roots in innumerable cross-cutting ways, which brought the political crisis of 1640–2 home to many localities and facilitated the eventual drift into war.

The disorders and social protests of the half-century before the civil war may seem mild in comparison with continental peasant furies, but many of them were more sophisticated, making use of the law, petitioning, and appeals to the ideology of good government, even to the 'moral economy' which historians have identified as an important theme in later centuries, resorting to violence only as one of a number of possible tactics. This background was probably more dangerous in the circumstances of 1642 than cruder outbursts of violent and localized resentment might have been, and it made the civil war a very different conflict from the medieval baronial revolts, which had not involved lower-class participation in the aristocratic business of making political choices. The 'middling sort' of seventeenth-century England were prepared to sign political petitions, attend meetings and demonstrations, and ultimately to arm for one side or the other (or even against both) in the English civil war because they had become accustomed to regarding themselves as participants in government rather than the dependants of feudal overlords.

6

Causes and Theories

In the light of what has been discussed so far, it would seem reasonable to agree that we are not looking for a single cause of the civil war. The Scottish and Irish rebellions need to be related to English grievances, some of which were a legacy of the conflicts of the 1620s; religious divisions in all three countries were intertwined with political and social concerns; while changes in English society cannot be ignored in explaining why the outcome was a parliamentary civil war rather than an old-fashioned baronial revolt. A recent account of historical methodology has argued that 'most historians will go to some lengths to avoid a "monocausal" explanation. ... Generally, however, they see it as their duty to establish a hierarchy of causes and to explain if relevant the relationship of one cause to another'(Evans, 1997, p. 158).

Yet historians of the English civil war frequently seem to have been attracted by the prospect of cutting through all the problems and reducing the solution to a single cause which would make all previous answers obsolete. This has been most tempting to those who believe in short-term causes only, and are dazzled by the concept of one accidental, avoidable event or coincidence whose absence could have prevented the civil war and altered the whole course of English history. Some examples of this 'virtual history' were mentioned in chapter 1, and a more sophisticated one will be dealt with below. Marxists, on the other hand, have been accused of reductionism because they see economic or social change as the ultimate single cause of all major events in history, and tend to explain other manifestations of conflict, such as constitutional or religious ideas, as reflections of the class conflicts produced by social and economic change. Meanwhile, many historians dealing with religion or political ideas see ideological conflict as the primary cause of the civil war, without which social, economic and cultural changes would have been accommodated peacefully by English society and the Stuart state. In order to assess these claims for ideology as the key, we must look at what the history of ideas has to say about meaning and context, and whether principles which are opposed to one another in modern thinking were incompatible at that time. In examining these cases of explanations which compete for sole attention, we shall have to give their theoretical underpinnings and implications more consideration than we have done so far.

There is also one 'monocausal' explanation which is widely popular, and has been so since the time of the civil war itself: a wide range of historians agree in placing the blame for the conflict on one individual, Charles I. Revisionist historians are far from revising this traditional view, though they disagree as to whether his responsibility for the conflict was short-term, being largely a matter of misjudgements and miscalculations between 1639 and 1642, or rooted in his whole approach to government since 1625 (Young, 1997, pp. 5–6). Any discussion of the king's responsibility for the war must be related to the general question of the role of the individual in history, and it has sometimes also involved uses of psychology in history which are worth examining. This chapter will, therefore, begin with an examination of the role of Charles I, before going on to look at the role of ideas as possible causes of the war, and theories of social change which portray it as part of a major social and political revolution.

Charles I: Generator of Conflict?

The twentieth century has seen intense debate about the role of the individual in history. On the one hand, the view that history is made by a few powerful individuals or 'great men' has been associated with an élitist and narrowly political approach to history. On the other, those historians who believe in the priority of impersonal social forces have argued that historical conditions impose narrow limits on what individuals can intend or achieve; that those few who influenced historical events 'gave expression to their times, and were always representative of wider historical forces'(Evans, 1997, pp. 161–5, 186–9). No historian of the English civil war, however, would deny an important place among its causes to Charles I, and this is partly because in an age of personal monarchy the individual ruler was bound to have great scope for imposing his (or occasionally her) personal choices on events. It was an age in which, for all monarchs, 'character was destiny'(Carlton, 1995, p. xviii). Very few would blame the war entirely on Charles's attitudes and decisions: even Russell would include long-term structural problems in the government of England among its causes (Russell 1990a, p. 213). But for most, Charles Stuart played the major part in precipitating the conflict, whether this arose from his character or from a single fatal decision, such as not fighting the Scottish covenanting army when he encountered it in the first Bishops'War (Adamson, 1997).

There is widespread agreement about Charles I's character. According to Michael Young, he was stubborn and self-righteous, and had a confrontational style (Young 1997, pp. 49–50, 70). Conrad Russell suggests that he had an 'ability to rub people up the wrong way' which we cannot grasp directly, since in face-to-face politics personality may have an impact not conveyed by the written word (Russell 1990a, p. 185). Charles Carlton believes he was a lazy ruler, but most historians disagree, though they see the king's energy as misdirected. He was 'wholly incompetent' (Morrill, 1993, p. 69), 'a man thoroughly ill-equipped to be king' (Reeve, 1989, p. 174); he was 'a stubborn, combative, and high-handed king who generated conflict' (Young, 1997, p. 70); he 'invited resistance in all of his three kingdoms, and got what he was asking for' (Russell, 1987, p. 412). Most historians agree that his basic problem was an underlying personal insecurity, and those who recognize in him some virtues stress that these were mainly of a domestic kind, ill-suited to the public role of a king.

There have been some attempts to discuss how Charles got to be the kind of person he was, the most sustained being Carlton's (1995) essay in psychoanalytical biography. Unfortunately, this is flawed in many ways. On Charles's childhood it is inconsistent: Carlton notes, as most historians do, that his being fostered out was normal for royal children and relatively stable (with a Scots noble family until he was four and an English gentry one until he was twelve), but insists that he lacked a satisfactory mother substitute 'such as the proverbial English nanny' (ibid., pp. 4–15). Worse, Carlton has a marked insensitivity to the context and culture of the time, describing Charles's relations with Buckingham as going 'further even than those normal between the deepest of male friends' (ibid., p. 107), though there is abundant evidence that expressions of attachment between men which we would interpret as signs of homosexuality were not abnormal in early modern England (Bray, 1990). The conventions of heterosexual platonic love, a major preoccupation of court culture in Renaissance Europe, are dismissed as 'a non-adult, almost pre-adolescent stage in emotional development', attributable to Charles and Henrietta Maria's shared immaturity (Carlton, 1995, pp. 130–1). It is hardly easier to believe that Charles's suspicion of his opponents was based on a projection onto them of his own desire to change the constitution, that his collecting works of art was a manifestation of his authoritarian personality, or that he found it hard to cope with his problems from 1637 on because of the mid-life crisis which 'men often experience' in their late thirties – notwithstanding the shorter expectation of life and different attitudes to youth and age in the seventeenth century (ibid., pp. 83–4, 144, 206).

Charles's relations with his father were no doubt strained and awkward until his late teens, but this was not unusual in the royal and noble families of the time (Houlbrooke, 1984, pp. 179–80). Compared with his immediate predecessors, he had a remarkably sheltered childhood, for Elizabeth's mother was executed by her father and James's was driven into exile after being implicated in the murder of his father. His brother-in-law, Louis XIII of France, grew up in a court environment where he spent more time in his father's mistress's household than in his mother's, and was subjected in front of courtiers to what we would now consider sexual abuse (Aries, 1979, pp. 98–100). If we are looking for what made Charles an insecure person, Carlton does not provide evidence that his childhood was any more likely to generate such a pattern than that of other rulers of the period.

Nor can Charles's marriage explain his relations with his

parliaments, despite Buckingham's allegedly joking, 'If he could not control his wife how then could he expect to control parliament?' (Carlton, 1995, p. 78). Although, as previously said, this reflects the ideas of the time about relations between men and women, it is an unsatisfactory explanation. The sixteen-year-old Henrietta Maria was fully backed by French male priests and courtiers in her refusal to attend Charles's coronation or give up her Catholic priests and servants. Charles did not want or expect at this point to live a private family life with his wife, which was still unusual for European monarchs and had not been the case with his own parents or hers. The expectations of a royal marriage were aptly stated by the French minister Richelieu: 'We made that alliance expecting to marry England to France, more than to marry individuals' (ibid., p. 89). It was only after the death of Buckingham three years later that Charles sought an intimate personal relationship with his wife. The domestic happiness which they then discovered was unusual for any royal couple, and they were 'the first English royal couple to be glorified as husband and wife in the domestic sense' (Young, 1997, pp. 61, 74, 82). Needless to say, Charles's relations with parliament did not improve with his marital satisfaction. Indeed, his attachment to Henrietta Maria is often blamed for his intransigence in the 1640s, since the advice she gave him was usually to harden up. Russell remarks that one of the queen's letters 'could easily have been signed "Lady Macbeth"' (Russell 1990a, p. 206)! It has been pointed out, however, that Charles consistently chose to listen to such strong-minded advice, whether from men or from women (Young, 1997, p. 175).

It has been suggested that the domestic life of the royal court after 1629 had a wider political impact, especially during the period of personal rule, in that it utilized the seventeenth-century fondness for analogies between the family and the state by presenting a model of harmony and order for the whole of society (Sharpe, 1992, pp. 222–35). But the famous masques which showed the royal couple as bringers of peace and harmony through their love for each other were seen only by a narrow circle of courtiers, and Charles's expectation of strict domestic privacy, novel for an English ruler, was associated with a renewed emphasis on formality and distance (Sharpe, 1989, p. 160). While his court was ruled by ritual and ceremony, he avoided public celebrations and displays, crowds were not permitted to follow his progresses around the country, and soon after his accession he issued a proclamation 'for restraint of disorderly and unnecessary resort to the court'. This distancing probably had a negative effect: such remoteness was not what people expected of a caring monarch (Richards, 1986, p. 77). While it is easy in personal terms to attribute his 'sense of decorum and authority' to his insecure and authoritarian personality (Carlton, 1995, p. 108), we must remember that there was a crucially important ideological dimension to all this. For Charles, divine right was not so much a political theory as a way of life: he was working at enhancing 'the "mystery" of kingship as he understood it', and this distanced him from the mass of his subjects politically as well as physically (Richards, 1986, p. 80).

It is hard to pin an explicit political theory of absolutism on Charles, but his implicit views on authority, obedience, loyalty and trust are very clear. He expected to be obeyed, and once told his councillors that 'the question was of obeying the king, not of counselling' (Cust, 1987, p. 82). He expected demonstrations of loyalty (especially in the form of willing financial contributions) as his due, not as the outcome of negotiation and compromise. His announcement in 1629 that he would call another parliament only when 'our people shall see more clearly into our intents and actions and ... shall come to a better understanding of us and themselves' was typical: the idea that he was the one who needed to understand his people better does not seem to have crossed his mind (Reeve, 1989, p. 111). Charles 'wanted to get things under control, arrange them his way. ... The orders came from the top down, and reality was expected to obligingly conform. ... Charles thought purely in terms of descending authority, never ascending authority' (Young, 1997, p. 81). Russell suggests that Charles had 'a mistaken definition of loyalty' (1990a, p. 202), but the vital mistake was in his definition of authority. He was not prepared to recognize, as even absolute monarchs usually did, that his government ultimately rested on consent.

Despite his insistence that the law was on his side, Charles seems to have believed that he was on a mission from above which enabled him to bend the rules. He declared his intention not to use this power 'beyond the just rule of moderation' (Burgess, 1992, p. 201), but his attempt to meddle with the judicial record in the Five Knights' case, his suppression of the first printing of the Petition of Right in favour of his own edition, and his refusal to allow the MPs imprisoned after the 1629 parliament to attend a bail hearing, simply gave the impression that he was not to be trusted (Young, 1997, pp. 52–3, 59–60, 76). He, on the other hand, appeared not to trust his people: he 'had a deep-seated suspicion, bordering on paranoia, of popular sentiment and the popular voice' (Quintrell, 1993, p. 89), and saw the widespread refusal to finance his wars in the mid-1620s as 'a "popular" assault on the very foundation of monarchy' (Cust, 1987, p. 87).

It may have been because of Charles's sense of divine right as a personal mission that he refused to allow his servants to take the blame for his policies, whether it was a case of his favourite Buckingham, his privy councillors, or the customs officers who collected tonnage and poundage on his behalf (Reeve, 1989, pp. 29–31; Cust, 1987, pp. 88–9; Russell, 1979, pp. 402–3). Strafford was the only servant whom he was forced, with great misgivings, to sacrifice to the doctrine of the evil counsellor's responsibility. Everyone else, even humble food rioters who blamed bad advisers for shortages and high prices, seems to have grasped that letting others take the blame kept the monarch safe from dangerous direct attacks. Charles did not accept the theory that he had two bodies, his natural one as an individual human being and his political one as a king. Refusing to recognize this piece of medieval mystification may have been his one genuinely modern attitude, but it led in the end to his downfall.

The king's attempt to impose a ceremonial and clerical version of Protestantism on his people increased the potential for confrontation. Though his views were not very different from those of Elizabeth, the church and people of England were more polarized in the 1620s than they had been at her death in 1603. No doubt there would have been both Puritan evangelism and an anti-Puritan reaction in the English church without Charles, and there clearly were differences in cultural attitudes towards ritual and ceremony within English society. But perhaps these would not have led to major political conflict if the king had not been so blatantly partisan. Charles politicized religious issues even more than was normal in the seventeenth century. His spiritualized view of his own role as supreme head of the church under God reflected his personalization of divine right, his preference for ceremony over sermons paralelled his insistence on ritualized behaviour at court, and he strongly believed, like most anti-Puritans, that rejection of the bishops' authority in the church implied rejection of the king's authority in the state. While Charles feared that all Puritans were republicans, his opponents believed that he intended to take the English church back to Rome. Charles was never a Roman Catholic, however. His personal view of theology drew a narrow but very clear line between his own beliefs and the doctrines of the Roman church, though he invited confusion by insisting that he, as well as the pope, had the right to call himself a Catholic (Carlton, 1995, pp. 138–9). Soon after his accession he ordered the laws against Roman Catholics in England to be strictly enforced (ibid., p. 66), though he later relaxed them. His personal tolerance of Catholics has been seen as a positive characteristic, opposed to the 'self-righteous zeal and ugly religious hatreds' of his subjects (Young, 1997, p. 178). But Charles was hardly lacking in self-righteous zeal, and his hatred of Puritans was real. As argued in chapter 3, these animosities cannot be judged out of their context.

If Charles I generated conflict among his people, would a different king have done any better? There is an intriguing alternative possibility here: Charles had an older brother, Henry, who died in 1612 at the age of eighteen. Henry was warmly praised in his lifetime, and after his death, as a staunch Calvinist and a martial youth committed to the international crusade against the Catholic Habsburgs. He opposed his father's plans to marry him to a Spanish Catholic princess, though he would probably have married an anti-Spanish Catholic Italian one if he had lived (Strong, 1986, pp. 1–85). Had he survived, it is said, he could have united the nation behind his aggressive Protestant policies, and a group of young nobles attached to his court who later became opponents of the king in the civil war, including the Earl of Essex, would have supported his Protestant absolutism (Hunt, 1988). Not all historians agree with this vision: one has suggested that a major intervention by England in the continental religious wars would have been expensive and possibly disastrous (Morrill, 1993, p. 2). It is hard to find any information on

Henry's attitudes to royal authority or the role of parliament, and he seems to have had the same kind of cold, authoritarian personality as his brother. Macaulay also believed that a more heroic Stuart monarch would have become absolutist, imposing taxation without consent to finance his wars. 'Had James been ... a valiant, active and politic ruler, had he put himself at the head of the Protestants of Europe, had he gained great victories ... at the head of fifty thousand troops, brave, well disciplined, and devotedly attached to his person, the English parliament would soon have been nothing more than a name' (Macaulay 1913, p. 59). Macaulay possibly had in mind the analogy of the French monarchy in the seventeenth century. Louis XIII and his son Louis XIV used war and absolutism to reinforce each other, and were successful despite the political resistance and social problems they encountered.

Charles has been compared with Louis XIII and XIV surprisingly rarely. Many parallels could be drawn: of Louis XIV especially it has been said that he was 'always quick to assert his authority, he would not tolerate defiance, dissent or even reasoned criticism. ... Wary of possible betrayal, he placed his trust in a few chosen ministers ... he tolerated incompetence more readily than disloyalty'. Though his enemies claimed that he was manipulated by evil counsellors, 'this fiction became hard to sustain when he came of age and declared his will' (Miller, 1987, pp. 160, 162). Both French kings faced noble dissidence, popular revolts, problems raising money, religious minorities and resistance from the provinces, but successfully overcame all of these and extended the powers of the French absolute monarchy. The nobles who challenged Louis XIV in the revolt known as the Fronde in 1648 demanded a meeting of the estates general (the equivalent of the English parliament), more high offices for nobles, and the removal of the king's most unpopular adviser, making Henrietta Maria fear that the English civil war was about to be repeated (ibid., pp. 154–5, 162). One of the few modern studies comparing the Stuart and Bourbon kings attributes the difference in outcomes to the different 'personal abilities' of Charles I and Louis XIV. But French society and institutions were different from English, so different that the kind of unity which held sections of the English nobility, gentry and middling sorts together was not found in France, and the

Fronde collapsed because they were disunited rather than because the monarch was strong or capable (ibid., pp. 14, 159). To some extent this was because England was a smaller, more unified and more centralized kingdom (Hughes, 1991, pp. 32–6), but the different relations between nobles, peasants and middling sorts in the two kingdoms are also relevant considerations.

To suggest that perhaps Charles I would have been more successful as a king of France than of England is to make the same point as Michael Young does when he suggests that rather than Charles being unfit to be a king, 'the problem lay not so much with Charles alone but with the fit between the monarchy and the people at the time when he happened to come to the throne' (Young 1997, p. 178). Charles displayed attitudes and pursued policies which might well have worked in a different kingdom or at a different time, and to explain the civil war it is necessary to consider what it was about his people, as well as himself, that brought about the conflict.

Though few historians have a positive view of Charles's character, there are some who suggest that it was not his personality or patterns of behaviour which caused the civil war, but one or more ill-judged decisions, such as calling a second parliament in 1640, or gathering an army of his own in 1642 (Russell, 1984a, 1984b). In both these cases, as discussed in chapter 2, it is hard to see what else he could have done. A more thoughtful exercise in virtual history is John Adamson's (1997) speculation that if Charles had fought the rebel Scots army in 1639, instead of negotiating with the Covenanters, he would have won the first Bishops' War, avoided calling parliament at all in 1640, and seen off the threats of constitutional and Puritan opposition as the older generation of gentlemen and lawyers who were attached to these ideas died off. This argument manages to ignore not only the deep roots of presbyterianism in the most populous parts of Scotland, but the importance of popular Puritanism and the political role of the middling sort in England. In effect, it discounts the presence of anyone below the rank of gentleman in seventeenth-century Britain. Behind the argument about the contingency of specific decisions and the events which followed them, there is always another argument, in this case one about the state of the political nation in 1639. Despite Adamson's speculations, the suspicion remains 'that Charles failed to vanquish the Scots because his English subjects were disaffected' (Sommerville, 1986, p. 236).

A Conflict of Ideas?

The notion that the English civil war was caused by a fundamental ideological conflict is still a popular one. Even Marxists, though they argue that ideology is merely a reflection of material social conflicts, are usually quite eager to find an ideological dimension in the English civil war because they tend to regard certain ideas, such as liberty and property rights, as 'bourgeois values', and this helps to confirm for them that they are dealing with a bourgeois revolution. It is not historical materialism, but the new history of ideas associated with Quentin Skinner and the Cambridge school of thought which has most radically undermined old assumptions about the role of ideas in society (Tully, 1988). Ideas, these historians point out, do not do battle with one another; an idea does not originate, grow or triumph in an essential, unchanged form; principles cannot be independent of the minds, the societies, the languages and discourses within which they are expressed. To describe the civil war as a conflict between two opposing ideas, such as freedom and authority, or absolutism and constitutionalism, runs the risk of excessive abstraction, in which past ideas are packaged by the historian's mind into products bearing little relation to the way people thought in the past. Yet the ideas with which the civil war was made must engage our attention if we are to debate its causes. Christopher Hill's memorable image, of ideas as the steam without which the engine of history would not have moved, may be too mechanical, but he is right to point out that the civil war was made by thinking people even though it was not made by intellectuals (Hill, 1997, p. 5).

Although early revisionist historians tended to dismiss all political ideas as a cover for immediate aims and interests, most of their followers now hold the view that ideological consensus, rather than ideological conflict, prevailed in early Stuart England. If some historians' accounts of ideological polarization oversimplify the rich turmoil of ideas in early seventeenth-century England, some revisionist accounts of consensus threaten to simplify it still further, denying that alternatives to the official court ideology had any impact at all (Sharpe, 1989, pp. 3–71). Although the consensus was weakened by the late 1620s, they argue, it was followed not by the development of new ideas, but by 'confusion, fear and doubt' (Burgess, 1992, p. x). On the other hand there are anti-revisionist historians who see theoretical tensions as the main cause of conflict between Charles and his parliaments, insisting even that debates on the role of parliament were 'subordinate to the more general dispute between absolutists and their opponents' (Sommerville, 1986, p. 174). We have seen in chapter 4 that there are problems about defining the early Stuart monarchs' position as absolutist, and to take the discussion further we will now have to examine the ideas of their opponents.

To avoid misleading anachronisms, the ideas of seventeenth-century parliamentarians must be located in their contemporary context. This can be illustrated by some problems surrounding the concept of liberty, which Charles I's opponents undoubtedly held to be an important principle. Contemporaries argued over its meaning themselves: Clarendon remarked that 'though the name of liberty be pleasant to all kinds of people, yet all men do not understand the same thing by it'(Richardson and Ridden, 1986, p. 153). Later generations assumed their own definitions: the eighteenth-century philosopher David Hume remarked, 'These people were extremely fond of liberty; but seem not to have understood it very well' (Wootton, 1986, p. 21). In the nineteenth century, Whig historians identified seventeenth-century liberty with projects of constitutional reform in their own time, and in the twentieth century there has been a tendency to define liberty as freedom of choice and personal autonomy. Legal historians have pointed out, however, that in the Middle Ages the word had a different meaning: a liberty was a special privilege bestowed on a particular individual, corporation or estate – such as the 'liberty'of the archbishopric of Durham – rather than a common right (Richardson and Ridden, 1986, p. 7). Long before 1600, however, other meanings of the word had proliferated. When associated with guild privileges, it had overtones of self-interest and exclusiveness, but also of self-government by common consent. When related to the medieval urban commune, it embraced concepts of individual security and property later associated with the idea of civil society (Black, 1984). In the context of late medieval Italian city-states opposed to the rise of despotism, it came to imply 'a heightened self-consciousness about the special value of political independence and republican self-government'(Skinner, 1978a, p. 26).

Many historians have seen in the seventeenth century a transition from the concept of liberties as corporate privileges, to that of liberty as a set of individual rights (Wood and Wood, 1997, pp. 61–4). They are not agreed on when this happened, however. That the traditional idea of parliamentary liberties as a body of specific privileges could still have wide appeal is suggested by the appearance of the term 'prerogative of parliament' in the oppositional political literature of 1628 (Beer, 1997, p. 115), and 'privileges of parliament' as a slogan in the London demonstrations of January 1642 (Lindley, 1997, p. 121). One important link between the medieval and the modern concept of liberty may be that the concept of self-government in privileged towns and corporations was related to the idea of the whole commonweal, or state, as a corporate body of subjects possessing the privilege of constitutional government. In this sense, the liberties of the subject meant 'the specific rights and freedoms that followed from being a freeman under the English common law'(Sacks, 1992b, p. 94).

When early seventeenth-century members of parliament referred to the 'liberties of parliament'they were sometimes using the word to mean the privileges they enjoyed as individuals while parliament was in session. It is, however, hard to justify the view that this was the only thing they ever meant by it (Morrill, 1996). When they claimed, as they frequently did, that their privileges 'belonged' not to themselves alone but to the whole English nation, they were relating their rights as members to the benefits which the whole nation received from having parliaments. If members were not free to speak their minds without fear of arrest or harassment, they could not represent their constituents: 'We are intrusted for our country', said one member in 1621; 'if we lose our privileges we betray it' (Sommerville, 1992, pp. 69–70). In 1628, following the imprisonment of the forced loan refusers and the disputes over billeting and martial law, the Petition of Right defended some of the principles that constitute civil rights in the modern sense: freedom from arbitrary arrest and from invasion of privacy, and free access to the law of the land at all times. Concern for the 'liberties of the subject' in individual terms did not completely replace the idea of specific privileges which were the freeborn Englishman's 'birthright and inheritance', but by the late 1620s these two concepts of liberty were closely associated (Sommerville, 1992). The rights of freeborn Englishmen were associated with 'the ideal of community and a sense of participation in its public business'. Personal independence – especially the right to make a living from a craft or trade – was also valued as part of the liberties of the subject, but not in the modern sense of personal autonomy; for freedom under the law was mainly valued as 'a liberty to pursue one's godly obligations and positive social duties'(Sacks, 1992b, pp. 110–11).

It is a popular argument among revisionist historians that rather than defending political principles which we might see as progressive, the people who opposed Charles I in the late 1620s and the early 1640s were conservatives who saw the king as an innovator and wanted a return to the fundamental constitutional principles which they believed were under threat (Ashton, 1978, p. 20). The king was, of course, as anxious as his opponents to condemn innovation and present himself as the defender of tradition. Before 1642, all the participants in political debate in England shared an ideology of tradition, order and harmony. It has been alleged that the opposing sides in 1642 'did not go to war because they articulated fundamentally opposed ideologies', but 'because they could not trust each other to maintain what they still believed to be common values and ideals'. In this view, there was no revolution in political ideas until the early 1640s, and when it did come it was a result of the outbreak of civil war, not a cause of it (Sharpe, 1989, pp. 63–71).

At one level, it is a truism that Charles I and his opponents shared a common language of political discourse: they could hardly have communicated with each other if they had not. It is also recognized by all recent historians that almost everyone at the time endorsed the view that innovation was evil and moderation was the chief virtue in political argument. The ideas expressed in the language of moderation were, however, sometimes highly combative ones. Among anti-Catholic writers, 'claims to moderation, charity and irenicism were increasingly seen as trumps in the struggle to cast

the other side as the innovative, schismatic and disruptive party',
and being able to label one's opponents as extremists was 'a very
valuable polemical commodity' (Lake, 1995, p. 57). It has also
been suggested that most parliamentary speeches on political principles were 'avowedly short-term political polemic, in which tacti-
cal considerations were strongly present' (Tuck, 1993, p. 222). This
does not necessarily mean that all expressions of the ideology of
tradition and moderation were a cover for other, more radical ideas.
Fear of disorder was a genuine problem for men with families,
property and local influence who were trying to find ways of criticizing Charles I's government without endangering the principle of
order on which they believed their own position depended (Wood
and Wood, 1997, pp. 74–8).

The cultural context of early modern conservatism was very different from that of our own time, when conservatism implies resistance to an ideology of modernization which did not exist in the
seventeenth century. The principle of improving things by returning
to the distant past was one of the key ideas of early modern Western
Europe. Not only the Protestant Reformation (as discussed in
chapter 3) but the renaissance of classical learning and the visual
arts was justified by an ideology of return to the sources, or reno-
vation. This was only much later replaced by the ideology of modernization, or improvement by innovation. One of the passages
most frequently cited as an expression of conservatism is John
Pym's speech in the parliament of 1628 in which he said, 'It is
observed by the best writers upon this subject that those common-
wealths have been most durable and perpetual which have often
reformed and recomposed themselves according to their first institution and ordinance; for by this means they repair the breaches and
counterwork the ordinary and natural effects of time' (Kenyon,
1986, p. 15). Though often seen as expressing primarily a conservative fear of change and decay, this is actually an indirect quotation
from the *Discourses* of Machiavelli, a work regarded as so danger-
ously innovatory that it was not even published in English until
1638. Yet many educated Englishmen were familiar with
Machiavelli's ideas, and admired his analysis of history while shun-
ning his recommendations for political conduct (Raab, 1964).
Justifying controversial changes by appealing to the past could

allay fears about innovation or alteration in the minds of those who used such ideas, as well as those of their audience. Sometimes, the appeal was to a mythical past which had never really existed, opening up the possibility of alternative visions of society, as we have seen in the case of popular protests (see above, p. 132).

The question of the ancient constitution in early Stuart politics must be seen in this context. The early Stuart kings and their parliamentarians both expressed reverence for the ancient constitution and the common law of England, and in this sense, all of the participants believed in the 'politics of the ancient constitution' (Burgess, 1992). But they disagreed about what it was and how it came into existence. Many upholders of parliament's claims believed that the origins of parliament itself were lost in the mists of time, and greeted with hostility and even outrage the historical research which showed that the House of Commons was not originally part of parliament, but was first summoned in the thirteenth century (Sommerville, 1992, pp. 82–3). It has been said that members of the Commons were unable to accept a historical account of their own origins because they adhered to a legal ideology, in which prescriptive rights were an essential concept (Weston, 1991). But common lawyers were troubled by similar arguments about whether the origins of English law were immemorial and its essential content was unchangeable, or whether it had grown and developed over time (Burgess, 1992, pp. 58–78). Both James I and Charles I insisted that kings had called parliaments into existence, either in the beginning or in the Middle Ages. For them, this indicated that the kings of England had chosen to rule with the consent of their people, not that they were obliged to do so. Their opponents tended to the view that parliaments, and even monarchy itself, had been set up by an act of popular consent, however long ago, which was not a matter of documentary record, but could be deduced from current laws and constitutional practices (Sommerville, 1986, p. 64).

The parliamentarians'ideas of the ancient constitution were thus different from the monarchy's. These were real ideological differences, though they were concentrated on a fairly narrow area of the discussion. It is important to realize that English constitutionalism before the civil war also differed from the constitutionalism of sixteenth-century French and Scottish writers which is well known in the history of political thought (Skinner, 1978b). Just as the positions of James and Charles and their allegedly absolutist supporters fail to show clearly that they believed the king to be above the law, so two ideas often associated with constitutionalism, the right of resistance to tyranny and the sovereignty of the people, were rarely expressed in England before 1642. Resistance theories continued to be associated with Catholicism, and were shunned even by those who believed that the English monarchy was a limited one. The few Protestant intellectuals bold or incautious enough to defend resistance theory in England before 1639 did not prosper, and from 1639 to 1642 the main proponents of resistance theory in English were Scots defending the National Covenant (Sommerville, 1986, pp. 69–77). Supporters of the early Stuart monarchs sometimes appealed to the concept of sovereignty, or a single ultimate authority in the state. But their opponents among parliamentarians and common lawyers disliked the idea and did not try before the civil war to argue that the people, or parliament itself, held sovereign power instead (Wood and Wood, 1997, pp. 75–8). It was Charles I's public repudiation of the idea of absolutism in June 1642, in favour of mixed monarchy and the necessity of a balance of powers between the king, Lords and Commons, which released a flood of new and more radical political ideas among the parliamentarians who were now taking up arms against him (Weston, 1991, p. 396).

The strength and volume of radical writings in defence of parliament from mid-1642 was remarkable. Works such as Henry Parker's *Observations upon some of His Majesty's late Answers*, Stephen Marshall's *Plea for Defensive Arms*, William Prynne's *The Sovereign Power of Parliaments* and numerous other pamphlets defended the right of the king's subjects to resist him (Sanderson, 1989, pp. 10–37). Parker claimed, moreover, that 'power is originally inherent in the people', and argued that parliament without the king could be considered to be the whole body of the state 'by virtue of representation' (Wood and Wood, 1997, pp. 77–8). The floodgates were opened to an unprecedented torrent of discussion about parliamentary sovereignty and the 'ascending theory' of political authority which derived all political power from the people. The ideas expressed in print in 1642–3 went much further than defending parliament's right to resist the king; some of them even anticipated the radical arguments of 1647–9 regarding parliament's right to depose the king and the people's right to set up a new constitution (Wootton, 1990). These revolutionary developments in political thinking present historians of English political ideas with a major problem. While some insist that they show that ideological conflict was not a cause of the war, but a result of it (Russell, 1990a, pp. 131–60; Morrill, 1993, pp. 285–306), others disagree. The traditional view is that there was, long before 1642, an inherent conflict between essentially irreconcilable ideas, but this was not fully grasped by the participants. 'Neither side presented its case clearly and fully; for neither side saw it whole' (Allen, 1967, p. 3).The assumption here is that historians, like the pamphleteers of 1642–3, do see it whole. Sovereignty is an issue which many political theorists, from the 1640s onwards, have held to be necessary for any systematic theory of the modern state; as long as political debate failed to recognize this, it was defective. This interpretation does seem to give political principles an existence independent of human beings, which seems questionable.

According to some historians, ideological confrontation was avoided before 1642 chiefly because of censorship, including self-censorship induced by the climate of repression in early Stuart England (Hill, 1997, pp. 390–2). Revisionist historians, however, deny the importance of censorship, claiming that 'there were no adequate institutions or mechanisms through which to exercise it, [it] was largely ineffective even when attempted and the evidence suggests it was attempted only in extreme cases' (Sharpe, 1989, p. 9). Perhaps a few extreme cases could be as effective as modern bureaucratic methods. Since the ear-cropping shears used by order of Star Chamber in the 1630s were inherently more intimidating than the blue pencil, a few examples would do to discourage the open expression of dangerous ideas (Sommerville, 1986, p. 118). It is also possible that people consciously limited what they said because they were concerned with discussing what was practicable rather than what was desirable (Tuck, 1993, p. 222). We have seen above that opponents of Ship Money expressed their dissent mainly in private, and that the necessity of winning the moderate middle ground was an important motivation of both sides in the months preceding the outbreak of war.

Some innovatory ideas were, nevertheless, put forward in the House of Commons before they were widely disseminated in print. In 1628, a leading member referred to 'the original contract between king and people' as a well-known fact (Sommerville, 1986, p. 64; cf. Burgess, 1992, p. 96). By the spring of 1642, radical constitutionalist ideas were appearing in the commons' debates. One member asserted that 'the king is derivative from the parliament and not the parliament from the king', and the whole house passed a resolution stating that the king was bound by his coronation oath to assent to all Bills agreed by the two houses of parliament (Fletcher, 1981, pp. 235, 238). In May 1642, the remonstrance of both houses against the king's attempt to claim his 'property' in Hull stated that the town and the arms magazine did not belong to the king, but were 'entrusted unto him' for the common good, and that 'as this trust is for the use of the kingdom, so ought it to be managed by the advice of the houses of parliament, whom the kingdom hath trusted for that purpose'. It explicitly attacked the belief that kingdoms are the property of kings, 'as if their kingdoms were for them, and not they for their kingdoms', which was such a well-known definition of tyranny from Aristotle onwards that surely no parliamentarian could have missed the implication (Kenyon, 1986, pp. 221–2). It is true that parliamentarians also continued to argue, right up to the outbreak of the war, that they were acting in self-defence, to save themselves and the English people from evil counsellors, popish plotters and Irish rebels (Morrill, 1993, pp. 285–306). Such arguments had a part to play in defending themselves against royalist accusations that they were fomenting a popular revolution from below, but they did not exclude the development of more radical ideas.

Radical constitutionalist ideas were not the only novelty in parliamentarian thinking in 1642–3. Under pressure, the rule of law and the ancient constitution were sometimes abandoned in favour of new ideas such as reason of state, necessity being above the law, or *salus populi suprema lex* (the safety of the people is the highest law). These ideas had developed in the Renaissance circles of late sixteenth- and early seventeenth-century Europe, and university-educated Englishmen, such as many MPs were, would be familiar with this neo-classical rhetoric. While most historians stress the absence of republican or democratic views in England before the civil war, Richard Tuck suggests that the way in which parliamentarian writers were willing to discuss these possibilities in 1643–4 shows that the ground had been prepared by classical humanist as well as constitutionalist ideas. 'Constitutionalism,', he says, 'gave way to a wholly different mode of discourse', when the parliamentarians took the decision to raise their own army under the Militia Ordinance (Tuck, 1993, pp. 224–32). Constitutionalist ideas and the ascending theory of political power were not abandoned, however. Philip Hunton's *Treatise of Monarchy* (1643), for example, was a defence of parliament still formulated in these terms (Wootton, 1986, pp. 175–211).

The way in which political ideas developed rapidly in the hothouse atmosphere of the early months of the civil war suggests that acute ideological polarization did not occur until 1642. This does not mean, however, that there was nothing but a conservative consensus before then. Rather than a conflict between two clearly identified schools of political thought, there was in early seventeenth-century England a many-sided contest of ideas both old and new, which were used by participants in politics in a wide variety of ways. Christopher Hill's (1997) classic attempt to line up all new ideas in early Stuart England – in science as well as politics – on the side of the coming revolution has been much condemned as selective and simplistic, but the recent reissue of this book can be read as a much-needed reminder of how rich and varied intellectual discussion was in the decades before the civil war. 'The most striking feature … of the intellectual life of pre-revolutionary England', Hill tells us, 'was its confusion and ferment'(ibid., p. 9). Renaissance humanism, the new science, the use of history as a source of lessons for the present, and debates about the origins and nature of law, had influenced many literate people, from among the middling sort as well as the gentry and professionals. This intellectual turmoil coexisted with the expressions of conservatism and deference which a revisionist historian has identified as the ruling consensus in early Stuart England (Sharpe, 1989, pp. 3–71). Though no one set of ideas caused the civil war, the presence of many alternative ideas about politics and society was one of the factors which made it possible.

A Social Conflict?

The idea that the English civil war was caused by the impact of long-term changes in society on the political structure did not begin with Marx and has not been limited to Marxist circles. In the 1650s the republican James Harrington believed that changes in the distribution of landed property had upset the balance of the state, and it followed that 'the dissolution of this government caused the war, not the war the dissolution of this government'. This theme was taken up by eighteenth-century authors such as David Hume and Catherine Macaulay, who placed more emphasis on industry and commerce as forces for change. By the early nineteenth century the French historian Guizot was arguing that the decline of the feudal aristocracy, and in general 'the struggle of the various classes for influence and power', was the underlying cause of the English revolution as it was of the later French one (Richardson, 1988, pp. 16, 54, 78). When Karl Marx and Friedrich Engels asserted in the *Communist Manifesto* of 1848 that 'the bourgeoisie, historically, has played a most revolutionary part', they were reformulating, with new socialist aims, a historical theory of social change and revolution which was already a familiar part of European intellectual culture. Marx and Engels labelled the English civil war a bourgeois revolution, though it was not made by the bourgeoisie alone. Sometimes they stressed the alliance of the bourgeoisie with the 'big landlords'whose estates were 'not feudal but bourgeois property'; sometimes the leading role of the middling sort or 'plebeian element' (Marx and Engels, 1971, pp. 92–3; 1962, vol. II, pp. 104–5). Most importantly, they placed bourgeois revolutions such as the English civil war in the longer-term context of a transition from feudalism to capitalism in Western Europe which spanned many centuries, from the late Middle Ages to the industrial revolution of their own day. Much of the argument about the social causes of the English civil war, especially among English-speaking Marxists, has to be placed in this context, though non-Marxists such as Stone and Trevor-Roper have also advanced theories of social causation, as will be seen below.

Maurice Dobb's classic Marxist study of the transition from feudalism to capitalism in England, originally published in 1946, stressed the conservatism of the merchant class, which many historians of social change both before and after Marx had held to be the main agent of social transformation, and argued instead that capitalist enterprises emerged mainly from among the independent small producers in town and countryside (Dobb, 1963; Hilton, 1978). But Dobb's work had little to say directly about political history, and its main impact on Marxist explanations of the civil war was to reinforce the view that it was not caused by merchants. The ideas of R. H. Tawney, who did not consider himself a Marxist but a Christian socialist, had a more direct impact, through his early work on relations between landlords and tenants in the sixteenth century, his *Religion and the Rise of Capitalism*, and his important thesis on the 'rise of the gentry'in the hundred years before the civil war. The rise of the gentry, rather than the bourgeoisie, became the characteristic social explanation of the civil war among English-speaking Marxists; and it has been accompanied by the view that agrarian capitalism, rather than mercantile or industrial, was the key to the English transition from a feudal to a capitalist society. Thus Marxists have tended to identify the gentry (or a section of it) as a capitalist class and a revolutionary one, or even to claim that 'the rising gentry, then, was the English bourgeoisie, by and for whom the Great Revolution of 1640 was made' (Callinicos, 1989, p. 117). For most Marxists, however, the eruption of the gentry in the years 1640–2 was only the first stage of a revolution which was later pushed in a more radical direction by the pressure of lower social layers, not the bourgeoisie as such but the independent small producers in town and countryside, or 'middling sort'.

The writings of Christopher Hill, England's leading Marxist historian, have varied considerably on the class character of the civil war. He started with a view that the war was initiated by 'the progressive section of the gentry and the bourgeoisie' (Hill, 1940, p. 55), but by 1961 had adopted Zagorin's opinion that it began as 'a quarrel between two groups of the ruling class', the court and the country (Hill, 1961, p. 105). Later, he argued that the term 'bourgeois revolution' 'in Marxist usage does *not* mean a revolution made or consciously willed by the bourgeoisie', and that 'it was the structures, fractures and pressures of the society, rather than the wishes of leaders, which dictated the outbreak of revolution and shaped the state which emerged from it', without the intervention of any consciously revolutionary class or classes (Hill, 1987, pp. 95–7). Many Marxists agree that bourgeois revolutions are not always made by the bourgeoisie, especially since the Prussian state in Marx's own lifetime appeared to have made the transition to a capitalist regime without any revolution from below. If not made by the bourgeoisie, such revolutions may be identified by their bourgeois aims, such as freeing or encouraging the advance of capitalism; or by their promotion of bourgeois values, such as individualism, liberty and property. This identification of social class with a specific set of values, which has been important to followers of Weber as well as Marx, is one of the reasons why Marxists are usually keen to defend the idea that there was an ideological conflict in early Stuart England.

Although Hill has written literally volumes on the ideas which he believes inspired the middling sort to intervene in the revolution (Hill, 1969, 1993, 1997), his major interpretative essays have repeatedly returned to the idea that it was the gentry who initiated the civil war, as they also brought about the restoration of monarchy in 1660, with the motive of defending their local power as the 'natural rulers' of English rural society (Hill, 1961, p. 103; 1987, pp. 104, 107, 114). From revolutionary class to natural rulers is quite a conceptual leap, but it is one of several that recent Marxists have been surprisingly willing to make, arguing for example that 'the aristocracy was as capitalist as the bourgeoisie' and that 'the revolutionary inclinations of the English ruling class' were directed towards changing the role of the state (Wood, 1991, pp. 31, 39). The best-known advocate of such views is Robert Brenner, who has long argued that it was changes in relations between landlords and peasants which brought about the revolutions of early modern Western Europe (Brenner, 1987). According to Brenner's most recent work, it was 'the self-transformation of the landed classes' from feudal lords into agrarian capitalists which brought about the transition to capitalism in England, 'to the benefit of the landed aristocracy', and it was their dissatisfaction with the attempts of the early Stuart monarchy to encroach on private property that led the landed classes into the confrontation of 1640 (Brenner, 1993, pp. 649–88).

The idea that the civil war was a conflict between two landed classes, gentry and aristocracy, has been widely abandoned, after much argument over whether the gentry constituted a class, whether their interests conflicted with those of the aristocracy, and whether they were typically engaged in a capitalist transformation of agriculture. Some of this background has been discussed in chapter 5 above. For Tawney (1941), the gentry were a new social class, distinguished from the aristocracy not only by their recent origins, but by their commercial and improving attitude towards land, and close family and business links with the merchant class. For Stone (1965a), the peerage was an 'aristocracy in crisis', not so much because of the rise of the gentry as because of the decline of the nobility's own independent judicial and military powers under the Tudor and Stuart monarchy. For Trevor-Roper (1953), only those of the gentry who had access to income from trade or office-holding rose, while the 'mere' gentry – those who had no other source of income than land – were in decline, and ready to revolt in protest at the financial demands of the overgrown Stuart court. Many Marxists, like Hill, assume that there was a difference in outlook between 'progressive'gentry who improved their lands by enclosures and estate reorganization, and 'unprogressive' gentry who defended the old feudal ways (Hill, 1940, p. 55). Though the terminology of 'progress'is outdated , it may be that differences in the use of landed property were more important and more divisive than the distinction between the gentry and the peerage.

Lawrence Stone (1985) has claimed that the capitalist exploitation of landed estates was not associated with pro-parliamentarian allegiance in the civil war, on the basis of evidence from a 1630s list of landlords fined for reducing the number of peasant holdings on their estates by enclosures. But of the 600 names from five midland counties, he is able to find information on the civil war allegiance of only 54, and if Stone's own breakdown of these figures by rank has any statistical significance at all, it shows that peers and baronets fined for enclosing were more likely to be royalists than knights and wealthy squires who were fined for it (ibid., p. 51). Like the notorious counting of manors with which Tawney claimed to back up his rise of the gentry thesis, this supposedly statistical analysis does not amount to much. There were substantial

regional as well as individual differences in the ways in which
nobles and gentlemen exploited their estates, and it is perhaps sug-
gestive that in the northern counties, where some agricultural historians have seen rent increases and enclosures as an indication of
'fiscal seigneurialism' rather than agrarian capitalism (above, p.
115), there were more royalist than parliamentarian gentry in the
civil war (Morrill, 1993, pp. 191–213). Roger Manning has suggested that fiscal seigneurialism was more likely to be practised by
the owners of large estates than those of 'medium-sized estates
where resident landlords more generally farmed their own
demesnes and introduced new techniques in husbandry' (Manning,
1988, pp. 153–4). The crucial question, however, may not be the
incidence of enclosure or rent increases, but how these affected
relations between the landlords and their tenants and neighbours.
Historians have recognized that where enclosure was by agreement
and favourable to the larger tenant farmers, it cemented the alliance
between the better-off villagers and their landlords; fiscal seigneurialism, on the other hand, tended to worsen landlord–tenant relations
(ibid., pp. 108–54). This could answer a question asked long ago by
Conrad Russell, about why the gentry was apparently divided by
the rise of the yeomanry, rather than united against it (Russell,
1973, p. 9).

The study of tenant farmers brings our attention back to the
rising capitalists among the middling sort: the larger farmers regularly hiring wage labour, the clothiers who employed cottage
workers, the artisans who owned larger workshops with greater
numbers of journeymen. Brian Manning has argued that the 'main
changes in society were taking place in its middle ranks', and that
the two new classes of bourgeoisie and proletariat were both
emerging from among the small producers, as they polarized
increasingly between the richer, who were the employers, and the
poorer, who were the wage labourers (Manning, 1996, p. 8).
Prosperous capitalist farmers provided their landlords with rising
rents, collaborated in enclosure by agreement, held leading positions in village society, and demanded effective control of the 'disorderly' poor. They were part of 'a self-conscious elite of
substantial craftsmen, husbandmen, yeomen and some minor
gentry who dominated the community through their monopoly of

such positions of authority as jurymen, constables, churchwardens and overseers of the poor', and they showed a strong inclination 'to maintain hierarchy and good order in the face of disorder and chaos' (Sharp, 1988, p. 108). We have seen that members of village and small-town élites became involved in the political crisis of 1640–2 through news, petitioning and demonstrations, and that in appealing to these people more and more as the crisis developed the opponents of the king came to be characterized as the 'popular party' who betrayed traditional values of hierarchy and obedience. Hill has also argued that parliament could never have defeated the king without backing from merchants, artisans and yeomen, and has claimed that 'the expansion of these classes, in numbers and in wealth ... offers the most obviously *new* social fact in England during the century before 1640' (Hill, 1997, p. 8). While the radicalization of the revolution from 1647 is widely attributed to pressure from members of these social groups – including London merchants and craftsmen, and the rank and file of the New Model Army – it is also true that in some areas, members of village and small-town élites supported royalism or became active neutralist 'clubmen' later in the civil war. The socio-economic and cultural background to these differences in allegiance among the middling sort have been explored by David Underdown (1987, 1996) in his work on the southwest of England.

Merchants are also finding their way back into social explanations of the English civil war, though in a qualified way. It has long been clear that some of the leading merchant groups of early Stuart England, such as those who dominated the City of London up to 1641 or the Newcastle Hostmen who monopolized the coal trade, took the royalist side in the civil war, confirming for Marxists Dobb's view that the merchant class typically 'compromised with feudal society once its privileges had been won' and that merchants were 'essentially parasites on the old economic order' (Dobb, 1963, pp. 120–1). Robert Brenner has argued that 'far from transforming the old system economically or subverting it politically, the merchant class ... tended to live off the old socio-economic order and to constitute one of its main bulwarks' (Brenner, 1989, p. 291). In their own cities, merchant oligarchies were often a narrow élite who sought to exclude other citizens and inhabitants from the benefits of privileged trade. In the important provincial port of Bristol, for example, the Society of Merchant Venturers excluded retailers and craftsmen from membership and 'conceived of the economy as a great chain of being with themselves at the top mediating between the domestic and international markets' (Sacks, 1986, p. 90). Brenner argues that such privileged merchant oligarchies were linked to the crown by a community of interests, and that any opposition they showed in the 1620s (especially in the 1629 controversy over tonnage and poundage) was exceptional and temporary (Brenner, 1993, pp. 199–315). In the decades preceding the civil war, the government of London had come to be dominated by members of the privileged corporations which enjoyed monopolies in long-distance trade, the Levant and East India Companies, and the city's official support for the parliamentary opposition in late 1641 and 1642 was secured only by the ousting of this group from control by the more radical citizens (Pearl, 1961, pp. 197–275; Brenner, 1993, pp. 319–55). Brenner goes on to argue that a different set of overseas merchants, the 'new men'who were excluded from oligarchical and monopoly privileges, and traded instead with the new colonies across the Atlantic or challenged the monopolists by interloping in Far Eastern trade, played a crucial role in the London events of 1640–2. They 'stood at the head of the City [of London] popular movement and played a critical role in connecting that movement to the national parliamentary opposition', which they were able to do through their links with colonizing aristocrats such as Lords Brooke and Saye, and their associates in the House of Commons such as Pym (Brenner, 1993, p. 316). While this colonial connection has in the past been offered as proof that the events of 1640–2 were dominated by a faction of the aristocracy (Farnell, 1977), Brenner argues that these new merchants' links with London's non-merchant citizens in political agitation within the city were equally important. He goes on to show that many of the same 'new merchants' played an active part in the republican regime after 1649, when their old aristocratic patrons, incidentally, had disappeared from the political scene.

Revisionist historians have shown remarkably little interest in these new social interpretations of the civil war, which is surprising, as Conrad Russell's oft-quoted claim that, 'For the time being, then, social change explanations of the English civil war must be regarded as having broken down', was followed by the prediction that any new social change explanation 'will have to be based on the power of these people (yeomen, tradesmen and artificers) who were rising, not so much at the expense of the gentry, as at the expense of smallholders and the labouring poor'(Russell, 1973, pp. 8–9). Revisionists often claim that they do not have a social explanation for the civil war, but they have in practice taken up the suggestion made long ago by Jack Hexter (nowadays, ironically, an opponent of revisionists) that the nobility of Renaissance Europe, having lost their independent military power, 'were seeking ... to exercise power in a changed world through new channels', and that any revaluation of the social structure of early modern Western Europe should 'start ... by thinking in terms not of the decline of the aristocracy but of its reconstruction' (Hexter, 1961, pp. 69–70). Revisionist accounts of the causes of the civil war do describe the parliamentarian nobles, deprived of their former military strength, seeking to recover power by allying with the armed Scottish Covenanters, manipulating their 'dutiful subordinates'in the House of Commons, using their contacts with colonial merchants in the City of London, and adopting the political stance of aristocratic ancient Roman republicans, when they were not mining the archives for medieval precedents (Farnell, 1977; Russell, 1984a, 1993a; Adamson, 1990). The problem is, not that this was not happening – for there is quite a lot of evidence that it was – but that the efforts of these aristocrats to keep control of the situation failed almost from the start, when not only the House of Commons, but the citizens of London and even the rural electorate, through mass petitioning, entered the field and wrested control of the political situation out of their hands.

If explanations of the English civil war in terms of social change are worth pursuing – even for revisionists – it is not because they can reduce the complex question of causality to a simple, agreed formula of bourgeois revolution, or for their supposedly scientific borrowing from the social sciences, but because they can still attempt to bring together the different strands of explanation; to mediate, in effect, between long-term changes in the economy and short-term political events, and even to aim at that 'integrating or totalizing role'towards which social history has frequently aspired, and repair the breach between the history of society and the history of the state (Wilson, 1993, pp. 20–1). As Christopher Hill put it at the end of a similar exercise to this one, 'In the three preceding chapters our arbitrary division between economics, politics and ideas continually broke down. ... This impossibility of shutting off "religious", "constitutional", and "economic" causes of the civil war corresponds to the complexity of life in seventeenth-century England' (Hill, 1961, p. 101). If it is true that the social history approach is basically a unifying one, it is no accident – though I have to say it was not fully planned in advance – that each of the preceding chapters of this book tends towards one thesis more than any other, that of the importance of the middling sort as a catalyst which polarized the divisions over religion, politics and government in 1640–2. Religious activism in the local community, participation in local government (which also brought them into political controversies over the forced loan and Ship Money), and agitation around elections and petitions during the first two years of the Long Parliament, brought the leaders of local communities into political relations with the regional and national ruling class. These relations made it impossible for the opposition in the Long Parliament to back down, or for the king to disperse the latter by force, because the middling sort were the embodiment of the 'ascending' political theory. In other words, their presence forced the nobility and gentry to decide whether their authority as a ruling class depended on the king or on the people, on God or on the godly. Not all the nobility and gentry – nor all the middling sort – chose to believe that government in England had come to rest on the consent of these people, but perhaps it is more than an accident that those who chose to believe it did not were the losers in the civil war.

Guide to Further Reading

Note: where full bibliographical details are given in the Bibliography, they are not repeated here.

The English civil war and its causes are among the most intensively studied subjects in English history, and new general books as well as more detailed research appear every year. Similar titles may conceal very different approaches, and this is especially true of the two recent works with the same title as this volume. While Ann Hughes's *The Causes of the English Civil War* ranges from European problems and long-term social and cultural change, to an analysis of Charles I's reign, Conrad Russell's *The Causes of the English Civil War* argues a revisionist case focused on the causes of seven specific events which he believes led directly to the outbreak of war in 1642. Lawrence Stone's *The Causes of the English Revolution 1559–1642* earlier offered a theory of short-, medium- and long-term causes influenced by sociological theories. Works with less specific titles which discuss the causes of the war are Christopher Hill's *The Century of Revolution*, Robert Ashton's *The English Civil War: Conservatism and Revolution* and Barry Coward's *The Stuart Age*, with some significant changes in the second edition (1994). The revisionist case against long-term social and political causes is most clearly put in the title piece of John Morrill's collected essays, *The Nature of the English Revolution*, while Conrad Russell's *Unrevolutionary England* includes reprints of some of his ground-breaking articles of the 1970s and 1980s.

Three collections of essays by various authors which discuss the causes of the war, spanning three decades of historiography, are *The Origins of the English Civil War*, edited by Conrad Russell; Howard Tomlinson's *Before the English Civil War*, and the counter-revisionist collection edited by Richard Cust and Ann Hughes, *Conflict in Early Stuart England*. None of these works, however, deals with recent controversies about the validity of the enquiry into causation as such: for these problems, see Keith Jenkins's *Rethinking History*, and the 'realist' defences by Joyce Appleby, Lynn Hunt and Margaret Jacob, *Telling the Truth about History*, and Richard Evans's *In Defence of History*.

For good, readable narratives of the whole civil war period, see Martyn Bennett's *The Civil Wars in Britain and Ireland, 1638–1651* and Mark Kishlansky's *A Monarchy Transformed: Britain 1603–1714*. For greater detail, which allows students to formulate their own interpretations even in the face of the author's opinions, Anthony Fletcher's *The Outbreak of the English Civil War* and Conrad Russell's *The Fall of the British Monarchies* are excellent. The different analyses of the Scottish Covenanting revolution by Alan Macinnes in *Charles I and the Making of the Covenanting Movement 1625–1641* and Keith Brown in *Kingdom or Province? Scotland and the Regal Union, 1603–1715,* show that there is much argument about the causes of these events, while Peter Donald's work, *An Uncounselled King: Charles I and the Scottish Troubles, 1637–1641,* takes a wider British perspective, and a full account of Charles I's campaigns against the Covenanters is provided by Mark Fissel in *The Bishops' Wars.* Brendan Fitzpatrick in *Seventeenth Century Ireland: The War of Religions* interprets the rebellion in Ireland from a contemporary Irish perspective and challenges several myths which are staples of both British and Irish historiography. Further coverage of the debate about its causes can be obtained by reading Aidan Clarke's article in *Plantation to Partition,* edited by Peter Roebuck, Michael Perceval-Maxwell's *The Outbreak of the Irish Rebellion of 1641* and Nicholas Canny's piece in Jane Ohlmeyer (ed.), *Ireland from Independence to Occupation, 1641–1660.*

Kevin Sharpe deals fully with the Short Parliament in the concluding section of *The Personal Rule of Charles I.* For some key documents of the Long Parliament, J. P. Kenyon's *The Stuart Constitution* is useful, though his commentary has swung dramatically from a traditional to a revisionist position between the 1966 and 1986 editions. For two contrasting interpretations of political polarization in the country as a whole in 1640–2, see John Morrill's *Revolt of the Provinces* and Brian Manning's *The English People and the English Revolution,* each with additional comment in its second edition (1980 and 1991 respectively). The study of London's role in the crisis, initiated by Valerie Pearl's *London and the Outbreak of the Puritan Revolution,* is broadened and radicalized by Keith Lindley's recent *Popular Politics and Religion in Civil War London.*

The indispensable guide to the development of the Church of England from the Reformation to the civil war (and beyond) is Susan Doran and Christopher Durston's *Princes, Pastors and People.* Leo F. Solt's *Church and State in Early Modern England 1509–1640* is also useful, though its focus is narrower. Patrick Collinson's *The Religion of Protestants* should not be missed by anyone studying this subject. The collection of essays edited by Kenneth Fincham, *The Early Stuart Church,* brings together a number of different views, while Christopher Hill's incomparable *The English Bible and the Seventeenth-Century Revolution* is essential reading for any student harbouring doubts about how seriously religion was taken in early Stuart England.

Students may have encountered Weber's 'Protestant ethic' in sociology classes, but R. H. Tawney's *Religion and the Rise of Capitalism* is a much better starting point for seventeenth-century English Puritanism, and William Haller's *Rise of Puritanism* is another classic. Nicholas Tyacke, who revolutionized views on the nature of Puritanism, followed up his important article of 1973 with *Anti-Calvinists* some years later, and this has been opposed by Peter White in *Predestination, Policy and Polemic*. On the social implications of religion, the second volume of Christopher Hill's collected essays, *Religion and Politics in Seventeenth-Century England*, supplements his sometimes simplistic approach in *Society and Puritanism in Pre-Revolutionary England*. An alternative social interpretation of religious differences is offered by David Underdown in *Revel, Riot and Rebellion*, while detailed studies of grassroots Puritanism include Keith Wrightson and David Levine's pioneering *Poverty and Piety in an English Village*, William Hunt's *The Puritan Moment* and Underdown's *Fire from Heaven*. Some interesting insights into Puritan mentalities are suggested by Stephen Baskerville in *Not Peace but a Sword*, though this work needs to be handled with care in the context of causation. William Lamont's *Puritanism and Historical Controversy* challenges the more traditional views of Puritanism.

Many of the above works are also useful for an understanding of Arminianism, while very different interpretations of this subject are given by Peter White in *Predestination, Policy and Polemic* and Julian Davies in *The Caroline Captivity of the Church*. Peter Lake argues in defence of a more traditional position in his *Past and Present* article, 'Calvinism and the English Church 1570–1635' (1987). On the importance of understanding anti-Catholicism, Hill's *Antichrist in Seventeenth-Century England* made an important breakthrough, and Peter Lake's article, 'Anti-Popery: The Structure of a Prejudice' in Cust and Hughes (1989) shows the usefulness of this approach. Michael Finlayson, in *Historians, Puritanism and the English Revolution*, argues that it was mainly anti-Catholicism, rather than any other religious difference, that distinguished Puritans from the mainstream of the Church of England. Indispensable evidence for the reality behind Puritan fears is provided by Caroline Hibbard's *Charles I and the Popish Plot*.

Problems in the interpretation of constitutional conflict which were first discussed in Margaret Attwood Judson's *Crisis of the Constitution* have contributed to Glenn Burgess's analyses in *The Politics of the Ancient Constitution* and *Absolute Monarchy and the Stuart Constitution*. The view that there was a fundamental ideological conflict between kings and parliaments is argued by Johann Sommerville, in *Politics and Ideology in England 1603–1640* and David Wootton in his preface to *Divine Right and Democracy*. James Daly's 1978 article, 'The Idea of Absolute Monarchy in Seventeenth-century England', demonstrates the usefulness of detailed research into the changing meanings of political concepts.

Conrad Russell's *Parliaments and English Politics 1621–1629* stands at the centre of all discussions of the parliaments of the 1620s, and some of his earlier articles on these themes are reprinted in *Unrevolutionary England*. Serious criticisms of Russell's view have been put forward by Richard Cust in *The Forced Loan and English Politics*, L. J. Reeve in *Charles I and the Road to Personal*

Rule, Christopher Thompson's *Parliamentary History in the 1620s: In or Out of Perspective?* and the first two chapters of Michael Young's *Charles I*. Different analyses of the implications of the electoral process are offered by Derek Hirst, *The Representative of the People?* and Mark Kishlansky, *Parliamentary Selection*. The politics of the personal rule, and relations between central and local government during that period, are dealt with in Kevin Sharpe's *The Personal Rule of Charles I*, Esther Cope's *Politics Without Parliaments* and Perez Zagorin's *The Court and the Country*. Anthony Fletcher's *Reform in the Provinces* and Buchanan Sharp's *In Contempt of All Authority* provide more detailed and thought-provoking information and analysis on questions of local government and the maintenance of order.

For the study of English society in the century before the civil war, Keith Wrightson's *English Society 1580–1650* and Barry Coward's *Social Change and Continuity in Early Modern England* both offer useful assessments of the balance between change and continuity, while C. G. A. Clay's *Economic Expansion and Social Change*, in two volumes, is still the best economic history. Joan Thirsk's collected essays in *The Rural Economy of England* offer a variety of local and thematic studies for consideration, while the collection edited by R. C. Richardson, *Town and Countryside in the English Revolution*, provides some recent thinking on both rural and urban change. Sybil Jack, in *Towns in Tudor and Stuart Britain*, gives the best overview from an urban historian's point of view, while Beier and Finlay's collection *London 1500–1700: The Making of the Metropolis*, Jonathan Barry's *The Tudor and Stuart Town* and Peter Clark and Paul Slack's *English Towns in Transition 1500–1700* will provide further food for thought on urban change. *The Crisis of the Aristocracy* by Lawrence Stone is still immensely valuable for its detailed study of noble property and lifestyles, while a traditional approach to the gentry exemplified by G. E. Mingay, *The Gentry: The Rise and Fall of a Ruling Class*, can be compared with a more recent one by Felicity Heal and Clive Holmes, *The Gentry in England and Wales, 1500–1700*. For discussion of the labouring classes, Alan Everitt's article on farm labourers in Thirsk's *The Agrarian History of England and Wales*, vol. IV, should still be read, along with A. L. Beier's study of vagrancy, *Masterless Men*.

On questions of social order and disorder, there are several important contributions which have been much discussed, in Fletcher and Stevenson (eds), *Order and Disorder in Early Modern England*. Roger Manning, in *Village Revolts*, covers a wide range of popular protests, including London apprentice riots; this work is not to be confused with Brian Manning's *The English People and the English Revolution*, which offers a more radical interpretation of such disorders. Provincial riots are further discussed in Buchanan Sharp's *In Contempt of All Authority*, David Underdown's *Revel, Riot and Rebellion* and Keith Lindley's *Fenland Riots and the English Revolution*. Unfortunately, John Walter's forthcoming work on popular violence in the civil war and revolution, to be titled *Understanding Popular Violence in the English Revolution*, was not available at the time of this book's going to press. The relationship between gender and order is discussed most explicitly by Susan Amussen in *An Ordered Society* and by David Underdown in *A Freeborn People*, while some background on the wide variety of interpretations of the history of the family can be gained from Ralph Houlbrooke's *The English Family 1450–1700*.

Almost all books on the English civil war offer some interpretation of Charles I's role, but the most thought-provoking biographies are *Charles I: The Personal Monarch* by Charles Carlton and Michael Young's short but sharp *Charles I*. A recent and thought-provoking argument about the importance of the decisions made by Charles in 1639–40 appears in the piece by John Adamson, in Niall Ferguson (ed.), *Virtual History*, which can usefully be compared with Russell's speculations in two articles written in 1984, 'Why did Charles I fight the Civil War?' and 'Why did Charles I call the Long Parliament?'

Further perspectives on the English use of concepts such as liberty and the ancient constitution are provided by a number of authors in *Parliament and Liberty from the Reign of Elizabeth to the English Civil War*, edited by J. H. Hexter, and a Marxist perspective is offered by Ellen Meiksins Wood and Neal Wood in *A Trumpet of Sedition*. John Sanderson argues strongly in *'But the People's Creatures'*, which is subtitled *The Philosophical Basis of the English Civil War*, that revolutionary ideas were of central importance to the development of the civil war and revolution, arguing against Conrad Russell in chapter 6 of *The Causes of the English Civil War* and John Morrill in chapter 15 of *The Nature of the English Revolution.* A more theoretical perspective on the problem of ideological conflict may be provided by the two volumes of Quentin Skinner's *Foundations of Modern Political Thought* though they do not deal directly with this period; these should be read, or at least sampled, before tackling Richard Tuck's *Philosophy and Government*.

Extracts from the classic contributions to the debate over the rise of the gentry are provided in the collection *Social Change and Revolution in England 1540–1640* edited by Lawrence Stone in 1965, though this debate now needs to be read in the light of more recent work referred to in the section on social change. Essential works of Christopher Hill on the social nature of the civil war include *The English Revolution, 1640*, *The Century of Revolution* and the article 'A Bourgeois Revolution?' which is reprinted in *People and Ideas in Seventeenth-Century England* with an interesting postscript. For illustrations of how far recent Marxists have developed the concept of bourgeois revolution into something distinctly different, see Ellen Meiksins Wood, *The Pristine Culture of Capitalism*, Robert Brenner, *Merchants and Revolution* and Colin Mooers, *The Making of Bourgeois Europe* (London: Verso, 1991). Brian Manning's Marxist interpretation is more solidly rooted in the English 'middling sort' and the most recent version of this is to be found in *Aristocrats, Plebeians and Revolution in England*. David Underdown's most recent work, *A Freeborn People*, is full of valuable insights into the political culture and consciousness of the middling sort, though his earlier *Revel, Riot and Rebellion* makes a more direct contribution to the debate on the causes of the war.

Bibliography

Adamson, John 1990: 'The baronial context of the English civil war.' *Transactions of the Royal Historical Society,* 5th Series, 40, 93–120.

Adamson, John 1997: 'England without Cromwell: what if Charles I had avoided the civil war? In Niall Ferguson (ed.) *Virtual History: Alternatives and Counterfactuals.* London: Macmillan.

Allen, John William 1967: *English Political Thought, 1603–1644.* Hamden, Connecticut: Methuen.

Allen, Robert C. 1992: *Enclosure and the Yeoman: The Agricultural Development of the South Midlands 1450–1850.* Oxford: Clarendon Press.

Amussen, Susan Dwyer 1988: *An Ordered Society: Gender and Class in Early Modern England.* Oxford: Blackwell Publishers.

Amussen, Susan Dwyer and Kishlansky, Mark (eds) 1995: *Political Culture and Cultural Politics in Early Modern England.* Manchester: Manchester University Press.

Appleby, Andrew B. 1975: 'Agrarian capitalism or seigneurial reaction? The Northwest of England, 1500–1700.' *American Historical Review,* 80, 574–94.

Appleby, Joyce, Hunt, Lynn and Jacob, Margaret 1994: *Telling the Truth about History.* New York: Norton.

Aries, Philippe 1979: *Centuries of Childhood.* Harmondsworth: Penguin.

Ashton, Robert 1978: *The English Civil War: Conservatism and Revolution.* London: Weidenfeld and Nicolson.

Aylmer, G. E. 1980: 'The meaning and definition of "property" in seventeenth-century England.' *Past and Present,* 86, 87–97.

Barry, Jonathan (ed.) 1990: *The Tudor and Stuart Town: A Reader in English Urban History 1530–1688.* London: Longman.

Baskerville, Stephen 1993: *Not Peace but a Sword: The Political Theology of the English Revolution.* London: Routledge.

Beer, Anna R. 1997: *Sir Walter Ralegh and his Readers in the Seventeenth Century.* Basingstoke: Macmillan.

Beier, A. L. 1985: *Masterless Men: The Vagrancy Problem in England 1560–1640.* London: Methuen.

Beier, A. L. 1986: 'Engine of manufacture: the trades of London.' In Beier and Finlay (eds) *London 1500–1700: The Making of the Metropolis.* London: Longman.

Beier, A. L. and Finlay, Roger (eds) 1986: *London 1500–1700: The Making of the Metropolis*. London: Longman.

Beier, A. L., Cannadine, David and Rosenheim, James M. 1989: *The First Modern Society: Essays in Honour of Lawrence Stone*. Cambridge: Cambridge University Press.

Bennet, Judith M. 1991: 'Misogyny, popular culture and women's work.' *History Workshop Journal* 31, 166–88.

Bennett, Martyn 1997: *The Civil Wars in Britain and Ireland, 1638–1651.* Oxford: Blackwell Publishers.

Black, Antony 1984: *Guilds and Civil Society in European Political Thought from the Twelfth Century to the Present*. London: Methuen.

Bottigheimer, Karl 1971: *English Money and Irish Land: The 'Adventurers' in the Cromwellian Settlement of Ireland*. Oxford: Oxford University Press.

Bray, Alan 1990: 'Homosexuality and the signs of male friendship in Elizabethan England.' *History Workshop Journal* 29, 1–19.

Brenner, Robert 1987: 'Agrarian class structure and economic development in pre-industrial Europe.' In Aston, Trevor H. and Philpin, C. H. E. (eds) *The Brenner Debate*. Cambridge: Cambridge University Press.

Brenner, Robert 1989: 'Bourgeois revolution and transition to capitalism.' In Beier, A. L., Cannadine, David and Rosenheim, James M. (eds) *The First Modern Society: Essays in English History in Honour of Lawrence Stone*. Cambridge: Cambridge University Press.

Brenner, Robert 1993: *Merchants and Revolution: Commercial Change, Political Conflict, and London's Overseas Traders, 1550–1653*. Cambridge: Cambridge University Press.

Brown, Keith M. 1992: *Kingdom or Province? Scotland and the Regal Union, 1603–1715*. Basingstoke: Macmillan.

Burgess, Glenn 1990: 'On revisionism: an analysis of early Stuart historiography in the 1970s and 1980s.' *Historical Journal* 33, 609–27.

Burgess, Glenn 1992: *The Politics of the Ancient Constitution: An Introduction to English Political Thought, 1603–1642.* London: Macmillan.

Burgess, Glenn 1996: *Absolute Monarchy and the Stuart Constitution*. London and New Haven, Conn.: Yale University Press.

Callinicos, Alex 1989: 'Bourgeois revolutions and historical materialism.' *International Socialism* 43, 113–71.

Canny, Nicholas 1995: 'What really happened in Ireland in 1641?' In Ohlmeyer, Jane H. (ed.) *Ireland from Independence to Occupation, 1641–1660*. Cambridge: Cambridge University Press.

Carlton, Charles 1995: *Charles I, The Personal Monarch*, 2nd edn. London: Routledge.

Carlyle, Thomas 1888: *Oliver Cromwell's Letters and Speeches.*

Carr, E. H. 1961: *What is History?* London: Penguin.

Charlesworth, Andrew (ed.) 1983: *An Atlas of Rural Protest in Britain 1548–1900*. London: Croom Helm.

Christianson, Paul 1977: 'The peers, the people and parliamentary management in the first six months of the Long Parliament.' *Journal of Modern History* 49, 575–99.

Clark, Jonathan Charles Douglas 1986: *Revolution and Rebellion: State and Society in England in the Seventeenth and Eighteenth Centuries*. Cambridge:

Cambridge University Press.

Clark, Peter 1976a: 'Popular protest and disturbances in Kent, 1558–1640.' *Economic History Review*, 2nd series, 29, 365–81.

Clark, Peter (ed.) 1976b: *The Early Modern Town: A Reader*. London: Longman/Open University Press.

Clark, Peter 1979: '"The Ramoth–Gilead of the good": urban change and political radicalism at Gloucester 1540–1640.' In Clark, Peter, Smith, Alan G. R. and Tyacke, Nicholas (eds) *The English Commonwealth 1547–1640: Essays in Politics and Society*. Leicester: Leicester University Press.

Clark, Peter and Slack, Paul 1976: *English Towns in Transition 1500–1700*. Oxford: Oxford University Press.

Clarke, Aidan 1970: 'Ireland and the General Crisis.' *Past and Present* 48, 79–99.

Clarke, Aidan 1981: 'The genesis of the Ulster rising of 1641.' In Roebuck, Peter (ed.) *Plantation to Partition: Essays in Ulster History in Honour of J. L. McCracken*. Belfast: Blackstaff Press.

Clarkson, Leslie Albert 1985: *Proto-industrialization: The First Phase of Industrialization?* Basingstoke: Macmillan.

Clay, C. G. A. 1984: *Economic Expansion and Social Change: England 1500–1700*, 2 vols. Cambridge: Cambridge University Press.

Cliffe, J. T. 1984: *The Puritan Gentry: The Great Puritan Families of Early Stuart England*. London: Routledge and Kegan Paul.

Clifford, C. A. 1982: 'Ship money in Hampshire: collection and collapse.' *Southern History* 4, 91–106.

Clifton, Robin 1973: 'Fear of Popery.' In Russell (ed.) *The Origins of the English Civil War*. London: Macmillan.

Cogswell, Thomas 1989: *The Blessed Revolution: English Politics and the Coming of War, 1621–1624*. Cambridge: Cambridge University Press.

Collinson, Patrick 1982: *The Religion of Protestants: The Church in English Society 1559–1625*. Oxford: Clarendon Press.

Collinson, Patrick 1983: *Godly People*. London: Hambledon.

Cope, Esther 1987: *Politics Without Parliaments*. London: Allen and Unwin.

Corfield, Penelope 1976: 'Urban development in England and Wales in the sixteenth and seventeenth centuries.' Reprinted in Barry (ed.) 1990: *The Tudor and Stuart Town: A Reader in English Urban History 1530–1688*. London: Longman.

Coward, Barry 1980: *The Stuart Age*. London: Longman.

Coward, Barry 1988: *Social Change and Continuity in Early Modern England 1550–1750*. London: Longman.

Coward, Barry 1994: *The Stuart Age*, 2nd edn. London: Longman.

Cust, Richard 1986: 'News and politics in early seventeenth-century England.' *Past and Present* 112, 60–90.

Cust, Richard 1987: *The Forced Loan and English Politics 1626–1628*. Oxford: Clarendon Press.

Cust, Richard 1989: 'Politics and the electorate in the 1620s.' In Cust and Hughes (eds) *Conflict in Early Stuart England: Studies in Religion and Politics 1603–1642*. London: Longman.

Cust, Richard and Hughes, Ann 1989: *Conflict in Early Stuart England: Studies in Religion and Politics 1603–1642*. London: Longman.

Daly, James 1978: 'The idea of absolute monarchy in seventeenth-century

England.' *Historical Journal* 21, 227–50.

Davies, Julian 1992: *The Caroline Captivity of the Church*. Oxford: Clarendon Press.

De Vries, Jan 1984: *European Urbanization 1500–1800*. London: Methuen.

Dobb, Maurice 1963: *Studies in the Development of Capitalism*, 2nd edn. London: Routledge and Kegan Paul.

Donald, Peter 1989: 'New light on the Anglo-Scottish contacts of 1640.' *Historical Research* 62, 221–9.

Donald, Peter 1990a: *An Uncounselled King: Charles I and the Scottish Troubles, 1637–1641*. Cambridge: Cambridge University Press.

Donald, Peter 1990b: 'The Scottish national Covenant and British politics.' In Morrill (ed.) *The Scottish National Covenant in its British Context*. Edinburgh: Edinburgh University Press.

Doran, Susan and Durston, Christopher 1991: *Princes, Pastors and People: The Church and Religion in England 1529–1689*. London: Routledge.

Durston, Christopher 1989: *The Family in the English Revolution*. Oxford: Blackwell Publishers.

Durston, Christopher 1992: '"Wild as colts untamed": radicalism in the Newbury area in the early-modern period.' In Barry Stapleton (ed.) *Conflict and Community in Southern England*. Stroud: Alan Sutton.

Eley, Geoff and Hunt, Willliam (eds) 1988: *Reviving the English Revolution: Reflections and Elaborations on the Work of Christopher Hill*. London: Verso.

Elton, Geoffrey 1960: *The Tudor Constitution*. Cambridge: Cambridge University Press.

Elton, Geoffrey 1966: 'Ahigh road to civil war?'In C. H. Carter (ed.) *From the Renaissance to the Counter-Reformation: Essays in Honor of Garrett Mattingly*. London: Cape.

Evans, John T. 1979: *Seventeenth-Century Norwich: Politics, Religion and Government 1620–1690*. Oxford: Clarendon Press.

Evans, Richard J. 1997: *In Defence of History*. London: Granta Books.

Everitt, Alan 1966: *The Community of Kent and the Great Rebellion, 1640–1660*. Leicester: Leicester University Press.

Everitt, Alan 1967: 'Farm Labourers.'In Thirsk, Joan (ed.) *The Agrarian History of England and Wales, IV, 1500–1640*. Cambridge: Cambridge University Press.

Everitt, Alan 1969a: *Change in the Provinces: The Seventeenth Century*. Leicester: Leicester University Press.

Everitt, Alan 1969b: *The Local Community and the Great Rebellion*. London: The Historical Association.

Farnell, J. T 1977: 'The social and intellectual basis of London's role in the English civil wars.' *Journal of Modern History* 49, 641–60.

Fincham, Kenneth 1984: 'The judges'decision on ship money in February 1637: the reaction of Kent.' *Bulletin of the Institute of Historical Research* 57, 230–7.

Finlay, Roger and Shearer, Beatrice 1986: 'Population growth and suburban expansion.' In Beier and Finlay (eds) *London 1500–1700: The Making of the Metropolis*. London: Longman.

Finlayson, Michael G. 1983: *Historians, Puritanism and the English Revolution: The Religious Factor in English Politics before and after the Interregnum*. Toronto: University of Toronto Press.

Fisher, F. J. 1971: 'London as an "engine of economic growth"'. In J. S. Bromley and E. H. Kossman (eds) *Britain and the Netherlands*, vol. 4. London: Macmillan.

Fissel, Mark Charles 1994: *The Bishops' Wars: Charles I's Campaigns against Scotland 1638–1640*. Cambridge: Cambridge University Press.

Fitzpatrick, Brendan 1988: *Seventeenth Century Ireland: The War of Religions*. Dublin: Gill and Macmillan.

Fletcher, Anthony 1981: *The Outbreak of the English Civil War*. London: Edward Arnold.

Fletcher, Anthony 1983: 'National and local awareness in the county communities.' In Tomlinson (ed.) *Before the English Civil War: Essays on Early Stuart Politics and Government*. London: Macmillan.

Fletcher, Anthony 1986: *Reform in the Provinces: The Government of Stuart England*. New Haven, Conn. and London: Yale University Press.

Fletcher, Anthony and Stevenson, John (eds)1985: *Order and Disorder in Early Modern England*. Cambridge: Cambridge University Press.

Foster, Andrew 1989: 'Church policies of the 1630s.' In Cust and Hughes (eds) *Conflict in Early Stuart England: Studies in Religion and Politics 1603–1642*. London: Longman.

Fraser, Antonia 1984: *The Weaker Vessel: Women's Lot in Seventeenth-Century England*. London: Weidenfeld and Nicolson.

Gardiner, Samuel Rawson 1906: *Constitutional Documents of the Puritan Revolution*, 3rd edn. Oxford: Clarendon Press.

George, C. H. 1968: 'Puritanism as history and historiography.' *Past and Present* 41, 77–104.

Grell, Ole Peter 1996: 'Introduction.' In Grell, Ole Peter and Scribner, Bob, *Tolerance and Intolerance in the European Reformation*. Cambridge: Cambridge University Press.

Goodare, Julian 1995: 'The Scottish parliament of 1621.' *Historical Journal* 38, 29–51.

Goose, Nigel 1982: 'English pre-industrial urban economies.' *Urban History Yearbook*. Leicester: Leicester University Press. Reprinted in Barry (ed.) 1990: *The Tudor and Stuart Town: A Reader in English Urban History 1530–1688*. London: Longman.

Haller, William 1957: *The Rise of Puritanism*, 2nd edn. New York: Harper and Row.

Heal, Felicity 1984: 'The idea of hospitality in early modern England.' *Past and Present* 102, 66–93.

Heal, Felicity and Holmes, Clive 1994: *The Gentry in England and Wales, 1500–1700*. Basingstoke: Macmillan.

Herrup, Cynthia 1983: 'The counties and the country: some thoughts on seventeenth-century historiography.' *Journal of Modern History* 8, 169–81.

Hexter, J. H. 1941: *The Reign of King Pym*. Cambridge, Mass.: Harvard University Press.

Hexter, J. H. 1961: *Reappraisals in History*. London: Longman.

Hexter, J. H. (ed.) 1992: *Parliament and Liberty from the Reign of Elizabeth to the English Civil War*. Stanford, Calif.: Stanford University Press.

Hibbard, Caroline 1983: *Charles I and the Popish Plot*. Chapel Hill: University of North Carolina.

Hill, Christopher 1940: 'The English Revolution.' In Hill, Christopher (ed.) *The English Revolution 1640: Three Essays*. London: Lawrence and Wishart.

Hill, Christopher 1961: *The Century of Revolution, 1603–1714*. London: Nelson.

Hill, Christopher 1969: *Society and Puritanism in Pre-Revolutionary England*, 3rd edn. London: Panther.

Hill, Christopher 1986: *Religion and Politics in Seventeenth-Century England. Collected Essays, Volume Two*. Brighton: Harvester.

Hill, Christopher 1987: *People and Ideas in Seventeenth-Century England. Collected Essays, Volume Three*. Brighton: Harvester.

Hill, Christopher 1990: *Antichrist in Seventeenth-Century England*. London: Verso.

Hill, Christopher 1993: *The English Bible and the Seventeenth-Century Revolution*. London: Allen Lane.

Hill, Christopher 1997: *Intellectual Origins of the English Revolution Revisited*. Oxford: Clarendon Press.

Hilton, Rodney (ed.) 1978: *The Transition from Feudalism to Capitalism*. London: Verso.

Hindle, Steve 1998: 'Persuasion and protest in the Caddington Common enclosure dispute 1635–1639.' *Past and Present* 158, 37–78.

Hirst, Derek 1975: *The Representative of the People? Voters and Voting in England under the Early Stuarts*. Cambridge: Cambridge University Press.

Hirst, Derek 1992: 'Freedom, revolution and beyond.' In Hexter (ed.) *Parliament and Liberty from the Reign of Elizabeth to the English Civil War*. Stanford, Calif.: Stanford University Press.

Holmes, Clive 1980: 'The county community in Stuart historiography.' *Journal of British Studies* 19, 54–73.

Holmes, Clive 1985: 'Drainers and fenmen: the problem of popular political consciousness in the seventeenth century.' In Fletcher and Stevenson (eds) *Order and Disorder in Early Modern England*. Cambridge: Cambridge University Press.

Holt, Mack P. 1995: *The French Wars of Religion 1562–1629*. Cambridge: Cambridge University Press.

Houlbrooke, Ralph 1984: *The English Family 1450–1700*. London: Longman.

Hughes, Ann 1989: 'Local history and the origins of the civil war.' In Cust and Hughes (eds) *Conflict in Early Stuart England: Studies in Religion and Politics 1603–1642*. London: Longman.

Hughes, Ann 1991: *The Causes of the English Civil War*. Basingstoke: Macmillan.

Hughes, Ann 1992: 'Coventry and the English revolution.' In Richardson (ed.) *Town and Countryside in the English Revolution*. Manchester: Manchester University Press.

Hunt, William 1983: *The Puritan Moment: The Coming of Revolution in an English County*. Cambridge, Mass.: Harvard University Press.

Hunt, William 1988: 'Spectral origins of the English revolution: a legitimation crisis in early Stuart England.' In Eley and Hunt (eds) *Reviving the English Revolution: Reflections and Elaborations on the Work of Christopher Hill*. London: Verso.

Hutton, Ronald 1982: 'The royalist war effort.' In Morrill, John (ed.) *Reactions to the English Civil War*. London: Macmillan.

Jack, Sybil 1996: *Towns in Tudor and Stuart Britain.* London: Macmillan.

Jenkins, Keith 1991: *Rethinking History.* London: Routledge.

Judson, Margaret Attwood 1949: *The Crisis of the Constitution.* London and New Brunswick: Rutgers University Press.

Kendall, R. T. 1979: *Calvin and English Calvinism to 1649.* Oxford: Oxford University Press.

Kenyon, J. P. 1966: *The Stuart Constitution.* Cambridge: Cambridge University Press.

Kenyon, J. P. 1986: *The Stuart Constitution,* 2nd edn. Cambridge: Cambridge University Press.

Kenyon, J. P. 1988: *The Civil Wars of England.* London: Weidenfeld and Nicolson.

Kermode, Jenny and Walker, Garthine (eds) 1994: *Women, Crime and the Courts in Early Modern England.* London: UCL Press.

Kishlansky, Mark 1986: *Parliamentary Selection: Social and Political Choice in Early Modern England.* Cambridge: Cambridge University Press.

Kishlansky, Mark 1996: *A Monarchy Transformed: Britain 1603–1714.* London: Allen Lane.

Lake, Peter 1981: 'The collection of ship money in Cheshire during the 1630s: a case study of relations between central and local government.' *Northern History* 17, 44–71.

Lake, Peter 1987: 'Calvinism and the English Church 1570–1635.' *Past and Present* 114, 32–76.

Lake, Peter 1989: 'Anti-popery: the structure of a prejudice.'In Cust and Hughes (eds) *Conflict in Early Stuart England: Studies in Religion and Politics 1603–1642.* London: Longman.

Lake, Peter 1995: 'The moderate and irenic case for religious war: Joseph Hall's *Via Media* in context.'In Amussen and Kishlansky (eds) *Political Culture and Cultural Politics in Early Modern England.* Manchester: Manchester University Press.

Lamont, William 1996: *Puritanism and Historical Controversy.* London: UCL Press.

Laslett, Peter 1965: *The World We Have Lost.* London: Methuen.

Laslett, Peter 1983: *The World We Have Lost, Further Explored.* London: Methuen.

Levack, Brian P. 1987: *The Formation of the British State: England, Scotland and the Union 1603–1707.* Oxford: Clarendon Press.

Levine, David 1987: *Reproducing Families: The Political Economy of English Population History.* Cambridge: Cambridge University Press.

Lindley, Keith 1982: *Fenland Riots and the English Revolution.* London: Heinemann.

Lindley, Keith 1997: *Popular Politics and Religion in Civil War London.* Aldershot: Scolar Press.

Macaulay, Thomas Babington (Lord) 1913: *The History of England from the Accession of James II,* ed. C. H. Firth. London: Macmillan.

Macfarlane, Alan 1978: *The Origins of English Individualism.* Oxford: Blackwell Publishers.

McFarlane, K. B. 1973: *The Nobility of Later Medieval England.* Oxford: Oxford University Press.

Macinnes, Alan 1991: *Charles I and the Making of the Covenanting Movement 1625–1641*. Edinburgh: John Donald.

Mack, Phyllis 1992: *Visionary Women: Ecstatic Prophecy in Seventeenth-Century England*. Berkeley and Los Angeles: California University Press.

Maclachlan, Alistair 1996: *The Rise and Fall of Revolutionary England: An Essay on the Fabrication of Seventeenth-Century History*. Basingstoke: Macmillan.

Makey, Walter H. 1979: *The Church of the Covenant, 1637–1651*. Edinburgh: Donald.

Malcolm, Joyce Lee 1978: 'A king in search of soldiers: Charles I in 1642.' *Historical Journal* 21, 251–73.

Malcolm, Joyce Lee 1983: *Caesar's Due: Loyalty and King Charles 1642–1646*. London: Royal Historical Society.

Manning, Brian 1991: *The English People and the English Revolution*, 2dn edn. London: Bookmarks.

Manning, Brian 1996: *Aristocrats, Plebeians and Revolution in England 1640–1660*. London: Pluto Press.

Manning, Roger B. 1988: *Village Revolts: Social Protests and Popular Disturbances in England 1509–1640*. Oxford: Clarendon Press.

Marshall, Rosalind K. 1984: 'Wet-nursing in Scotland: 1500–1800.' *Review of Scottish Culture* 1, 43–51.

Marx, Karl and Engels, Frederick 1962: *Selected Works in Two Volumes*. Moscow: Foreign Languages Publishing House.

Marx, Karl and Engels, Frederick 1971: *Articles on Britain*. Moscow: Progress Publishers.

Miller, John 1987: *Bourbon and Stuart: Kings and Kingship in France and England in the Seventeenth Century*. London: George Philip.

Mingay, G. E. 1976: *The Gentry: The Rise and Fall of a Ruling Class*. London: Longman.

Morrill, John 1980: *The Revolt of the Provinces: Conservatives and Radicals in the English Civil War 1630–1650*, 2nd edn. London: Longman.

Morrill, John (ed.) 1990: *The Scottish National Covenant in its British Context*. Edinburgh: Edinburgh University Press.

Morrill, John 1993: *The Nature of the English Revolution*. London: Longman.

Morrill, John 1995: 'The unweariableness of Mr Pym: influence and eloquence in the Long Parliament.' In Amussen and Kishlansky (eds) *Political Culture and Cultural Politics in Early Modern England*. Manchester: Manchester University Press.

Morrill, John 1996: 'Taking liberties with the seventeenth century.' *Parliamentary History* 15, 379–91.

Morrill, John and Walter, John 1985: 'Order and disorder in the English Revolution.' In Fletcher and Stevenson (eds) *Order and Disorder in Early Modern England*. Cambridge: Cambridge University Press.

Mousnier, Roland 1971: *Peasant Uprisings in Seventeenth-Century France, Russia and China*, trans. Brian Pearce. London: Allen and Unwin.

Outhwaite, R. B. 1986: 'Progress and backwardness in English agriculture, 1500–1650.' *Economic History Review* 2nd series, 39, 1–18.

Parker, Kenneth L. 1988: *The English Sabbath: A Study of Doctrine and Discipline from the Reformation to the English Civil War*. Cambridge: Cambridge University Press.

Pearl, Valerie 1961: *London and the Outbreak of the Puritan Revolution.* Oxford: Oxford University Press.

Perceval-Maxwell, Michael 1994: *The Outbreak of the Irish Rebellion of 1641.* Dublin: Gill and Macmillan.

Pocock, J. G. A. 1957: *The Ancient Constitution and the Feudal Law: A Study of English Historical Thought in the Seventeenth Century.* Cambridge: Cambridge University Press.

Pocock, J. G. A. 1974: *The Ancient Constitution and the Feudal Law.* Bath: Chivers.

Popofsky, Linda S. 1990: 'The crisis over tonnage and poundage in parliament in 1629.' *Past and Present* 126, 44–75.

Pugh, T. B. 1972: 'The magnates, knights and gentry.' In Chrimes, S. B., Ross, C. D. and Griffiths, R. A. (eds) *Fifteenth-Century England, 1399–1509.* Manchester: Manchester University Press.

Quintrell, Brian 1993: *Charles I, 1625–1640.* London: Longman.

Raab, Felix 1964: *The English Face of Machiavelli: A Changing Interpretation.* London: Routledge and Kegan Paul.

Reay, Barry 1988: 'The world turned upside down: a retrospect.' In Eley and Hunt (eds) *Reviving the English Revolution: Reflections and Elaborations on the Work of Christopher Hill.* London: Verso.

Reeve, L. J. 1989: *Charles I and the Road to Personal Rule.* Cambridge: Cambridge University Press.

Richards, Judith 1986: '"His nowe majestie" and the English monarchy: the kingship of Charles I before 1640.' *Past and Present* 113, 70–96.

Richardson, R. C. 1988: *The Debate on the English Revolution Revisited.* London: Routledge.

Richardson, R. C. (ed.) 1992: *Town and Countryside in the English Revolution.* Manchester: Manchester University Press.

Richardson, R. C. and Ridden, G. M. (eds) 1986: *Freedom and the English Revolution: Essays in History and Literature.* Manchester: Manchester University Press.

Richet, Denis 1973: *La France moderne: l'esprit des institutions.* Paris: Flammarion.

Rigby, S. H. 1995: 'Historical causation: is one thing more important than another?' *History* 80, 227–42.

Russell, Conrad 1965: 'The theory of treason in the trial of Strafford.' *English Historical Review* 80, 30–50. Reprinted in Russell, 1990b: *Unrevolutionary England, 1603–1642.* London: Hambledon Press.

Russell, Conrad (ed.) 1973: *The Origins of the English Civil War.* London: Macmillan.

Russell, Conrad 1976: 'Parliamentary history in perspective, 1604–1629.' *History* 61, 1–27.

Russell, Conrad 1979: *Parliaments and English Politics 1621–1629.* Oxford: Clarendon Press.

Russell, Conrad 1983: 'The nature of a parliament in early Stuart England.' In Tomlinson (ed.) *Before the English Civil War: Essays on Early Stuart Politics and Government.* London: Macmillan.

Russell, Conrad 1984a: 'Why did Charles I fight the civil war?' *History Today* June, 31–4.

Russell, Conrad 1984b: 'Why did Charles I call the Long Parliament? *History* 69, 375–83.

Russell, Conrad 1987: 'The British problem and the English civil war.' *History* 72, 395–415.

Russell, Conrad 1990a: *The Causes of the English Civil War*. Oxford: Oxford University Press.

Russell, Conrad 1990b: *Unrevolutionary England, 1603–1642*. London: Hambledon Press.

Russell, Conrad 1991: *The Fall of the British Monarchies*. Oxford: Oxford University Press.

Russell, Conrad 1993a: 'The Scottish party in English parliaments 1640–42, or The myth of the English revolution.' *Historical Research* 66, 35–52.

Russell, Conrad 1993b: 'Divine rights in the early seventeenth century.' In Morrill, John, Slack, Paul and Woolf, Daniel (eds) *Public Duty and Private Conscience in Seventeenth-Century England*. Oxford: Clarendon Press.

Sacks, David Harris 1986: 'The corporate town and the English state: Bristol's "little businesses" 1625–1641.' *Past and Present* 110, 69–105.

Sacks, David Harris 1992a: 'Bristol's "wars of religion".' In Richardson (ed.) *Town and Countryside in the English Revolution*. Manchester: Manchester University Press.

Sacks, David Harris 1992b: 'Parliament, liberty and the commonweal.' In Hexter (ed.) *Parliament and Liberty from the Reign of Elizabeth to the English Civil War*. Stanford, Calif.: Stanford University Press.

Salt, S. P. 1994: 'Sir Simonds D'Ewes and the levying of ship money, 1635–1640.' *Historical Journal* 37, 253–87.

Sanderson, John 1989: *'But the People's Creatures': The Philosophical Basis of the English Civil War*. Manchester: Manchester University Press.

Sanderson, John 1993: 'Conrad Russell's ideas.' *History of Political Thought* 14, 85–102

Scott, David 1992: 'Politics and government in York, 1640–1662.' In Richardson (ed.) *Town and Countryside in the English Revolution*. Manchester: Manchester University Press.

Scott, David 1997: '"Hannibal at our gates": loyalists and fifth-columnists during the Bishops' Wars – the case of Yorkshire.' *Historical Research* 70, 269–93.

Seaver, Paul 1980: 'The Puritan work ethic reconsidered.' *Journal of British Studies* 19, 35–53.

Sharp, Buchanan 1980: *In Contempt of All Authority: Rural Artisans and Riot in the West of England, 1586–1660*. Berkeley and Los Angeles: University of California Press.

Sharp, Buchanan 1988: 'Common rights, charities and the disorderly poor.' In Eley and Hunt (eds) *Reviving the English Revolution: Reflections and Elaborations on the Work of Christopher Hill*. London: Verso.

Sharpe, J. A. 1987: *Early Modern England: A Social History 1550–1760*. London: Edward Arnold.

Sharpe, Kevin (ed.) 1978: *Faction and Parliament: Essays on Early Stuart History*. Oxford: Clarendon Press.

Sharpe, Kevin 1983: 'The personal rule of Charles I.' In Tomlinson (ed.) *Before the English Civil War: Essays on Early Stuart Politics and Government*. London: Macmillan.

Sharpe, Kevin 1989: *Politics and Ideas in Early Stuart England.* London: Pinter.

Sharpe, Kevin 1992: *The Personal Rule of Charles I.* New Haven, Conn. and London: Yale University Press.

Skinner, Quentin 1969: 'Meaning and understanding in the history of ideas.' *History and Theory* 8, 3–53.

Skinner, Quentin 1978a: *The Foundations of Modern Political Thought. Volume One: The Renaissance.* Cambridge: Cambridge University Press.

Skinner, Quentin 1978b: *The Foundations of Modern Political Thought. Volume Two: The Age of Reformation.* Cambridge: Cambridge University Press.

Smith, Alan G. R. 1984: *The Emergence of a Nation State.* London: Longman.

Solt, Leo F. 1990: *Church and State in Early Modern England 1509–1640.* Oxford: Oxford University Press.

Sommerville, J. P. 1986: *Politics and Ideology in England 1603–1640.* London: Longman.

Sommerville, J. P. 1989: 'Ideology, property and the constitution.' In Cust and Hughes (eds) *Conflict in Early Stuart England: Studies in Religion and Politics 1603–1642.* London: Longman.

Sommerville, J. P. 1992: 'Parliament, privilege, and the liberties of the subject.' In Hexter (ed). *Parliament and Liberty from the Reign of Elizabeth to the English Civil War.* Stanford, Calif.: Stanford University Press.

Sommerville, Margaret R. 1995: *Sex and Subjection: Attitudes to Women in Early-Modern Society.* London: Arnold.

Spufford, Margaret 1974: *Contrasting Communities.* Cambridge: Cambridge University Press.

Spufford, Margaret 1985: 'Puritanism and social control?' In Fletcher and Stevenson (eds) *Order and Disorder in Early Modern England.* Cambridge: Cambridge University Press.

Stone, Lawrence 1965a: *The Crisis of the Aristocracy, 1558–1641.* Oxford: Clarendon Press.

Stone, Lawrence (ed.) 1965b: *Social Change and Revolution in England 1540–1640.* London: Longman.

Stone, Lawrence 1967: *The Crisis of the Aristocracy, 1558–1641,* abridged edn. Oxford: Oxford University Press.

Stone, Lawrence 1972: *The Causes of the English Revolution 1559–1642.* London: Routledge and Kegan Paul.

Stone, Lawrence 1977: *The Family, Sex and Marriage in England, 1500–1800.* London: Weidenfeld and Nicolson.

Stone, Lawrence 1985: 'The bourgeois revolution of seventeenth-century England revisited.' *Past and Present* 109, 44–54.

Stone, Lawrence and Stone, Jeanne C. Fawtier 1984: *An Open Elite? England 1540–1880.* Oxford: Oxford University Press.

Strong, Roy 1986: *Henry, Prince of Wales and England's Lost Renaissance.* London: Thames and Hudson.

Supple, B. E. 1959: *Commercial Crisis and Change in England 1600–1642.* Cambridge: Cambridge University Press.

Tanner, J. R. 1928: *English Constitutional Conflicts of the Seventeenth Century.* Cambridge: Cambridge University Press.

Tawney, R. H. 1936: *Religion and the Rise of Capitalism,* 3rd edn. London: John Murray.

Tawney, R. H. 1941: 'The rise of the gentry, 1558–1640.' *Economic History Review* 11, 1–38.

Thirsk, Joan (ed.) 1967: *The Agrarian History of England and Wales, IV, 1500–1640.* Cambridge: Cambridge University Press.

Thirsk, Joan 1978: *Economic Policy and Projects: The Development of a Consumer Society in Early Modern England.* Oxford: Clarendon Press.

Thirsk, Joan 1984: *The Rural Economy of England: Collected Essays.* London: Hambledon Press.

Thomas, Keith 1971: *Religion and the Decline of Magic: Studies in Popular Beliefs in Sixteenth- and Seventeenth-Century England.* London: Weidenfeld and Nicolson.

Thompson, Christopher 1986: *Parliamentary History in the 1620s: In or Out of Perspective?* Wivenhoe: Orchard Press.

Thompson, Christopher 1989: 'Court politics and parliamentary conflict in 1625.' In Cust and Hughes (eds) *Conflict in Early Stuart England: Studies in Religion and Politics 1603–1642.* London: Longman.

Tolmie, Murray 1977: *The Triumph of the Saints: The Separate Churches of London 1616–1649.* Cambridge: Cambridge University Press.

Tomlinson, Howard (ed.) 1983: *Before the English Civil War: Essays on Early Stuart Politics and Government.* London: Macmillan.

Trevor-Roper, Hugh R. 1953: 'The gentry, 1540–1640.' Supplement to *Economic History Review* 1.

Trevor-Roper, Hugh R. 1967: 'Scotland and the Puritan revolution.' In *Religion, the Reformation and Social Change.* London: Macmillan.

Tuck, Richard 1993: *Philosophy and Government 1572–1651.* Cambridge: Cambridge University Press.

Tully, James (ed.) 1988: *Meaning and Context: Quentin Skinner and his Critics.* Cambridge: Cambridge University Press.

Tyacke, Nicholas 1973: 'Puritanism, Arminianism and counter-revolution.' In Russell (ed.) *The Origins of the English Civil War.* London: Macmillan.

Tyacke, Nicholas 1987: *Anti-Calvinists: The Rise of English Arminianism, c. 1590–1640.* Oxford: Clarendon Press.

Underdown, David 1987: *Revel, Riot and Rebellion: Popular Politics and Culture in England 1603–1660.* Oxford: Oxford University Press.

Underdown, David 1993: *Fire From Heaven: Life in an English Town in the Seventeenth Century.* London: Fontana.

Underdown, David 1996: *A Freeborn People: Politics and the Nation in Seventeenth-Century England.* Oxford: Clarendon Press.

Vincent, John 1996: *An Intelligent Person's Guide to History.* London: Duckworth.

Walter, John 1985: 'A "rising of the people"? The Oxfordshire rising of 1596.' *Past and Present* 107, 90–143.

Walter, John and Wrightson, Keith 1976: 'Dearth and the social order in early modern England.' *Past and Present* 71, 22–42.

Walzer, Michael 1966: *The Revolution of the Saints: A Study in the Origins of Radical Politics.* New York: Atheneum.

Wanklyn, M. D. G and Young, Brigadier P. 1981: 'A king in search of soldiers: Charles I in 1642. A rejoinder.' *Historical Journal* 24, 147–54.

Weber, Max 1930: *The Protestant Ethic and the Spirit of Capitalism.* London:

Allen and Unwin.

Weston, Corinne C. 1991: 'England: the ancient constitution and the common law.' In Burns, J. H. and Goldie, Mark: *The Cambridge History of Political Thought, 1450–1700*. Cambridge: Cambridge University Press.

White, Peter 1992: *Predestination, Policy and Polemic: Conflict and Consensus in the English Church from the Reformation to the Civil War*. Cambridge: Cambridge University Press.

White, Peter 1993: 'The via media in the early Stuart church.' In Kenneth Fincham (ed.) *The Early Stuart Church*. London: Macmillan.

White, Stephen D. 1979: *Sir Edward Coke and the Grievances of the Commonwealth*. Manchester: Manchester University Press.

Wilson, Adrian 1993 (ed.): *Rethinking Social History: English Society 1570–1920 and its Interpretation*. Manchester: Manchester University Press.

Wood, Andy 1997: 'Beyond post-revisionism? The civil war allegiances of the miners of the Derbyshire "peak country".' *Historical Journal* 40, 23–40.

Wood, Ellen Meiksins 1991: *The Pristine Culture of Capitalism*. London: Verso.

Wood, Ellen Mieksins and Wood, Neal 1997: *A Trumpet of Sedition: Political Theory and the Rise of Capitalism*. London: Pluto Press.

Wootton, David 1986: *Divine Right and Democracy: An Anthology of Political Writing in Stuart England*. London: Penguin.

Wootton, David 1990: 'From rebellion to revolution, 1642–43.' *English Historical Review* 195, 654–69.

Wrightson, Keith 1982: *English Society 1580–1650*. London: Hutchinson.

Wrightson, Keith 1987: 'Estates, degrees and sorts.' *History Today* January, 17–21.

Wrightson, Keith and Levine, David 1979: *Poverty and Piety in an English Village: Terling, 1525–1700*. London: Academic Press.

Young, Michael B. 1989: 'Revisionism and the Council of War, 1624–26.' *Parliamentary History* 8, 1–27.

Young, Michael B. 1997: *Charles I*. London: Macmillan.

Zagorin, P. 1969: *The Court and the Country: The Beginning of the English Revolution*. London: Routledge and Kegan Paul.

Glossary

Note: while every effort has been made to explain terms which may be unfamiliar to students the first time they appear in the course of the book, the following list offers a quick checking facility. In many cases, fuller explanations of the concepts are given in the text.

Absolutism   A term used by historians to describe the growing power of early modern monarchies, especially those in which the monarch made laws and levied taxation without the participation of representative assemblies. What contemporaries meant by 'absolute monarchy'is discussed in chapter 4.

Agrarian capitalism   Agricultural production for the market by larger farmers using hired labour.

Anglocentrism   An exclusive preoccupation with England, to the neglect of Scotland and Ireland in this context.

Arminianism   Theological revision of Calvinist ideas on predestination put forward by the Dutch scholar Jacob Hermandzoon, or Arminius; discussed in chapter 3.

Attainder   An Act of parliament declaring someone guilty of treason without trial; used against the Earl of Strafford in 1641.

Calvinism   The doctrines of the sixteenth-century French Protestant leader John Calvin; discussed in chapter 3.

Canons   Church laws, passed by a Convocation; see below.

Catechism   A book from which religious doctrine is taught by learning questions and answers.

Convocation   The assembly of the English clergy in each province (Canterbury and York), consisting of an upper house of bishops and lower house of other clergy.

Copyhold   A form of land tenure in England, registered in the local manor court and often inheritable.

Covenanters   Supporters of the Scottish national covenant of 1638. See chapter 2.

Episcopacy   The system of church government by bishops.

Evangelical   Stressing preaching and the Bible as central to religious experience.

Fiscal seigneurialism   A term used by some historians to mean the policy of landlords who increased their income from land by traditional means rather than by promoting agricultural improvement and increased production.

Forced loan   The raising of compulsory contributions to the king's finances, to be repaid at some future date.

Gentry   The class or status of gentlemen; discussed in chapter 5.

Impeachment   Trial by parliament, with the Commons prosecuting and the Lords judging.

Kirk   Scots for 'church'; the name for the established church in Scotland.

Laudian   Having to do with the reforms in religious discipline and practice promoted by William Laud, Archbishop of Canterbury 1633–45.

Manorialism   The medieval system of local society and government whereby landlords had judicial authority over their tenants as well as property in their land.

Manufacture   The production of non-agricultural commodities for sale, especially on a large scale, but not in this period the modern industrial system.

Non-conformity   Before the civil war, this meant refusal to follow the full ceremonies of the Church of England's Prayer Book, not separatism (see below).

Old English   Descendants of medieval English settlers in Ireland; unlike the New English, they were mainly Catholics.

Peasant   A small to medium farmer producing primarily for family subsistence.

Predestination   The doctrine that God has selected some human beings to be saved by the gift of faith, which does not depend on their own actions; discussed in chapter 3.

Prerogative   Discretionary power, especially the king's.

Presbyterianism   A system of church government by ministers and elders, through a series of local and national assemblies. Deeply rooted in Scotland, but not in England in this period.

Proto-industrialization   A term sometimes used for the system of 'putting-out' manufactures to cottage workers.

Puritanism   The meanings of this term range from a movement for moral reform in everyday life to opposition to Charles I and Archbishop Laud's church policies in the 1630s. It is important to remember that Puritans wanted to change the Church of England from within, not to leave it.

Recusant   A person who refused to attend the Sunday services of the Church of England (or the Church of Ireland) as required by law. Most recusants were Roman Catholics.

Semi-separatist   Term used by historians to describe a congregation remaining within the Church of England but choosing its own way of worship and often having a select group of 'covenanted' members within the parish framework.

Separatist   Term used to describe a congregation or sect which has broken away from the Church of England; there were very few of these before the civil war, though many more by the mid-1640s.

Ship Money   Levy on property for the purpose of supporting the navy, imposed by Charles I on coastal counties in 1634 and on all counties annually from 1635 to 1640.

Subsidy   Tax on property granted to the monarch by parliament, often in multiples, e.g. five subsidies.

Index

Gardiner, Samuel R., 50, 73–4,
  99
gentry, 36–7, 41–2, 54, 58–9,
  84, 98, 100, 112, 114,
  119–20, 123, 131–2, 155–8,
  182
Gloucester, 55
Grand Remonstrance, 28, 30,
  31, 38, 76

Haller, William, 50
Hamilton, James Marquis of,
  14
Hampden's case, 101–2
Harrington, James, 1, 154
Harrison, William, 119, 120
hedge levelling, 40, 128
Henrietta Maria, Queen, 8–9,
  137–8, 142
Henry, Prince, 141–2
Hexter, J. H. (Jack), 161
Hill, Christoper, 4, 41, 47, 69,
  144, 153, 155–7, 159, 162
hospitality, 100, 117
Hull, 33, 152
Hunt, William, 71
Hunton, Philip, 153
husbandmen, 121

impositions, 80–1, 88, 89, 93
industry *see* manufactures
Ireland, 15, 21–4, 71;
  plantations in, 22–3;
  rebellion in, 8, 16, 22–4,
  32–3, 152

James VI and I, 15, 17, 53–4,
  62–3, 64, 68, 70, 76, 78, 81,

88–90, 95, 137, 142, 149
Justices of the Peace, 13,
  98–100

labourers, 58, 107, 115, 121–2,
  124
Lancashire, 41, 42
Laslett, Peter, 114
Laud, William, Archbishop of
  Canterbury, 20, 27, 29, 48,
  50–1, 54, 62, 64, 65–6, 68
Laudianism, 63–7, 72
liberty, 4, 145–7, 156
local government, 97–100
London, 31, 33, 43–5, 111–12,
  123, 130, 159–61
Lords, House of, 14, 28, 31,
  33, 44, 91, 116, 150
Louis XII, 137, 142
Louis XIV, 142–3
Lunsford, Thomas, 33, 44

Macaulay, Thomas Babington,
  Lord, 76, 142
Macfarlane, Alan, 114
Machiavelli, 148
Malthusian crisis, 106, 108
Manning, Brian, 127, 158
Manning, Roger, 128, 158
manufactures, 38, 108–10,
  112, 115, 123–4, 182
Manwaring, Roger, 67, 78–9,
  81, 93
Marshall, Stephen, 36–7, 150
Marxist interpretations, 10, 25,
  58, 104, 134, 144, 154–62
merchants, 17, 43, 122–3, 131,
  155, 159–60